Alexander Maclaren

The Secret of Power

And other Sermons

Alexander Maclaren

The Secret of Power
And other Sermons

ISBN/EAN: 9783744742283

Printed in Europe, USA, Canada, Australia, Japan

Cover: Foto ©Lupo / pixelio.de

More available books at **www.hansebooks.com**

THE
SECRET OF POWER,

AND

OTHER SERMONS.

BY

ALEXANDER MACLAREN, D.D.

London:
MACMILLAN AND CO.
1882.

MOST OF THE SERMONS IN THIS VOLUME HAVE ALREADY APPEARED IN LESS PERMANENT FORMS.

CONTENTS.

SERMON		PAGE
I.	THE SECRET OF POWER	1
II.	THE PATTERN OF SERVICE	26
III.	THE AWAKING OF ZION	58
IV.	"TIME FOR THEE TO WORK"	81
V.	THE EXHORTATION OF BARNABAS	107
VI.	MEASURELESS POWER AND ENDLESS GLORY	130
VII.	LOVE'S TRIUMPH	145
VIII.	THE GRAVE OF THE DEAD JOHN AND THE GRAVE OF THE LIVING JESUS	159
IX.	THE TRANSLATION OF ELIJAH AND THE ASCENSION OF CHRIST	174
X.	CAN WE MAKE SURE OF TO-MORROW?	187
XI.	THE SOLITARINESS OF CHRIST IN HIS TEMPTATIONS	201
XII.	THE WELLS OF SALVATION	212

CONTENTS.

XIII.	SEEKING THE FACE OF GOD	222
XIV.	CITIZENS OF HEAVEN	237
XV.	MOSES AND HOBAB	251
XVI.	THE OBSCURE APOSTLES	265
XVII.	THE SOUL'S PERFECTION	280
XVIII.	THE FIRST PREACHING AT ANTIOCH	294
XIX.	THE MASTER AND HIS SLAVES	304
XX.	A PRISONER'S DYING THOUGHTS	313

SERMON I.*

THE SECRET OF POWER.

ST. MATTHEW xvii. 19, 20.

Then came the disciples to Jesus apart, and said, Why could not we cast him out? And Jesus said unto them, Because of your unbelief.

"AND when He had called unto Him His twelve disciples, He gave them power against unclean spirits to cast them out." That same power was bestowed, too, on the wider circle of the seventy who returned again with joy, saying, "Lord, even the devils are subject unto us through Thy name." The ground of it was laid in the solemn words with which Christ met their wonder at their own strength, and told how He "beheld Satan as lightning fall from heaven." Therefore had they triumphed, showing the fruits of their Master's victory; and therefore had He a right to renew the gift, in the still more comprehensive promise, "I give unto you power—over all the power of the enemy."

What a commentary on such words this story affords! What has become of their supernatural might? Has it

* Preached before the Directors and Friends of the London Missionary Society.

ebbed away as suddenly as it flowed? Is their Lord's endowment a shadow—His assurances delusion? Has He taken back what He gave? Not so. And yet His servants are ignominiously beaten. One poor devil-ridden boy brings all their resources to nothing. He stands before them writhing in the gripe of his tormentor, but they cannot set him free. The importunity of the father's prayers is vain, and the tension of expectancy in his eager face relaxes into the old hopeless languor as he slowly droops to the conviction that they could not cast him out. The malicious scorn in the eyes of the Scribes, those hostile critics who "knew that it would be so," helps to produce the failure which they anticipated. The curious crowd buzz about them—and in the midst of it all the little knot of baffled disciples, possessors of power which seems to leave them when they need it most, with the unavailing spells dying half spoken on their lips, and their faint hearts longing that their Master would come down from the mount, and cover their weakness with His own great strength.

No wonder that, as soon as Christ and they are alone, they want to know how their mortifying defeat has come about. And they get an answer which they little expected, for the last place where men look for the explanation of their failures is within; and they will ascend into the heavens, and descend into the deeps for remote and recondite reasons, before they listen to the voice which says, "The fault is nigh thee—in thy heart." Christ's reply distinctly implies that the cause of their impotence lay wholly in themselves, not in any defect or withdrawal of power, but solely in that in them which grasped the power. They little expected, too, to be told that they had failed because they had not been sure they would succeed. They had thought they believed in their ability to cast out the demon. They had tried with some kind of anticipation that they could. They had been surprised when they found they could not. They had wonderingly asked why. And now Christ tells them that all along they had had no real faith in Him and in the reality of His gift. So subtly may unbelief steal into the heart, even while we fancy that we are working in faith. And a further portion of our Lord's reply points them to the great means by which this conquering faith can be maintained—namely, prayer and fasting. If, then, we put all these things together, we get a series of considerations, very simple and commonplace indeed, but all the better and truer therefore, which I venture to submit to you, as having a very important bearing on all our Christian work, and especially on the missionary work of the Church. The principles which the text suggests touch the perpetual possession of the power which conquers; the condition of its victorious exercise by us, as being our faith; the subtle danger of unsuspected unbelief to which we are exposed; and the great means of preserving our faith pure and strong. I ask your attention to a few considerations on these points in their order.

But first, let me say very briefly, that I would not be understood as, by the selection of such a text, desiring to suggest that we have failed in our work. Thank God!

we can point to results far, far greater than we have deserved, far greater than we have expected, however they may be beneath our desires, and still further below what the gospel was meant to accomplish. It may suit observers who have never done anything themselves, and have not particularly clear eyes for appreciating spiritual work, to talk of Christian missions as failures; but it would ill become us to assent to the lie. Failures indeed! with half a million of converts, with new forms of Christian life budding in all the wilderness of the peoples, with the consciousness of coming doom creeping about the heart of every system of idolatry! Is the green life in the hedges and in the sweet pastures starred with rathe primroses, and in the hidden copses blue with hyacinths a failure, because the east wind bites shrewdly, and " the tender ash delays to clothe herself with green "? No! no we have *not* failed. Enough has been done to vindicate the enterprise, more than enough to fill our lips with thanksgiving, enough to entitle us to say to all would-be critics—Do you the same with your enchantments. But, on the other hand, we have to confess that the success has been slow and small, chequered and interrupted, that often we have been foiled, that we have confronted many a demon whom we could not cast out, and that at home and abroad the masses of evil seem to close in around us, and we make but little impression on their serried ranks. We have had success enough to assure us that we possess the treasure, and failures enough to make us feel how weak are the earthen vessels which hold it.

And now let us turn to the principles which flow from this text.

I. *We have an unvarying power.*

No doubt the explanation of their defeat which most naturally suggested itself to these disciples would be that somehow or other—perhaps because of Christ's absence—they had lost the gift which they knew they once had. And the same way of accounting for later want of success lingers among Christian people still. You will sometimes hear it said :—" God sends forth His Spirit in special fulness at special times, according to His own sovereign will ; and till then we can only wait and pray." Or " The miraculous powers which dwelt in the early Church have been withdrawn, and therefore the progress is slow." The strong imaginative tendency to make an ideal perfect in the past leads us to think of the primitive age of the Church as golden, in opposition to the plain facts of the case. We fancy that because apostles were its teachers, and the Cross within its memory, the infant society was stronger, wiser, better than any age since, and had gifts which we have lost. What had it which we do not possess? The power of working miracles. What have we which it did not possess? A completed Bible, and the experience of eighteen centuries to teach us to understand it, and to confirm by facts our confidence that Christ's gospel is for all time and every land. What have we in common with it? The same mission to fulfil, the same wants in our brethren to meet, the same gospel, the same spirit, the same immortal Lord. All that any age has possessed to fit it for the task of witnessing for Christ we too possess. The Church has in it a power which is ever adequate to the conquest of the world; and that power is constant through all time, whether we consider it as recorded in an unvarying gospel, or as energized by an abiding spirit, or as flowing from and centred in an unchangeable Lord.

We have a gospel which never can grow old. Its adaptation to the deepest needs of men's souls remains constant with these needs. These vary not from age to age. No matter what may be the superficial differences of dress the same human heart beats beneath every robe. The great primal wants of men's spirits abide as the great primal wants of their bodily life abide. Food and shelter for the one,—a loving, pardoning God, to know and love, for the other—else they perish. Wherever men go they carry with them a conscience which needs cleansing, a sense of separation from God joined with a dim knowledge that union with Him is life, a will which is burdened with its own self-hood, an imagination which paints the misty walls of this earthly prison with awful shapes that terrify and faint hopes that mock, a heart that hungers for love, and a reason which pines in atrophy without light. And all these the gospel which is lodged in our hands meets. It addresses itself to nothing in men that is not in Man. Surface differences of position, culture, clime, age, and the like, it brushes aside as unimportant and it goes straight to the universal wants. People tell us it has done its work, and much confident dogmatism proclaims that the world has outgrown it. We have a right to be confident also, with a confidence born of our knowledge, that it has met and satisfied for us the wants which are ours and every man's, and to believe that as long as men live by bread, so long will this word which proceedeth out of the mouth of God be the food of their souls. Areopagus and Piccadilly, Benares and Oxford, need the same message and will find the same response to all their wants in the same word.

Much of the institutions in which Christendom has embodied its conceptions of God's truth will crumble away. Many of the conceptions will have to be modified, neglected truths will grow, to the dislocation of much systematic theology, and the Word better understood will clear away many a portentous error with which the Church has darkened the word. Be it so. Let us be glad when "the things which can be shaken are removed," like mean huts built against the wall of some cathedral, masking and marring the completeness of its beauty; "that the things which cannot be shaken may remain," and all the clustered shafts, and deep-arched recesses, and sweet tracery may stand forth freed from the excrescences which hid them. "The grass withereth, and the flower thereof falleth away. But the word of the Lord endureth for ever."

We have an abiding Spirit, the Giver to us of a power without variableness or the shadow of turning, " I will pray the Father, and He shall give you another Paraclete, that He may abide with you for ever." The manner of His operations may vary, but the reality of His energy abides. The "works" of wonder which Jesus did on earth may no more be done, but the greater works than these are still the sign of *His* presence, without whom no spiritual life is possible. Prophecies may fail, tongues may cease, but the more excellent gifts are poured out now as richly as ever. We are apt to look back to Pentecost and think that that marked a height to which the tide has never reached since, and therefore we are stranded amidst the ooze and mud. But the river which proceeds from the throne of God and of the Lamb is not like one of our streams on earth, that leaps to the light and dashes rejoicingly down the hillside, but creeps along sluggish in its level course, and dies away at last in the sands. It pours along the ages the same full volume with which it gushed forth at first. Rather, the source goes with the Church in all ages, and we drink not of water that came forth long ago in the history of the world, and has reached us through the centuries, but of that which wells out fresh every moment from the Rock that follows us. The Giver of all power is with us.

We have a Lord, the same yesterday, and to-day, and for ever. " Lo, I am with you always, even to the end of the world." We have not merely to look back to the life and death of Christ in history, and recognise there the work, the efficacy of which shall endure for ever. But whilst we do this, we have also to think of the Christ " that is risen again, who is even at the right hand of God, who also maketh intercession for us." And the one thought, as the other, should strengthen our confidence in our possession of all the might that we need for bringing the world back to our Lord.

A work in the past which can never be exhausted or lose its power is the theme of our message. The mists of gathering ages wrap in slowly thickening folds of forgetfulness all other men and events in history, and make them ghostlike and shadowy; but no distance has yet dimmed or will ever dim that human form divine. Other names are like those stars that blaze out for a while, and then smoulder down into almost complete invisibility; but He is the very Light itself, that burns and is not consumed. Other landmarks sink below the horizon as the tribes of men pursue their solemn march through the centuries, but the Cross on Calvary " shall stand for an ensign of the people, and to it shall the Gentiles seek." To proclaim that accomplished salvation, once for all lodged in the heart of the world's history, and henceforth for ever valid, is our unalterable duty. The message carries in itself its own immortal strength.

A living Saviour in the present, who works with us, confirming the word with signs following, is the source of our power. Not till He is impotent shall we be weak. The unmeasurable measure of the gift of Christ defines the degree, and the unending duration of His life who continueth for ever sets the period, of our possession of the grace which is given to every one of us. He is ever bestowing. He never withdraws what He once gives. The fountain sinks not a hair's breadth, though eighteen centuries have drawn from it. Modern astronomy begins to believe that the sun itself by long expense of light will be shorn of its beams and wander darkling in space, circled no more by its daughter planets. But this Sun of our souls rays out for ever the energies of life and light and love, and after all communication possesses the infinite fulness of them all. "His name shall be continued as long as the sun, all nations shall call Him blessed."

Here then, brethren, are the perpetual elements of our constant power, an eternal Word, an abiding Spirit, an unchanging Lord.

II. *The condition of exercising this power is Faith.*

With such a force at our command—a force that could shake the mountains and break the rocks—how come we ever to fail? So the disciples asked, and Christ's answer cuts to the very heart of the matter. Why could you not cast him out? For one reason only, because you had lost your hold of My strength, and therefore had lost your confidence in your own derived power, or had forgotten that it was derived, and essayed to wield it as if it were your own. You did not trust Me, so you did not believe that you could cast him out; or you believed that you could by your own might, therefore you failed. He throws them back decisively on themselves as solely responsible. Nowhere else, in heaven or in earth or hell, but only in us, does the reason lie for our breakdown, if we have broken down. Not in God, who is ever with us, ready to make all grace abound in us, whose will is that all men should be saved and come to the knowledge of the truth; not in the gospel which we preach, for "it is the power of God unto salvation;" not in the demon might which has overcome us, for "greater is He that is in us than he that is in the world." We are driven from all other explanations to the bitterest and yet the most hopeful of all, that we only are to blame.

And what in us is to blame? Some of us will answer —Our modes of working; they have not been free enough, or not orderly enough, or in some way or other not wisely adapted to our ends. Some will answer—Our forms of presenting the truth; they have not been flexible enough, or not fixed enough; they have been too much a reproduction of the old; they have been too licentious a departure from the old. Some will answer—Our ecclesiastical arrangements; they have been too democratic; they have been too priestly. Some will answer—Our intellectual culture; it has been too great, obscuring the simplicity that is in Christ; it has been too small, sending poorly furnished men into the field to fight with ordered systems of idolatry which rest upon a philosophical basis, and can only be overturned by undermining that. It is no part of my present duty to discuss these varying answers. No doubt there is room for improvement in all the fields which they indicate. But does not the spirit of our Lord's words here beckon us away from these purely secondary subjects to fix our self-examination on the depth and strength of our faith, as incomparably the most important element in the conditions which determine our success or our failure? I do not undervalue the worth of wise methods of action, but the history of the Church tells us that pretty nearly any methods of action are fruitful in the right hands, and that without living faith the best of them become like the heavy armour which half-smothered a feeble man. I do not pretend to that sublime indifference to dogma which is the modern form of supreme devotion to truth, but experience has taught us that wherever the name of Christ, as the Saviour of the world, has been lovingly proclaimed, there devils have been cast out, whatever private and sectional doctrines the exorciser has added to it. I do not disparage organization, but courage is more than drill; and there is such a thing as the very perfection of arrangement without life, like cabinets in a museum, where all the specimens are duly classified, and dead. I believe, with the old preacher, that if God can do without our learning, He needs our ignorance still less, but it is of comparatively little importance whether the draught of living water be brought to thirsty lips in an earthen cup or a golden vase.

> "The main thing is, does it hold good measure?
> Heaven soon sets right all other matters."

And therefore, while leaving full scope for all improvements in these subordinate conditions, let me urge upon you that the main thing which makes us strong for our Christian work is the grasp of living faith, which holds fast the strength of God. There is no need to plunge into the jungle of metaphysical theology here. Is it not a fact that the might with which the power of God has wrought for men's salvation has corresponded with the strength of the Church's desire and the purity of its trust in His power? Is it not a truth plainly spoken in Scripture and confirmed by experience, that we have the awful prerogative of limiting the Holy One of Israel, and quenching the Spirit? Was there not a time in Christ's life on earth when He could do no mighty works because of their unbelief? We receive all spiritual gifts in proportion to our capacity, and the chief factor in settling the measure of our capacity is our faith. Here on the one hand is the boundless ocean of the Divine strength, unfathomable in its depth, full after all draughts, tideless and calm, in all its movement never troubled, in all its repose never stagnating; and on the other side is the empty aridity of our poor weak natures. Faith opens these to the influx of that great sea, and "according to our faith," in the exact measure of our receptivity, does it enter our hearts. In itself the gift is boundless. It has no limit except the infinite fulness of the power which worketh in us. But in reference to our possession it is bounded by our capacity, and though that capacity enlarges by the very fact of being filled, and so every moment becomes greater through fruition, yet at each moment it is the measure of our possession, and our faith is the measure of our capacity. Our power is God's power in us, and our faith is the power with which we grasp God's power and make it ours. So then, in regard to God, our faith is the condition of our being strengthened with might by His Spirit.

Consider, too, how the same faith has *a natural operation on ourselves* which tends to fit us for casting out the evil spirits. Given a man full of faith, you will have a man tenacious in purpose, absorbed in one grand object, simple in his motives, in whom selfishness has been driven out by the power of a mightier love, and indolence stirred into unwearied energy. Such a man will be made wise to devise, gentle to attract, bold to rebuke, fertile in expedients, and ready to be anything that may help the aim of his life. Fear will be dead in him, for faith is the true anæsthesia of the soul; and the knife may cut into the quivering flesh, and the spirit be scarce conscious of a pang. Love, ambition, and all the swarm of distracting desires will be driven from the soul in which the lamp of faith burns bright. Ordinary human motives will appeal in vain to the ears which have heard the tones of the heavenly music, and all the pomps of life will show poor and tawdry to the sight that has gazed on the vision of the great white throne and the crystal sea. The most ignorant and erroneous "religious sentiment"—to use a modern phrase—is mightier than all other forces in the world's history. It is like some of those terrible compounds of modern chemistry, an inert, innocuous-looking drop of liquid. Shake it, and it flames heaven high, shattering the rocks and ploughing up the soil. Put even an adulterated and carnalised faith into the hearts of a mob of wild Arabs, and in a century they will stream from their deserts, and blaze from the mountains of Spain to the plains of Bengal. Put a living faith in Christ and a heroic confidence in the power of His gospel to reclaim the worst sinners into a man's heart, and he will out of weakness be made strong, and plough his way through obstacles with the compact force and crashing directness of lightning. There have been men of all sorts who have been honoured to do much in this world for Christ. Wise and foolish, learned and ignorant, differing in tone, temper, creed, forms of thought, and manner of working, in every conceivable degree;—but one thing, and perhaps one thing only, they have all had—a passion of enthusiastic personal devotion to their Lord, a profound and living faith in Him and in His salvation. All in which they differed is but the gay gilding on the soldier's coat. That in which they were alike is as the strong arm which grasps the sword, and has its muscles braced by the very clutch. Faith is itself a source of strength, as well as the condition of drawing might from heaven.

Consider, too, how faith has power over *men who see it*. The exhibition of our own personal convictions has more to do in spreading them than all the arguments which we use. There is a magnetism and a contagious energy in the sight of a brother's faith which few men can wholly resist. If you wish me to weep, your own tears must flow; and if you would have me believe, let me see your soul heaving under the emotion which you desire me to feel. The arrow may be keen and true, the shaft rounded and straight, the bow strong, and the arm sinewy; but unless the steel be winged it will fall to the ground long before it strikes the butt. Your arrows must be winged with faith, else orthodoxy, and wise arrangements, and force and zeal, will avail nothing. No man will believe in, and no demon will obey, spells which the would-be exorcist only half believes himself. Even if he speak the name of Christ, unless he speak it with unfaltering confidence, all the answer he will get will only be the fierce and taunting question, "Jesus I know, and Paul I know, but who are ye?" Brethren, let us give heed to the solemn rebuke which our Master lovingly reads to us in these words, and while we aim at the utmost possible perfection in all subordinate matters, let us remember that they all without faith are weak, as an empty suit of armour with no life beneath the corslet; and that faith without them all is strong, like the knight of old, who rode into the bloody field in simple silken vest, and conquered. That which determines our success or failure in the work of our Lord is our faith.

III. *Our faith is ever threatened by subtle unbelief.*

It would appear that the disciples were ignorant of the unbelief that had made them weak. They fancied that they had confidence in their Christ-given power, and they certainly had in some dull kind of fashion expected to succeed in their attempt. But He who sees the heart knew that there was no real living confidence in their souls; and His words are a solemn warning to us all, of how possible it is for us to have our faith all honeycombed by gnawing doubt while we suspect it not, like some piece of wood apparently sound, the whole substance of which has been eaten away by hidden worms. We may be going on with Christian work, and may even be looking for spiritual results. We may fancy ourselves faithful stewards of the gospel, and all the while there may be an utter absence of the one thing which makes our words more than so much wind whistling through an archway. The shorn Samson went out " to shake himself as at other times," and knew not that the Spirit of the Lord had departed from him. Who among us is not exposed to the assaults of that pestilence that walketh in darkness? and, alas! who among us can say that he has repelled the contagion? Subtly it creeps over us all, the stealthy intangible vapour, unfelt till it has quenched the lamp which alone lights the darkness of the mine, and clogged to suffocation the labouring lungs.

Our time, and the object in view, preclude my speaking of the general sources of danger to our faith, which are always in operation with a retarding force as constant as friction, as certain as the gravitation which pulls the pendulum to rest at its lowest point. But I may very briefly particularize two of the enemies of that faith, which have a special bearing on our missionary work, and may be illustrated from the narrative before us.

First, *all our activity* in spreading the gospel, whether by personal effort or by our gifts, like every form of outward action, *tends to become mechanical*, and to lose its connection with the motive which originated it. Of course it is also true, on the other side, that all outward action also tends to strengthen the motive from which it flows. But our Christian work will not do so, unless it be carefully watched, and pains be taken to keep it from slipping off its original foundation, and so altering its whole character. We may very easily become so occupied with the mere external occupation as to be quite unconscious that it has ceased to be faithful work, and has become routine, dull mechanism, or the result of confidence, not in Christ, whose power once flowed through us, but in ourselves the doers. So these disciples may have thought, "*We* can cast out this devil, for we have done the like already," and have forgotten that it was not they, but Christ in them, who had done it.

How widely this foe to our faith operates amid the multiplied activities of this busy age one trembles to think. We see all around us a Church toiling with unexampled expenditure of wealth, and effort, and time. It is difficult to repress the suspicion that the work is out of proportion to the life. Ah, brethren, how much of all this energy of effort, so admirable in many respects, will He whose fan is in His hand accept as true service— how much of it will be wheat for the garner, how much chaff for the fire? It is not for us to divide between the two, but it is for us to remember that it is not impossible to make of our labours the most dangerous enemy to the depth of our still life hidden with Christ in God, and that every deed of apparent service which is not the real issue of living faith is powerless for good to others, and heavy with hurt to ourselves. Brethren and fathers in the ministry! how many of us know what it is to talk and toil away our early devotion; and all at once to discover that for years perhaps we have been preaching and labouring from mere habit and routine, like corpses galvanised into some ghastly and transient caricature of life. Christian men and women, beware lest this great enterprise of missions, which our fathers began from the holiest motives and in the simplest faith, should in our hand, be wrenched away from its only true basis, and be done with languid expectation and more languid desires of success, from no higher motive than that we found it in existence, and have become accustomed to carry it on. If that be our reason, then we harm ourselves, and mask from our own sight our own unbelief. If that be the case the work may go on for a while, like a clock ticking with fainter and fainter beats for a minute after it has run down; but it will soon cease, and neither heaven nor earth will be much the poorer for its ending.

Again, *the atmosphere of scornful disbelief which surrounded the disciples made their faith falter.* It was too weak to sustain itself in the face of the consciousness that not a man in all that crowd believed in their power; and it melted away before the contempt of the scribes and the incredulous curiosity of the bystanders, without any reason except the subtle influence which the opinions and characters of those around us have on us all.

And, brethren, are not we in danger to-day of losing the firmness of our grasp on Christ, as our Saviour and the world's, from a precisely similar cause? We live in an atmosphere of hesitancy and doubt, of scornful rejection of His claims, of contemptuous disbelief in anything which a scalpel cannot cut. We cannot but be conscious that to hold by Jesus Christ as the Incarnate God, the supernatural Beginning of a new life, the sole Hope of the world, is to expose ourselves to the contempt of so-called advanced and liberal thinkers, and to be out of harmony with the prevailing set of opinions. The current of educated thought runs strongly against such beliefs, and I suppose that every thoughtful man among us feels that a great danger to our faith to-day comes from the force with which that current swings us round, and threatens to make some of us drag our anchors, and drift, and strike and go to pieces on the sands. For one man who is led by the sheer force of reason to yield to the intellectual grounds on which modern unbelief reposes, there are twenty who simply catch the infection in the atmosphere. They find that their early convictions have evaporated, they know not how; only that once the fleece was wet with dew and now it is dry. For unbelief has a contagious energy wholly independent of reason, no less than has faith, and affects multitudes who know nothing of its grounds, as the iceberg chills the summer air for leagues, and makes the sailors shiver long before they see its barren peaks.

Therefore, brethren, let us all take heed to ourselves, lest we suffer our grasp of our dear Lord's hand to relax for no better reason than because so many have left His side. To us all His pleading love, which knows how much we are moulded by the example of others, is saying, in view of the fashion of unbelief, "Will ye also go away?" Let us answer, with a clasp that clings the tighter for our danger of being sucked in by the strong current, "Lord, to whom shall we go? Thou hast the words of eternal life." We cannot help seeing that the creeping paralysis of hesitancy and doubt about even the power of Christ's name is stealing over portions of the Church, and stiffening the arm of its activity. Lips that once spoke with full confidence the words that cast out devils, mutter them now languidly with half belief. Hearts that were once full of sympathy with the great purpose for which Christ died are growing cold to the work of preaching the gospel to the heathen, because they are growing to doubt whether, after all, there is any gospel at all. This icy breath, dear brethren, is blowing over our Churches and over our hearts. And wherever it reaches, there labour for Jesus and for men languishes, and we recoil baffled with unavailing exorcisms dying in our throats, and the rod of our power broken in our hands. "Why could not we cast him out? Because of your unbelief."

IV. *Our faith can only be maintained by constant devotion and rigid self-denial.*

I have already detained you far too long, and can touch but very lightly on that solemn thought in which our Lord sets forth the condition of our faith, and therefore of our power. This kind goeth not out but by prayer and fasting. The discipline then which nurtures faith is mainly moral and spiritual—not as a substitute for, or to the exclusion of, the intellectual discipline, which is presupposed, not neglected, in these words.

The first condition of the freshness and energy of faith is constant devotion. The attrition of the world wears it thin, the distractions of life draw it from its clinging hold on Christ, the very toil for Him is apt to entice our thoughts from out of the secret place of the most High into the busy arena of our strife. Therefore we have ever need to refresh the drooping flowers of the chaplet by bathing them in the Fountain of Life, to rise above all the fevered toil of earth to the calm heights where God dwells, and in still communion with Him to replenish our emptied vessels and fill our dimly burning lamps with His golden oil. The sister of the cumbered Martha is the contemplative Mary, who sits in silence at the Master's feet and lets His words sink into her soul: the closest friend of Peter the apostle of action is John the Apostle of love. If our work is to be worthy, it must ever be freshened anew by our gaze into His face; if our communion with Him is to be deep, it must never be parted from outward service. Our Master has left us the example, in that, when the night fell and every man went to his own home, Jesus went to the Mount of Olives; and thence, after His night of prayer, came very early in the morning, to the temple, and taught. The stream that is to flow broad and life-giving through many lands must have its hidden source high among the pure snows that cap the mount of God. The man that would work for God must live with God. It was from the height of transfiguration that *He* came, before whom the demon that baffled the disciples quailed and slunk away like a whipped hound. This kind goeth not out but by prayer.

The second condition is rigid self-denial. Fasting is the expression of the purpose to control the lower life, and to abstain from its delights in order that the life of the spirit may be strengthened. As to the outward fact, it is nothing—it may be practised or not. If it be, it will be valuable only in so far as it flows from and strengthens that purpose. And such vigorous subordination of all the lower powers, and abstinence from many an inferior good, both material and immaterial, is absolutely necessary if we are to have any wholesome strength of faith in our souls. In the recoil from the false asceticism of Roman Catholicism and Puritanism, has not this generation of the Church gone too far in the opposite direction? and in the true belief that Christianity can sanctify all joys, and ensure the harmonious development of all our powers, have we not been forgetting that hand and foot may cause us to stumble, and that we had better live maimed than die with all our limbs? There is a true asceticism, a discipline—a "gymnastic unto godliness," as Paul calls it. And if our faith is to grow high and bear rich clusters on the topmost boughs that look up to the sky, we must keep the wild lower shoots close nipped. Without rigid self-control and self-limitation, no vigorous faith.

And without them no effectual work! It is no holiday task to cast out devils. Self-indulgent men will never do it. Loose-braced, easy souls, that lie open to all the pleasurable influences of ordinary life, are no more fit for God's weapons than a reed for a lance, or a bit of flexible lead for a spear-point. The wood must be tough and compact, the metal hard and close-grained, out of which God makes His shafts. The brand that is to guide men through the darkness to their Father's home must glow with a pallor of consuming flame that purges its whole substance into light. This kind goeth not out but by prayer and fasting.

Dear brethren, what solemn rebuke these words have for us all to-day! How they winnow these works of Christian activity which bring us here this morning! How they show us the hollowness of our services, the self-indulgence of our lives, the coldness of our devotion, the cowardice of our faith! How marvellous they make the fruits which God's great goodness has permitted us to see even from our doubting service! Let us turn to Him with fresh thankfulness that unto us, who are " less than the least of all saints, is this grace given, that we should preach among the nations the unsearchable riches of Christ." Let us not be driven from our confidence that we have a gospel to preach for all the world; but strong in the faith which rests on impregnable historical grounds, on our own experience of what Christ has done for us, and on eighteen centuries of growing power and unfolding wisdom, let us thankfully welcome all that modern thought may supply for the correction of errors in belief, in organization, and in life, that may have gathered round His perfect and eternal gospel—being assured, as we have a right to be, that all will but lift higher the Name which is above every name, and set forth more plainly that Cross which is the true tree of life to all the families of men. Let us cast ourselves before Him with penitent confession, and say,—O Lord, our strength! we have not wrought any deliverance on earth; we have been weak when all Thy power was at our command; we have spoken Thy word as if it were an experiment and a peradventure whether it had might; we have let go Thy hand and lost Thy garment's hem from our slack grasp;

we have been prayerless and self-indulgent. Therefore Thou hast put us to shame before our foes, and "our enemies laugh among themselves. Thou that dwellest between the cherubim shine forth; stir up Thy strength and come and save us!" Then will the last words that He spoke on earth ring out again from the throne: "All power is given unto Me in heaven and in earth. Go ye therefore and teach all nations; and lo, I am with you alway, even unto the end of the world."

SERMON II.*

THE PATTERN OF SERVICE.

St. Mark vii. 33, 34.

He touched his tongue; and looking up to heaven, He sighed, and saith, Ephphatha, that is, Be opened.

FOR what reason was there this unwonted slowness in Christ's healing works? For what reason was there this unusual emotion ere He spoke the word which cleansed.

As to the former question, a partial answer may perhaps be that our Lord is here on half-heathen ground, where aids to faith were much needed, and His power had to be veiled that it might be beheld. Hence the miracle is a process rather than an act; and, advancing as it does by distinct stages, is conformed in appearance to men's works of mercy, which have to adapt means to ends, and creep to their goal by persevering toil. As to the latter we know not why the sight of this one poor sufferer should have struck so strongly on the ever-tremulous chords of Christ's pitying heart; but we do know that it was the vision brought before His spirit by this single

* Preached before the Wesleyan Missionary Society.

instance of the world's griefs and sicknesses, in which mass, however, the special case before Him was by no means lost, that raised His eyes to heaven in mute appeal, and forced the groan from His breast.

The "Missionary spirit" is but one aspect of the Christian spirit. We shall only strengthen the former as we invigorate the latter. Harm has been done, both to ourselves and to this great cause, by seeking to stimulate compassion and efforts for heathen lands by the use of other excitements, which have tended to vitiate even the emotions they have aroused, and are apt to fail us when we need them most. It may therefore be profitable if we turn to Christ's own manner of working, and His own emotions in his merciful deeds, set forth in this remarkable narrative, as containing lessons for us in our missionary and evangelistic work. I must necessarily omit more than a passing reference to the slow process of healing which this miracle exhibits. But that, too, has its teaching for us, who are so often tempted to think ourselves badly used, unless the fruit of our toil grows up, like Jonah's gourd, before our eyes. If our Lord was content to reach His end of blessing step by step, we may well accept patient continuance in well-doing as the condition indispensable to reaping in due season.

But there are other thoughts still more needful which suggest themselves. Those minute details which this evangelist ever delights to give of our Lord's gestures, words, looks, and emotions, not only add graphic force to the narrative but are precious glimpses of the very heart of Christ. That fixed gaze into heaven, that groan which neither the glories seen above nor the conscious power to heal could stifle, that most gentle touch, as if removing material obstacles from the deaf ears, and moistening the stiff tongue that it might move more freely in the parched mouth, that word of authority which could not be wanting even when His working seemed likest a servant's, do surely carry large lessons for us. The condition of all service, the cost of feeling at which our work must be done, the need that the helpers should identify themselves with the sufferers, and the victorious power of Christ's word over all deaf ears—these are the thoughts which I desire to connect with our text, and to commend to your meditation to-day.

I. We have here set forth the foundation and condition of all true work for God *in the Lord's heavenward look.*

The profound questions which are involved in the fact that, as man, Christ held communion with God in the exercise of faith and aspiration, the same in kind as ours, do not concern us here. I speak to those who believe that Jesus is for us the perfect example of complete manhood, and who therefore believe that He is "the leader of faith," the head of the long procession of those who in every age have trusted in God and been lightened. But, perhaps, though that conviction holds its place in our creeds, it has not been as completely incorporated with our thoughts as it should have been. There has, no doubt, been a tendency, operating in much of our evangelical teaching, and in the common stream of orthodox opinion, to except, half unconsciously, the exercises of the religious life from the sphere of Christ's example, and we need to be reminded that Scripture presents His vow, "I will put my trust in Him," as the crowning proof of His brotherhood, and that the prints of His kneeling limbs have left their impressions where we kneel before the throne. True, the relation of the Son to the Father involves more than communion—namely, unity. But if we follow the teaching of the Bible, we shall not presume that the latter excludes the former, but understand that the unity is the foundation of perfect communion, and the communion the manifestation, so far as it can be manifested, of the unspeakable unity. The solemn words which shine like stars—starlike in that their height above us shrinks their magnitude and dims their brightness, and in that they are points of radiance partially disclosing, and separated by, abysses of unlighted infinitude—tell us that in the order of eternity, before creatures were, there was communion, for "the Word was with God," and there was unity, for "the Word was God." And in the records of the life manifested on earth the consciousness of unity loftily utters itself in the unfathomable declaration, "I and my Father are one;" whilst the consciousness of communion, dependent like ours on harmony of will and true obedience, breathes peacefully in the witness which He leaves to Himself: "The Father has not left Me alone for I do always the things that please Him."

We are fully warranted, then, in supposing that that wistful gaze to heaven means, and may be taken to symbolize, our Lord's conscious direction of thought and spirit to God as He wrought His work of mercy. There are two distinctions to be noted between His communion with God and ours before we can apply the lesson to ourselves. His heavenward look was not the renewal of interrupted fellowship, but rather, as a man standing firmly on firm rock may yet lift his foot to plant it again where it was before, and settle himself in his attitude before he strikes with all his might; so we may say Christ fixes Himself where He always stood, and grasps anew the hand that He always held, before He does the deed of power. The communion that had never been broken was renewed; how much more the need that in *our* work for God the renewal of the—alas! too sadly sundered—fellowship should ever precede and always accompany our efforts! And again, Christ's fellowship was with the Father. Ours must be with the Father through the Son. The communion to which we are called is with Jesus Christ, in whom we find God.

The manner of that intercourse, and the various discipline of ourselves with a view to its perfecting, which Christian prudence prescribes, need not concern us here. As for the latter, let us not forget that a wholesome and wide-reaching self-denial cannot be dispensed with. Hands that are full of gilded toys and glass beads cannot grasp durable riches, and eyes that have been accustomed to glaring lights see only darkness when they look up to the violet heaven with all its stars. As to the former, every part of our nature above the simply animal is capable of God, and the communion ought to include our whole being.

Christ is truth for the understanding, authority for the

will, love for the heart, certainty for the hope, fruition for all the desires, and for the conscience at once cleansing and law. Fellowship with Him is no indolent passiveness, nor the luxurious exercise of certain emotions, but the contact of the whole nature with its sole adequate object and rightful Lord.

Such intercourse, brethren, lies at the foundation of all work for God. It is the condition of all our power. It is the measure of all our success. Without it we may seem to realize the externals of prosperity, but it will be all illusion. With it we may perchance seem to spend our strength for naught; but heaven has its surprises; and those who toiled, nor left their hold of their Lord in all their work, will have to say at last with wonder, as they see the results of their poor efforts, "Who hath begotten me these? behold, I was left alone; these, where had they been?"

Consider in few words the manifold ways in which the indispensable pre-requisite of all right effort for Christ may be shown to be communion with Christ.

The heavenward look is the renewal of our own vision of the calm verities in which we trust, the recourse for ourselves to the realities which we desire that others should see. And what is equal in persuasive power to the simple utterance of your own intense conviction? He only will infuse his own religion into other minds, whose religion is not a set of hard dogmas, but is fused by the heat of personal experience into a river of living fire. It will flow then, not otherwise. The only claim which the hearts of men will listen to, in those who would win them to spiritual beliefs, is that ancient one : " That which we have seen with our eyes, which we have looked upon, declare we unto you." Mightier than all arguments, than all " proofs of the truth of the Christian religion," and penetrating into a sphere deeper than that of the understanding, is the simple proclamation, "We have found the Messias." If we would give sight to the blind, we must ourselves be gazing into heaven. Only when we testify of that which we see, as one might who, standing in a beleaguered city, discerned on the horizon the filmy dust-cloud through which the spearheads of the deliverers flashed at intervals, shall we win any to gaze with us till they too behold and know themselves set free.

The heavenward look draws new strength from the source of all our might. In our work, dear brethren, contemplating as it ought to do exclusively spiritual results, what we do depends largely on what we are, and what we are depends on what we receive, and what we receive depends on the depth and constancy of our communion with God. "The help which is done upon earth He doeth it all Himself." We and our organisations are but the channels through which this might is poured; and if we choke the bed with turbid masses of drift and heavy rocks of earthly thoughts, or build from bank to bank thick dams of worldliness compact with slime of sin, how shall the full tide flow through us for the healing of the salt and barren places? Will it not leave its former course silted up with sand, and cut for itself new outlets, while the useless quays that once rang with busy life stand silent, and "the cities are solitary that were full of people"? We are

> "The trumpet at thy lips, the clarion
> Full of thy cry, sonorous with thy breath."

Let us see to it that by fellowship with Christ we keep the passage clear, and become recipients of the inspiration which shall thrill our else-silent spirits into the blast of loud alarum and the ringing proclamation of the true King.

The heavenward look will guard us from the temptations which surround all our service, and the distractions which lay waste our lives. It is habitual communion with Christ alone that will give the persistency that makes systematic, continuous efforts for Him possible, and yet will keep systematic work from degenerating, as it ever tends to do, into mechanical work. There is no greater virtue in irregular desultory service than in systematized labour. The one is not freer from besetting temptations than the other, only the temptations are of different sorts. Machinery saves manual toil, and multiplies force. But we may have too heavy machinery for what engineers call the boiler power,—too many wheels and shafts for the steam we have to drive them with. What we want is not less organisation, or other sorts of it, but more force. Any organisation will do if we have God's Spirit breathing through it. None will be better than so much old iron if we have not.

We are ever apt to trust to our work, to do it without a distinct recurrence at each moment to the principles on which it rests, and the motives by which it should be actuated,—to become so absorbed in details that we forget the purpose which alone gives them meaning, to over-estimate the external aspects of it, to lose sight of the solemn truths which make it so grand, and to think of it as common-place because it is common, as ordinary because it is familiar. And from these most real dangers, which beset us all, there is no refuge but the frequent, the habitual, gaze into the open heavens, which will show us again the realities of things, and bring to our spirits, dwarfed even by habits of goodness, the freshening of former motives by the vision of Jesus Christ.

Such constant communion will further surround us with an atmosphere through which none of the many influences which threaten our Christian life and our Christian work can penetrate. As the diver in his bell sits dry at the bottom of the sea, and draws a pure air from the free heavens far above him, and is parted from that murderous waste of green death that clings so closely round the translucent crystal walls which keep him safe; so we, enclosed in God, shall repel from ourselves all that would overflow to destroy us and our work, and may by His grace lay deeper than the waters some courses in the great building that shall one day rise, stately and many-mansioned, from out of the conquered waves. For ourselves, and for all that we do for Him, living communion with God is the means of power and peace, of security and success.

It was never more needful than now. Feverish activity rules in all spheres of life. The iron wheels of the car which bears the modern idol of material progress whirl fast, and crush remorselessly all who cannot keep up the pace. Christian effort is multiplied and systematized beyond all precedent. And all these things make calm fellowship with God hard to compass. The measure of the difficulty is the measure of the need. I, for my part, believe that there are few Christian duties more neglected than that of meditation, the very name of which has fallen of late into comparative disuse,—that augurs ill for the frequency of the thing. We are so busy thinking, discussing, defending, inquiring; or preaching, and teaching, and working, that we have no time and no leisure of heart for quiet contemplation, without which the exercise of the intellect upon Christ's truth will not feed, and busy activity in Christ's cause may starve the soul. There are few things which the Church of this day in all its parts needs more than to obey the invitation, "Come ye yourselves apart into a lonely place, and rest awhile."

Christ has set us the example. Let our prayers ascend as His did, and in our measure the answers which came to Him will not fail us. For us, too, "praying, the heavens" shall be "opened," and the peace-bringing spirit fall dove-like on our meek hearts. For us, too, when the shadow of our cross lies black and gaunt upon our paths, and our souls are troubled, communion with heaven will bring the assurance, audible to our ears at least, that God will glorify Himself even in us. If, after many a weary day, we seek to hold fellowship with God as He sought it on the Mount of Olives, or among the solitudes of the midnight hills, or out in the morning freshness of the silent wilderness, like Him we shall have men gathering around us to hear us speak when we come forth from the secret place of the Most High. If our prayer, like His, goes before our mighty deeds, the voice that first pierced the skies will penetrate the tomb, and make the dead stir in their grave-clothes. If our longing trustful look is turned to the heavens, we shall not speak in vain on earth when we say, " Be opened."

Brethren, we cannot do without the communion which our Master needed. Do we delight in what strengthened Him ? Does our work rest upon the basis of inward fellowship with God which underlay His ? Alas ! that our Pattern should be our Rebuke, and the readiest way to force home our faults on our consciences should be the contemplation of the life which we say that we try to copy !

II. We have here pity for the evils we would remove set forth by *the Lord's sigh.*

The frequency with which this Evangelist records our Lord's emotions on the sight of sin and sorrow has been often noticed. In his pages we read of Christ's grief at the hardness of men's hearts, of His marvelling because of their unbelief, of His being moved with compassion for an outcast leper and a hungry multitude, of His sighing deeply in His spirit when prejudiced hostility, assuming the appearance of candid inquiry, asked of Him a sign from heaven. All these instances of true human feeling, like His tears at the grave of Lazarus, and His weariness as He sat on the well, and His tired sleep in the stern of the little fishing-boat, and His hunger and His thirst, are very precious as aids in realizing His perfect manhood; but they have a worth beyond even that. They show us how the manifold ills and evils of man's fate and conduct appealed to the only pure heart that ever beat, and how quickly and warmly it, by reason of its purity, throbbed in sympathy with all the woe. One might have thought that in the present case the consciousness that His help was so near would have been sufficient to repress the sigh. One might have thought that the heavenward look would have stayed the tears. But neither the happiness of active beneficence, nor the knowledge of immediate cure, nor the glories above flooding His vision, could lift the burden from the labouring breast. And surely in this, too, we may discern a law for all our efforts, that their worth shall be in proportion to the expense of feeling at which they are done. They predict the harvests in Egypt by the height which the river marks on the gauge of the inundation. So many feet there represents so much fertility. Tell me the depth of a Christian man's compassion, and I will tell you the measure of his fruitfulness.

What was it that drew that sigh from the heart of Jesus? One poor man stood before him, by no means the most sorely afflicted of the many wretched ones whom He healed. But He saw in him more than a solitary instance of physical infirmities. Did there not roll darkly before His thoughts that whole weltering sea of sorrow that moans round the world, of which here is but one drop that He could dry up? Did there not rise black and solid against the clear blue to which He had been looking, the mass of man's sin, of which these bodily infirmities were but a poor symbol as well as a consequence! He saw as none but He could bear to see, the miserable realities of human life. His knowledge of all that man might be, of all that the most of men were becoming, His power of contemplating in one awful aggregate the entire sum of sorrows and sins, laid upon His heart a burden which none but He have ever endured. His communion with Heaven deepened the dark shadow on earth, and the eyes that looked up to God and saw Him, could not but see foulness where others suspected none, and murderous messengers of hell walking in darkness unpenetrated by mortal sight. And all that pain of clearer knowledge of the sorrowfulness of sorrow, and the sinfulness of sin, was laid upon a heart in which was no selfishness to blunt the sharp edge of the pain nor any sin to stagnate the pity that flowed from the wound. To Jesus Christ, life was a daily martyrdom before death had "made the sacrifice complete," and He bore our griefs, and carried our sorrows through many a weary hour before He "bare them in His own body on the tree." Therefore, " Bear ye one another's burden, and so fulfil the law" which Christ obeyed, becomes a command for all who would draw men to Him. And true sorrow, a sharp and real sense of pain, becomes indispensable as preparation for, and accompaniment to, our work.

Mark how in us, as in our Lord, the sigh of compassion is connected with the look to heaven. It follows upon that gaze. The evils are more real, more terrible, by their startling contrast with the unshadowed light which lives above cloudracks and mists. It is a sharp shock to turn from the free sweep of the heavens, starry and radiant, to the sights that meet us in "this dim spot which men call earth." Thus habitual communion with God is the root of the truest and purest compassion. It does not withdraw us from our fellow feeling with our brethren, it cultivates no isolation for undisturbed beholding of God. It at once supplies a standard by which to measure the greatness of man's godlessness, and therefore of his gloom, and a motive for laying the pain of these upon our hearts, as if they were our own. He has looked into the heavens to little purpose who has not learned how bad and how sad the world now is, and how God bends over it in pitying love.

And that same fellowship which will clear our eyes and soften our hearts, is also the one consolation which we have when our sense of all the ills that flesh is heir to becomes deep to near despair. When one thinks of the real facts of human life, and tries to conceive of the frightful meanness and passion and hate and wretchedness that has been howling and shrieking and gibbering and groaning through dreary millenniums, one's brain reels, and hope seems to be absurdity, and joy a sin against our fellows, as a feast would be in a house next door to where was a funeral. I do not wonder at settled sorrow falling upon men of vivid imagination, keen moral sense, and ordinary sensitiveness, when they brood long on the world as it is. But I do wonder at the superficial optimism which goes on with its little prophecies about human progress, and its rose-coloured pictures of human life, and sees nothing to strike it dumb for ever in men's writhing miseries, blank failures, and hopeless end. Ah! brethren, if it were not for the heavenward look, how could we bear the sight of earth! "We see not yet all things put under Him." No, God knows, far enough off from that. Man's folly, man's submission to the creatures he should rule, man's agonies, and man's transgression, are a grim contrast to the Psalmist's vision. If we had only earth to look to, despair of the race, expressed in settled melancholy apathy, or in fierce cynicism, were the wisest attitude. But there is more within our view than earth; "we see Jesus;" we look to the heaven, and as we behold the true man, we see more than ever, indeed, how far from that pattern we all are; but we can bear the thought of what men as yet have been, when we see that perfect example of what men shall be. The root and the consolation of our sorrow for men's evils is communion with God.

Let me remind you, too, that still more dangerous than the pity which is not based upon, and corrected by, the look to heaven, is the pity which does not issue in strenuous work. It is easy to excite people's emotions; but it is perilous for both the operator and the subject, unless they be excited through the understanding, and pass on the impulse to the will and the practical powers. The surest way to petrify a heart is to stimulate the feelings, and give them nothing to do. They will never recover their original elasticity if they have been wantonly drawn forth thus. Coldness, hypocrisy, spurious sentimentalism, and a whole train of affectations and falsehoods follow the steps of an emotional religion, which divorces itself from active work. Pity is meant to impel to help. Let us not be content with painting sad and true pictures of men's woes,—of the gloomy hopelessness of idolatry, for instance,—but let us remember that every time our compassion is stirred, and no action ensues, our hearts are in some measure indurated, and the sincerity of our religion in some degree impaired. The white-robed Pity is meant to guide the strong powers of practical help to their work. She is to them as eyes to go before them and point their tasks. They are to her as hands to execute her gentle will. Let us see to it that we rend them not apart; for idle pity is unblessed and fruitless as a sigh cast into the fragrant air, and unpitying work is more unblessed and fruitless still. Let us remember, too, that Christlike and indispensable as Pity is, she is second, and not first. Let us take heed that we preserve that order in our own minds, and in our endeavours to stimulate one another. For if we reverse it, we shall surely find the fountains of compassion drying up long before the wide stretches of thirsty land are watered, and the enterprises which we have sought to carry on by appealing to a secondary motive, languishing when there is most need for vigour. Here is the true sequence which must be observed in our missionary and evangelistic work, " Looking up to heaven He sighed."

Dear brethren! must we not all acknowledge woful failures in this regard? How much of our service, our giving, our preaching, our planning, has been carried on without one thought of the ills and godlessness we profess to be seeking to cure! If some angel's touch could annihilate all that portion of our activity, what gaps would be left in all our subscription lists, our sermons, and our labours both at home and abroad! Annihilate, do I say? It is done already. Such work *is* nothing, and comes to nothing. "Yea, it shall not be planted; yea, it shall not be sown; and He shall also blow upon it, and it shall wither."

The hindrances to such abiding consciousness of and pity for the world's woes run all down to the one tap-root of all sin, selfishness. The remedies run all up to the common form of all goodness, the self-absorbing communion with Jesus Christ. And besides that mother-tincture of everything wrong, subsidiary impediments may be found in the small amount of time and effort which any of us give to bring the facts of the world's condition vividly before our minds. The destruction of all emotion is the indolent acquiescence in general statements which we are too lazy or busy to break up into individual cases. To talk about hundreds of millions of idolaters leaves the heart untouched. But take one soul out of all that mass, and try to feel what his life is in its pitchy darkness, broken only by lurid lights of fear and sickly gleams of hope, in its passions ungoverned by love, its remorse uncalmed by pardon, its affections feeling like the tendrils of some climbing plant for the stay they cannot find, and in the cruel blackness that swallows it up irrevocable at last. Follow him from the childhood that knows no discipline to the grave that knows no waking, and will not the solitary instance come nearer our hearts than the millions? But however that may be, the sluggishness of our imaginations, the very familiarity with the awful facts, our own feeble hold on Christ, our absorption in personal interests, the incompleteness and desultoriness of our communion with our Lord, do all concur with our natural selfishness to make a sadly large proportion of our apparent labours for God and men utterly cold and unfeeling, and therefore utterly worthless. Has the benighted world ever caused us as much pain as some trivial pecuniary loss has done? Have we ever felt the smart of the gaping wounds through which our brothers' blood is pouring forth as much as we do the tiniest scratch on our own fingers? Does it sound to us like exaggerated rhetoric when a prophet breaks out, "Oh that my head were waters, and mine eyes a fountain of tears, that I might weep night and day!" or when an apostle in calmer tones declares, "I have great heaviness and continual sorrow of heart"? Some seeds are put to steep and swell in water, that they may be tested before sowing. The seed which we sow will not germinate unless it be saturated with our tears. And yet the sorrow must be blended with joy; for it is glad labour which is ordinarily productive labour—just as the growing time is the changeful April, and one knows not whether the promise of harvest is most sure in the clouds that drop fatness, or in the sunshine that makes their depths throb with whitest light, and touches the moist-springing blades into emeralds and diamonds. The gladness comes from the heavenward look, the pain is breathed in the deep-drawn sigh; both must be united in us if we would "approve ourselves as the servants of God—as sorrowful, yet always rejoicing."

III. We have here loving contact with those whom we would help set forth in *the Lord's touch*.

The reasons for the variety observable in Christ's method of communicating supernatural blessing were, probably, too closely connected with unrecorded differences in the spiritual conditions of the recipients to be distinctly traceable by us. But though we cannot tell why a particular method was employed in a given case, why now a word, and now a symbolic action, now the touch of His hand, and now the hem of His garment, appeared to be the vehicles of His power we can discern the significance of these divers ways, and learn great lessons from them all.

His touch was sometimes obviously the result of what one may venture to call instinctive tenderness, as when He lifted the little children in His arms and laid His hands upon their heads. It was, I suppose, always the spontaneous expression of love and compassion, even when it was something more.

The touch of His hand on the ghastly glossiness of the leper's skin was, no doubt, His assertion of priestly functions, and of elevation above all laws of defilement; but what was it to the poor outcast, who for years had never felt the warm contact of flesh and blood? It always indicated that He Himself was the source of healing and life. It always expressed His identification of Himself with sorrow and sickness. So that it is in principle analogous to, and may be taken as illustrative of, that transcendent act whereby He became flesh, and dwelt among us. Indeed, the very word by which our Lord's taking the blind man by the hand is described in the chapter following our text, is that employed in the Epistle to the Hebrews when, dealing with the true brotherhood of Jesus, the writer says, " He took not hold of angels, but of the seed of Abraham He taketh hold." Christ's touch is His willing contact with man's infirmities and sins, that He may strengthen and hallow.

And the lesson is one of universal application. Wherever men would help their fellows, this is a prime requisite, that the would-be helper should come down to the level of those whom he desires to aid. If we wish to teach, we must stoop to think the scholar's thoughts. The master who has forgotten his boyhood will have poor success. If we would lead to purer emotions, we must try to enter into the lower feelings which we labour to elevate. It is of no use to stand at the mouth of the alleys we wish to cleanse, with our skirts daintily gathered about us, and smelling-bottle in hand, to preach homilies on the virtues of cleanliness. We must go in among the filth, and handle it, if we want to have it cleared away. The degraded must feel that we do not shrink from them, or we shall do them no good. The leper, shunned by all, and ashamed of himself because everybody loathes him, hungers in his hovel for the grasp of a hand that does not care for defilement, if it can bring cleansing. Even in regard to common material helps the principle holds good. We are too apt to cast our doles to the poor like the bones to a dog, and then to wonder at what we are pleased to think men's ingratitude. A benefit may be so conferred as to hurt more than a blow; and we cannot be surprised if so-called charity which is given with contempt and a sense of superiority, should be received with a scowl, and chafe a man's spirit like a fetter. Such gifts bless neither him who gives nor him who takes. We must put our hearts into them, if we would win hearts by them. We must be ready, like our Master, to take blind beggars by the hand, if we would bless or help them. The despair and opprobrium of our modern civilization, the gulf growing wider and deeper between Dives and Lazarus, between Belgravia and Whitechapel, the mournful failure of legalized help, and of delegated efforts to bridge it over, the darkening ignorance, the animal sensuousness, the utter heathenism that lives in every town of England, within a stone's throw of Christian houses, and near enough to hear the sound of public worship, will yield to nothing but that sadly forgotten law which enjoins personal contact with the sinful and the suffering, as one chief condition of rasing them from the black mire in which they welter.

But the same law has its special application in regard to the enterprise which summons us together to-day.

It defines the spirit in which Christian men should proclaim the Gospel. The effect of much well-meant Christian effort is simply to irritate. People are very quick to catch delicate intonations which reveal a secret sense, "how much better, wiser, more devout I am than these people!" and wherever a trace of that appears in our work, the good of it is apt to be marred. We all know how hackneyed the charge of spiritual pride and Pharisaic self-complacency is, and, thank God, how unjust it often is. But averse as men may be to the truths which humble, and willing as they may be to assume that the very effort to present these to others on our parts implies a claim which mortifies, we may at least learn from the threadbare calumny, what strikes men about our position, and what rouses their antagonism to us. It is allowable to be taught by our enemies, especially when it is such a lesson as this, that we must carefully divest our evangelistic work of apparent pretensions to superiority, and take our stand by the side of those to whom we speak. We cannot lecture men into the love of Christ. We can but win them to it by showing Christ's love to them; and not the least important element in that process is the exhibition of our own love. We have a Gospel to speak of which the very heart is, that the Son of God stooped to become one with the lowliest and most sinful; and how can that Gospel be spoken with power unless we, too, stoop like Him?

We have to echo the invitation, "Learn of me, for I am lowly in heart;" and how can such divine words flow from lips into which like grace has not been poured? Our theme is a Saviour who shrunk from no sinner, who gladly consorted with publicans and harlots, who laid His hand on pollution, and His heart, full of God and of love, on hearts reeking with sin, and how can our message correspond with our theme if, even in delivering it, we are saying to ourselves, "The Temple of the Lord are we: this people which knoweth not the law is cursed"? Let us beware of the very real danger which besets us in this matter, and earnestly seek to make ourselves one with those whom we would gather into Christ, by actual familiarity with their condition, and by identification of ourselves in feeling with them, after the example of that greatest of Christian teachers who became "all things to all men, that by all means he might gain some;" after the higher example, which Paul followed, of that dear Lord who, being highest, descended to the lowest, and in the days of his humiliation was not content with speaking words of power from afar, nor abhorred the contact of mortality and disease and loathsome corruption; but laid His hands upon death, and it lived; upon sickness, and it was whole; on rotting leprosy, and it was sweet as the flesh of a little child.

The same principle might be further applied to our Christian work, as affecting the form in which we should present the truth. The sympathetic identification of ourselves with those to whom we try to carry the Gospel will certainly make us wise to know how to shape our message. Seeing with their eyes, we shall be able to graduate the light. Thinking their thoughts, and having in some measure succeeded, by force of sheer community of feeling, in having as it were got inside their minds, we shall unconsciously, and without effort, be led to such aspects of Christ's all-comprehensive truth as they most need. There will be no shooting over people's heads, if we love them well enough to understand them. There will be no toothless generalities, when our interest in men keeps their actual condition and temptations clear before us. There will be no flinging fossil doctrines at them from a height, as if Christ's blessed Gospel were, in another than the literal sense, "a stone of offence," if we have taken our place on their level. And without such sympathy, these and a thousand other weaknesses and faults will certainly vitiate much of our Christian effort.

Let me not be misunderstood when I speak of adapting our presentation of the Gospel to the wants of those to whom we carry it. That general statement may express the plainest dictate of Christian prudence or the most dangerous practical error. The one great truth of the Gospel wants no adaptation by our handling to any soul of man. It is fitted for all, and demands only plain, loving, earnest statement. There must be no tampering with central verities, nor any diplomatic reserve on the plea of consulting the needs of the men whom we address. Every sinful spirit needs the simple Gospel of salvation by Jesus Christ more than it needs anything else. Nor does adaptation mean deferential stretching a point to meet man's wishes in our presentation of the truth. Their wishes have to be contravened, that their wants may be met. The truth which a man or a generation requires most is the truth which he or they like least; and the true Christian teacher's adaptation of his message will consist quite as much in opposing the desires and contradicting the lies, as in seeking to meet the felt wants of the world. Nauseous medicines or sharp lancets are adapted to the sick man, quite as truly as pleasant food and soothing ointment.

But remembering all this, we still have a wide field for the operation of practical wisdom and loving common sense, in determining the form of our message and the manner of our action. And not the least important of qualifications for solving the problems connected therewith is cheerful identification of ourselves with the thoughts and feelings of those whom we would fain draw to the love of God. Such contact with men will win their hearts, as well as soften ours. It will make them willing to hear, as well as us wise to speak. It will enrich our own lives with wide experience and multiplied interests. It will lift us out of the enchanted circle which selfishness draws around us. It will silently proclaim the Lord from whom we have learnt it. The clasp of the hand will be precious, even apart from the virtue that may flow from it, and may be to many a soul burdened with a consciousness of corruption, the dawning of belief in a love that does not shrink even from its foulness. Let us preach the Lord's touch as the source of all cleansing. Let us imitate it in our lives, that "if any will not hear the word, they may without the word be won."

IV. We have here the true healing power and the consciousness of wielding it set forth in *the Lord's authoritative word.*

All the rest of His action was either the spontaneous expression of His true participation in human sorrow, or a merciful veiling of His glory that sense-bound eyes might see it the better. But the word was the utterance of His will, and that was omnipotent. The hand laid on the sick, the blind or the deaf was not even the channel of His power. The bare putting forth of His energy was all-sufficient. In these we see the loving, pitying man. In this blazes forth, yet more loving, yet more compassionate, the effulgence of manifest God. Therefore so often do we read the very syllables with which His "voice then shook the earth," vibrating through all the framework of the material universe. Therefore do the Gospels bid us listen when He rebukes the fever, and it departs; when He says to the demons, "Go," and they go; when one word louder in its human articulation than the howling wind hushes the surges; when "Talitha cumi" brings back the fair young spirit from dreary wanderings among the shades of death. Therefore was it a height of faith not found in Israel when the Gentile soldier, whose training had taught him the power of absolute authority, as heathenism had driven him to long for a man who should speak with the imperial sway of a god, recognised in His voice an all-commanding power. From of old, the very signature of divinity has been declared to be, "He spake, and it was done;" and He, the breath of whose lips could set in motion material changes, is that Eternal Word, by whom all things were made.

What unlimited consciousness of sovereign dominion sounds in that imperative from His autocratic lips! It is spoken in deaf ears, but He knows that it will be heard. He speaks as the fontal source, not as the recipient channel of healing. He anticipates no delay, no resistance. There is neither effort nor uncertainty in the curt command. He is sure that He has power, and He is sure that the power is His own.

There is no analogy here between us and Him. Alone, fronting the whole race of man, He stands—utterer of a word which none can say after Him, possessor of unshared might, "and of His fulness do all we receive." But even from that Divine authority and solitary sovereign consciousness we may gather lessons not altogether aside from the purpose of our meeting here to-day. Of His fulness we *have* received, and the power of the word on His lips may teach us that of His word even on ours, as the victorious certainty with which He spake His will of healing may remind us of the confidence with which it becomes us to proclaim His name.

His will was almighty then. It is less mighty or less loving now? Does it not gather all the world in the sweep of its mighty purpose of mercy? His voice pierced then into the dull cold ear of death, and has it become weaker since? His word spoken *by* Him was enough to banish the foul spirits that run riot, swine-like, in the garden of God in man's soul, trampling down and eating up its flowers and fruitage; is the word spoken *of* Him less potent to cast them out? Were not all the mighty deeds which He wrought by the breath of His lips on men's bodies prophecies of the yet mightier which His Will of love, and the utterance of that Will by stammering lips, may work on men's souls. Let us not in our faintheartedness number up our failures, the deaf that will not hear, the dumb that will not speak His praise, nor unbelievingly say Christ's own word was mighty, but the word concerning Christ is weak on our lips. Not so; our lips are unclean, and our words are weak, but His word—the utterance of His loving Will that men should be saved—is what it always was and always will be. We have it, brethren, to proclaim. Did our Master countenance the faithless contrast between the living force of His word when He dwelt on earth, and the feebleness of it as He speaks through his servant? If He did, what did He mean when He said, "He that believeth on me, the works that I do shall he do also, and greater works than these shall he do, because I go unto the Father"?

And the reflection of Christ's triumphant consciousness of power should irradiate our spirits as we do His work, like the gleam from gazing on God's glory which shone on the lawgiver's stern face while he talked with men. We have everything to assure us that we cannot fail. The manifest fitness of the Gospel to be the food of all souls; the victories of eighteen centuries, which at least prove that all conditions of society, all classes of civilization, all varieties of race, all peculiarities of individual temperament, all depths of degradation and distances of alienation, are capable of receiving the word, which, like corn, can grow in every latitude, and though it be an exotic everywhere, can everywhere be naturalized; the firm promises of unchanging faithfulness, the universal aspect of Christ's work, the prevalence of His continual intercession, the indwelling of His abiding Spirit, and, not least, the unerring voice of our own experience of the power of the truth to bless and save,—all these are ours. In view of these, what have we to doubt? Unwavering confidence is the only attitude that corresponds to such certainties. We have a rock to build on; let us build on it *with* rock. Putting fear and hesitancy far from us, let us gird ourselves with the joyful strength of assured victory, striking as those who know that conquest is bound to their standard, and through all the dust of the field seeing the fair vision of the final triumph. The work is done before we begin it. "It is finished," was a clarion blast proclaiming that' all was won when all seemed lost. Weary ages have indeed to roll away before the great voice from heaven shall declare "It is done;" but all that lies between the two is but the gradual unfolding and appropriating of the results which are already secured. The strong man is bound; what remains is but the spoiling of his house. The head is bruised; what remains is but the dying lashing of the snaky horror's powerless coils. "I send you to reap that whereon ye bestowed no labour." The tearful sowing in the stormy winter's day has been done by the Son of man. For us there remains the joy of harvest— hot and hard work, indeed, but gladsome too.

Then, however languor and despondency may sometimes tempt us, thinking of slow advancement, and dying men who fade from the place of the living before the gradual light has reached their eyes, our duty is plain— to be sure that the word we carry cannot fail. You remember the old story, how when Jerusalem was in her hour of direst need, and the army of Babylon lay around her battered walls, the prophet was bid to buy " the field that is in Anathoth, in the country of Benjamin," for a sign that the transient fury of the invader would be beaten back, that Israel might again dwell safely in the land. So with us, the hosts of our king's enemies come up like a river strong and mighty; but all this world, held though it be by the usurper, is still " Thy land, O Immanuel," and over it all Thy peaceful rule shall be established !

Many things in this day tempt the witnesses of God to speak with doubting voice. Angry opposition, contemptuous denial, complacent assumption that a belief in old-fashioned evangelical truth is, *ipso facto*, a proof of mental weakness, abound. Let them not rob us of our confidence. Shame on us if we let ourselves be frightened from it by a sarcasm or a laugh ! Do you fall back on all these grounds for assured reliance to which I have referred, and make the good old answer, yours, " Why, herein is a marvellous thing, that ye know not whence He is, and yet—He hath opened mine eyes ? "

Trust the word you have to speak. Speak it and work for its diffusion as if you did trust it. Do not preach it as if it were a notion of your own. In so far as it is, it will share the fate of all human conceptions of Divine realities —" will have its day, and cease to be." Do not speak it as if it were some new nostrum for curing the ills of humanity, which might answer or might not. Speak it as if it were what it is—the word of God, which liveth and abideth for ever. Speak it as if you were what you are, neither its inventors nor its discoverers, but only its messengers, who have but to "preach the preaching which He bids" you. And to all the wide-spread questionings of this day, filmy and air-filling as the gossamers of an autumn evening, to all the theories of speculation, and all the panaceas of unbelieving philanthropy, present the solid certainties of our inmost experience, the yet more solid certainty of that all-loving name and all-sufficient work on which these repose. "*We know* that we are of God, and the whole world lieth in wickedness. And we know that the Son of God is come." Then our proclamation, "This is the true God and eternal life," will not be in vain; and our loving entreaty, "Keep yourselves from idols," will be heard and yielded to in many a land.

The sum of the whole matter is briefly this. The root of all our efficiency in this great task to which we, unworthy, have been called, is in fellowship with Jesus Christ. "The branch cannot bear fruit of itself; without me ye are nothing." Living near Him, and growing like Him by gazing upon him, His beauty shall pass into our faces, His tender pity into our hearts, his loving identification of Himself with men's pains and sins will fashion our lives; and the word which He spoke with authority and assured confidence will be strong when we speak it with like calmness of certain victory. If the Church of Christ will but draw close to its Lord till the fulness of His life and the gentleness of His pity flow into heart and limbs, she will then be able to breathe the life which she has received into the prostrate bulk of a dead world. Only she must do, as the meekest of the prophets did in a like miracle, she must not shrink from the touch of the cold clay, nor the odour of incipient corruption, but, lip to lip, and heart to heart, must lay herself upon the dead, and he will live.

The pattern for our work, dear brethren, is before us in the Lord's look, His sigh, His touch, His word. If we take Him for the example, and Him for the motive, Him for the strength, Him for the theme, Him for the reward of our service, we may venture to look to Him as the prophecy of our success, and to be sure that when our own faint hearts or an unbelieving world question the wisdom of our enterprise, or the worth of our efforts, we may answer as He did, "Go and show again those things which ye do hear and see; the blind receive their sight, and the lame walk, the lepers are cleansed, and the deaf hear, the dead are raised up, and the poor have the Gospel preached unto them."

SERMON III.

THE AWAKING OF ZION.*

ISAIAH li. 9.

Awake, awake, put on strength, O arm of the Lord; awake, as in the ancient days, in the generations of old.

ISAIAH lii. 1.

Awake, awake; put on thy strength, O Zion.

BOTH these verses are, I think, to be regarded as spoken by one voice, that of the servant of the Lord. His majestic figure, wrapped in a light veil of obscurity, fills the eye in all these latter prophecies of Isaiah. It is sometimes clothed with divine power, sometimes girded with the towel of human weakness, sometimes appearing like the collective Israel, sometimes plainly a single person.

We have no difficulty in solving the riddle of the prophecy by the light of history. Our faith knows One who unites these diverse characteristics, being God and man, being the Saviour of the body, which is part of Himself and instinct with His life. If we may suppose that He speaks in both verses, then, in the one, as priest

* Preached before the Baptist Missionary Society.

and intercessor, He lifts the prayers of earth to heaven in His own holy hands—and in the other, as messenger and Word of God, He brings the answer and command of heaven to earth on His own authoritative lips—thus setting forth the deep mystery of His person and double office as mediator between man and God. But even if we set aside that thought, the correspondence and relation of the two passages remain the same. In any case they are intentionally parallel in form and connected in substance. The latter is the answer to the former. The cry of Zion is responded to by the call of God. The awaking of the arm of the Lord is followed by the awaking of the Church. He puts on strength in clothing us with His might, which becomes ours.

The mere juxtaposition of these verses suggests the point of view from which I wish to treat them on this occasion. I hope that the thoughts to which they lead may help to further that quickened earnestness and expectancy of blessing, without which Christian work is a toil and a failure.

We have here a common principle underlying both the clauses of our text, to which I must first briefly ask your attention, namely—

I. *The occurrence in the Church's history of successive periods of energy and of languor.*

It is freely admitted that such alternation is not the highest ideal of growth, either in the individual or in the community. Our Lord's own parables set forth a more excellent way—the way of uninterrupted increase, whereof the type is the springing corn, which puts forth "first the blade, then the ear, after that the full corn in the ear," and passes through all the stages from the tender green spikelets that gleam over the fields in the spring-tide to the yellow abundance of autumn, in one unbroken season of genial months. So would our growth be best, healthiest, happiest. So *might* our growth be, if the mysterious life in the seed met no checks. But, as a matter of fact, the Church has not thus grown. Rather at the best, its emblem is to be looked for, not in corn, but in the forest tree—the very rings in whose trunk tell of recurring seasons when the sap has risen at the call of spring, and sunk again before the frowns of winter. I have not to do now with the causes of this. These will fall to be considered presently. Nor am I saying that such a manner of growth is inevitable. I am only pointing out a fact, capable of easy verification and familiar to us all. Our years have had summer and winter. The evening and the morning have completed all the days since the first.

We all know it only too well. In our own hearts we have known such times, when some cold clinging mist wrapped us round and hid all the heaven of God's love and the starry lights of His truth; when the visible was the only real, and He seemed far away and shadowy; when there was neither confidence in our belief, nor heat in our love, nor enthusiasm in our service; when the shackles of conventionalism bound our souls, and the fetters of the frost imprisoned all their springs. And we have seen a like palsy smite whole regions and ages of the Church of God, so that even the sensation of impotence was dead like all the rest, and the very tradition of spiritual power had faded away. I need not point to the signal historical examples of such times in the past. Remember England a hundred years ago—but what need to travel so far. May I venture to draw my example from nearer home, and ask, have we not been in such an epoch? I beseech you, think whether the power which the Gospel preached by us wields on ourselves, on our churches, on the world, is what Christ meant it and fitted to exercise. Why, if we hold our own in respect to the material growth of our population, it is as much as we do. Where is the joyful buoyancy and expansive power with which the Gospel burst into the world? It looks like some stream that leaps from the hills, and at first hurries from cliff to cliff full of light and music, but flows slower and more sluggish as it advances, and at last almost stagnates in its flat marshes. Here we are with all our machinery, our culture, money, organizations—and the net result of it all at the year's end is but a poor handful of ears. " Ye sow much and bring home little." Well may we take up the wail of the old Psalm, "We see not our signs. There is no more any prophet; neither is there any among us that knoweth how long—arise, O Lord, plead Thine own cause."

If then there be such recurring seasons of languor, they must either go on deepening till sleep becomes death, or they must be broken by a new outburst of vigorous life. It would be better if we did not need the latter. The uninterrupted growth would be best; but if that has not been, then the ending of winter by spring, and the suppling of the dry branches, and the resumption of the arrested growth is the next best, and the only alternative to rotting away.

And it is by such times that the Kingdom of Christ always has grown. Its history has been one of successive impulses gradually exhausted, as by friction and gravity, and mercifully repeated just at the moment when it was ceasing to advance and had begun to slide downwards. And in such a manner of progress, the Church's history has been in full analogy with that of all other forms of human association and activity. It is not in religion alone that there are "revivals," to use the word of which some people have such a dread. You see analogous phenomena in the field of literature, arts, social and political life. In them all there come times of awakened interest in long-neglected principles. Truths which for many years had been left to burn unheeded, save by a faithful few watchers of the beacon, flame up all at once the guiding pillars of a nation's march, and a whole people strike their tents and follow where they lead. A mysterious quickening thrills through society. A contagion of enthusiasm spreads like fire, fusing all hearts in one. The air is electric with change. Some great advance is secured at a stride; and before and after that supreme effort are years of comparative quiescence; on the farther side perhaps of preparation, on the nearer side possibly of fruition and exhaustion—but slow and languid compared with the joyous energy of that moment. One day may be as a thousand years in the history of a people, and a nation may be born in a day.

So also is the history of the Church. And thank God it is so, for if it had not been for the dawning of these times of refreshing, the steady operation of the Church's worldliness would have killed it long ago.

Surely, dear brethren, we ought to desire such a merciful interruption of the sad continuity of our languor and decay. The surest sign of its coming would be a widespread desire and expectation of its coming, joined with a penitent consciousness of our heavy and sinful slumber. For we believe in a God who never sends mouths but He sends meat to fill them, and in whose merciful providence every desire is a prophecy of its own fruition. This attitude of quickened anticipation, diffusing itself silently through many hearts, is like the light air that springs up before sunrise, or like the solemn hush that holds all nature listening before the voice of the Lord in the thunder.

And another sign of its approach is the extremity of the need. "If winter come, can spring be far behind?" For He who is always with Zion strikes in with His help when the want is at its highest. His "right early" is often the latest moment before destruction. And though we are all apt to exaggerate the need of the moment and the severity of *our* conflict, it certainly does seem that, whether we regard the languor of the Church or the strength of our adversaries, succour delayed a little longer would be succour too late. "The tumult of those that rise up against Thee increaseth continually. It is time for Thee to work."

The juxtaposition of these passages suggests for us—

II. *The twofold explanation of these variations.*

That bold metaphor of God sleeping and waking is often found in Scripture, and generally expresses the contrast between the long years of patient forbearance, during which evil things and evil men go on their rebellious road unchecked but by Love, and the dread moment when some throne of iniquity, some Babylon cemented by blood, is smitten to the dust. Such is the original application of the expression here. But the contrast may fairly be widened beyond that specific form of it, and taken to express any apparent variations in the forth-putting of His power The prophet carefully avoids seeming to suggest that there are changes in God Himself. It is not He but His arm, that is to say, His active energy, that is invoked to awake. The captive Church prays that the dormant might which could so easily shiver Her prison-house would flame forth into action.

We may, then, see here implied the cause of these alternations of which we have been speaking on its Divine side, and then, in the corresponding verse addressed to the Church, the cause on the human side.

As to the former. It is true that God's arm slumbers, and is not clothed with power. There are, as a fact, apparent variations in the energy with which He works in the Church and in the world. And they are real variations, not merely apparent. But we have to distinguish between the power, and what Paul calls "the might of the power." The one is final, constant, unchangeable. It does not necessarily follow that the other is. The rate of operation, so to speak, and the amount of energy actually brought into play may vary, though the force remains the same.

It is clear from experience that there are these variations; and the only question with which we are concerned is, are they mere arbitrary jets and spurts of a Divine power, sometimes gushing out in full flood, sometimes trickling in painful drops, at the unknown will of the unseen hand which controls the flow? Is the "law of the Spirit of Life" at all revealed to us; or are the reasons occult, if there be any reasons at all other than a mere will that it shall be so? Surely, whilst we never can know all the depths of His counsels and all the solemn concourse of reasons which, to speak in man's language, determine the energy of His manifested power, He has left us in no doubt that this is the weightiest part of the law which it follows—the might with which God works on the world through His Church varies according to the Church's receptiveness and faithfulness.

Our second text tells us that if God's arm seems to slumber, and really does so, it is because Zion sleeps. In itself that immortal energy knows no variableness. "He fainteth not, neither is weary." "The Lord's arm is not shortened that He cannot save." "He that keepeth Israel shall neither slumber nor sleep." But He works through us; and we have the solemn and awful power of checking the might which would flow through us; of restraining and limiting the Holy One of Israel. It avails nothing that the ocean stretches shoreless to the horizon; a jar can only hold a jarful. The receiver's capacity determines the amount received, and the

F

receiver's desire determines his capacity. The law has ever been, "according to your faith be it unto you." God gives as much as we will, as much as we can hold, as much as we use, and far more than we deserve. As long as we will bring our vessels the golden oil will flow, and after the last is filled, there yet remains more that we might have had, if we could have held it, and might have held if we would. "Ye are not straitened in Me, ye are straitened in yourselves."

So, dear brethren, if we have to lament times of torpor and small success, let us be honest with ourselves, and recognise that all the blame lies with us. If God's arm seems to slumber it is because we are asleep. His power is invariable, and the gospel which is committed to our trust has lost none of its ancient power, whatsoever men may say. If there be variations, they cannot be traced to the Divine element in the Church, which in itself is constant, but altogether to the human, which shifts and fluctuates, as we only too sadly know. The light in the beacon tower is steady, and the same; but the beam it throws across the waters sometimes fades to a speck, and sometimes flames out clear and far across the heaving waves, according to the position of the glasses and shades around it. The sun pours out heat as profusely and as long on the 22nd of December as on Midsummer-day, and all the difference between the frost and darkness and glowing brightness and flowering life, is simply owing to the earth's place in its orbit and angle at which the unalterable rays fall upon it. The changes are in the terrestrial sphere; the heavenly is fixed for ever the same.

May I not venture to point an earnest and solemn appeal with these truths? Has there not been poured over us the spirit of slumber? Does it not seem as if an opium sky had been raining soporifics on our heads? We have had but little experience of the might of God amongst us of late years, and we need not wonder at it. There is no occasion to look far for the reason. You have only to regard the low ebb to which religious life has been reduced amongst us to have it all and more than all accounted for. I fully admit that there has been plenty of activity, perhaps more than the amount of real life warrants, not a little liberality, and many virtues. But how languid and torpid the true Christian life has been! how little enthusiasm! how little depth of communion with God! how little unworldly elevation of soul! how little glow of love! An improvement in social position and circumstances, a freer blending with the national life, a full share of civic and political honours, a higher culture in our pulpits, fine chapels, and applauding congregations—are but poor substitutes for what many of us have lost in racing after them. We have the departed prophets' mantle, the outward resemblance to the fathers who have gone, but their fiery zeal has passed to heaven with them; and softer, weaker men, we stand timidly on the river's brink, invoking the Lord God of Elijah, and too often the flood that obeyed them has no ear for our feebler voice.

I speak to you, brethren, who are in some sort representatives of our churches throughout the land, and you can tell whether my words are on the whole true or overstrained. We who labour in our great cities, what say we? If one of the number may speak for the rest, we have to acknowledge that commercial prosperity and business cares, the eagerness after pleasure and the exigencies of political strife, diffused doubt and wide-spread artistic and literary culture, are eating the very life out of thousands in our churches, and lowering their fervour till, like molten iron cooling in the air, what was once all glowing with ruddy heat is crusted over with foul black scoriæ ever encroaching on the tiny central warmth. You from our rural churches, what say you? Have you not to speak of deepening torpor settling down on quiet corners, of the passing away of grey heads leaving no successors, of growing difficulties and lessened power to meet them, that make you sometimes all but despair?

I am not flinging indiscriminate censures. I know there are lights as well as shades in the picture. I am not flinging censures at all. But I am giving voice to the confessions of many hearts, that our consciousness of our blame may be deepened, and we may hasten back to that dear Lord whom we have left to serve alone, as His first disciples left Him once to agonise alone under the gnarled olives in Gethsemane, while they lay sleeping in the moonlight. Listen to His gentle rebuke, full of pain and surprised love, "What, could ye not watch with Me one hour?" Listen to His warning call, loving as the kiss with which a mother wakes her child, "Arise, let us be going"—and let us shake the spirit of slumber from our limbs, and serve Him as those unsleeping spirits do, who rest not day nor night from vision, and work, and praise.

III. *The beginning of all awaking is the Church's earnest cry to God.*

It is with us as with infants, the first sign of whose awaking is a cry. The mother's quick ear hears it through all the household noises, and the poor little troubled life that woke to a scared consciousness of loneliness and darkness, is taken up into tender arms, and comforted and calmed. So, when we dimly perceive how torpid we have been, and start to find that we have lost our Father's hand, the first instinct of that waking, which must needs be partly painful, is to call to Him, whose ear hears our feeble cry amid the sound of praise like the voice of many waters, that billows round His throne, and whose folding arms keep us as one whom his mother comforteth. The beginning of all true awaking must needs be prayer.

For every such stirring of quickened religious life must needs have in it bitter penitence and pain at the discovery flashed upon us of the wretched deadness of our past—and, as we gaze like some wakened sleep-walker into the abyss where another step might have smashed us to atoms, a shuddering terror seizes us that must cry, "Hold Thou me up, and I shall be safe." And every such stirring of quickened life will have in it, too, desire for more of His grace, and confidence in His sure bestowal of it, which cannot but breathe itself in prayer.

Nor is Zion's cry to God only the *beginning* and *sign*

of all true awaking; it is also the condition and indispensable precursor of all perfecting of recovery from spiritual languor.

I have already pointed out the relation between the waking of God and the waking of His Church, from which that necessarily follows. God's power flows into our weakness in the measure and on condition of our desires. We are sometimes told that we err in praying for the outpouring of His Holy Spirit, because ever since Pentecost His Church has had the gift. The objection alleges an unquestioned fact, but the conclusion drawn from it rests on an altogether false conception of the manner of that abiding gift. The Spirit of God, and the power which comes from Him, are not given as a purse of money might be put into a man's hand once and for all, but they are given in a continuous impartation and communication and are received and retained moment by moment, according to the energy of our desires and the faithfulness of our use. As well might we say, Why should I ask for natural life, I received it half a century ago? Yes, and at every moment of that half-century I have continued to live, not because of a past gift, but because at each moment God is breathing into my nostrils the breath of life. So is it with the life which comes from His Spirit. It is maintained by constant efflux from the fountain of Life, by constant impartation of His quickening breath. And as He must continually impart, so must we continually receive, else we perish. Therefore, brethren, the first step towards awaking, and the condition of all true revival in our own souls and in our churches, is this earnest cry, "Awake, awake, put on strength, O arm of the Lord."

Thank God for the outpouring of a long unwonted spirit of prayer in many places. It is like the melting of the snows in the high Alps, at once the sign of spring and the cause of filling the stony river beds with flashing waters, that bring verdure and growth wherever they come. The winter has been long and hard. We have all to confess that we have been restraining prayer before God. Our work has been done with but little sense of our need of His blessing, with but little ardour of desire for His power. We have prayed lazily, scarcely believing that answers would come; we have not watched for the reply, but have been like some heartless marksman who draws his bow and does not care to look whether his arrow strikes the target. These mechanical words, these conventional petitions, these syllables winged by no real desire, inspired by no faith, these expressions of devotion, far too wide for their real contents, which rattle in them like a dried kernel in a nut, are these prayers? Is there any wonder that they have been dispersed in empty air, and that we have been put to shame before our enemies? Brethren in the ministry, do we need to be surprised at our fruitless work, when we think of our prayerless studies and of our faithless prayers? Let *us* remember that solemn word, "The pastors have become brutish, and have not sought the Lord, therefore they shall not prosper, and all their flocks shall be scattered." And let us all, brethren, betake ourselves, with penitence and lowly consciousness of our sore need, to prayer, earnest and importunate, believing and persistent, like this heaven-piercing cry which captive Israel sent up from her weary bondage.

Look at the passionate earnestness of it—expressed in the short, sharp cry, thrice repeated, as from one in mortal need; and see to it that our drowsy prayers be like it. Look at the grand confidence with which it founds itself on the past, recounting the mighty deeds of ancient days, and looking back, not for despair, but for joyful confidence on the generations of old; and let our faint-hearted faith be quickened by the example, to expect great things of God. The age of miracles is not gone. The mightiest manifestations of God's power in the spread of the Gospel in the past remain as patterns for His future. We have not to look back as from low-lying plains to the blue peaks on the horizon, across which the Church's path once lay, and sigh over changed conditions of the journey. The highest water-mark that the river in flood has ever reached will be reached and overpassed again, though to-day the waters may seem to have hopelessly subsided. Greater triumphs and deliverances shall crown the future than have signalised the past. Let our faithful prayer base itself on the prophecies of history and on the unchangeableness of God.

Think, brethren, of the prayers of Christ. Even He, whose spirit needed not to be purged from stains or calmed from excitement, who was ever in His Father's house whilst He was about His Father's business, blending in one, action and contemplation, had need to pray. The moments of His life thus marked are very significant. When He began His ministry, the close of the first day of toil and wonders saw Him, far from gratitude and from want, in a desert place in prayer. When He would send forth His apostles, that great step in advance, in which lay the germ of so much, was preceded by solitary prayer. When the fickle crowd desired to make Him the centre of political revolution, He passed from their hands and beat back that earliest attempt to secularize His work, by prayer. When the seventy brought the first tidings of mighty works done in His name, He showed us how to repel the dangers of success, in that He thanked the Lord of heaven and earth who had revealed these things to babes. When He stood by the grave of Lazarus, the voice that waked the dead was preceded by the voice of prayer, as it ever must be. When He had said all that He could say to His disciples, He crowned all with His wonderful prayer for Himself, for them, and for us all. When the horror of great darkness fell upon His soul, the growing agony is marked by His more fervent prayer, so wondrously compact of shrinking fear and filial submission. When the cross was hid in the darkness of eclipse, the only words from the gloom were words of prayer. When, Godlike, He dismissed His spirit, manlike He commended it to His Father, and sent the prayer from His dying lips before Him to herald His coming into the unseen world.

One instance remains, even more to our present purpose than all these—" It came to pass, that Jesus also being baptized, and praying, the heaven was opened, and the Holy Ghost descended in a bodily shape like a dove upon Him." Mighty mystery! In Him, too, the Son's desire is connected with the Father's gift, and the unmeasured possession of the Spirit was an answer to *His* prayer.

Then, brethren, let us lift our voices and our hearts. That which ascends as prayer descends as blessing, like the vapour that is drawn up by the kiss of the sun to fall in freshening rain. "Call upon Me, and I will answer thee, and show thee great and hidden things which thou knowest not."

IV. *The answering call from God to Zion.*

Our truest prayers are but the echo of God's promises. God's best answers are the echo of our prayers. As in two mirrors set opposite to each other, the same image is repeated over and over again, the reflection of a reflection, so here, within the prayer, gleams an earlier promise, within the answer is mirrored the prayer.

And in that reverberation, and giving back to us of our petition transformed into a command, we are not to see a dismissal of it as if we had misapprehended our true want. It is not tantamount to, Do not ask me to put on my strength, but array yourselves in your own. The very opposite interpretation is the true one. The prayer of Zion is heard and answered. God awakes, and clothes Himself with might. Then, as some warrior king, himself roused from sleep and girded with flashing steel, bids the clarion sound through the grey twilight to summon the prostrate ranks that lie round his tent, so the sign of God's awaking and the first act of His conquering might is this trumpet call—" The night is far spent, the day is at hand "—" put off the works of darkness," the night gear that was fit for slumber—"and put on the armour of light," the mail of purity that gleams and glitters even in the dim dawn. God's awaking is our awaking. He puts on strength by making us strong; for His arm works through us, clothing itself, as it were, with our arm of flesh, and perfecting itself even in our weakness.

Nor is it to be forgotten that this, like all God's commands, carries in its heart a promise. That earliest word of God's is the type of all His latter behests—" Let there be light "—and the mighty syllables were *creative* and self-fulfilling. So ever with Him, to enjoin and to bestow are one and the same, and His command is His conveyance of power. He rouses us by His summons, He clothes us with power in the very act of bidding us put it on. So He answers the Church's cry by stimulating us to quickened zeal, and making us more conscious of, and confident in, the strength which, in answer to our cry, He pours into our limbs.

But the main point which I would insist on for the few moments that remain to me is the practical discipline which this Divine summons requires from us.

And first, let us remember that the chief means of quickened life and strength is deepened communion with Christ.

As we have been saying, our strength is ours by continual derivation from Him. It has no independent existence, any more than a sunbeam could have, severed from the sun. It is ours only in the sense that it flows through us, as a river through the land which it enriches. It is His whilst it is ours, it is ours when we know it to be His. Then, clearly, the first thing to do must be to keep the channels free by which it flows into our souls, and to maintain the connection with the great Fountain Head unimpaired. Put a dam across the stream, and the effect will be like the drying up of Jordan before Israel. "The waters that were above rose up upon an heap, and the waters that were beneath failed and were cut off," and the foul oozy bed was disclosed to the light of day. It is only by constant contact with Christ that we have any strength to put on.

That communion with Him is no mere idle or passive thing, but the active employment of our whole nature with His truth, and with Him whom the truth reveals. The understanding must be brought into contact with the principles of His word, the heart must touch and beat against His heart, the will meekly lay the hand in His, the conscience ever draw at once its anodyne and its stimulus from His sacrifice, the passions know His finger on the reins, and follow led in the silken leash of love. Then, if I may so say, the prophet's miracle will be repeated in nobler form, and from Himself, the Life, thus touching all our being, life will flow into our deadness. "He put his mouth upon his mouth, and his eyes upon his eyes, and his hands upon his hands, and he stretched himself upon the child, and the flesh of the child waxed warm."

So, dear brethren, all our practical duty is summed up in that one word, the measure of our obedience to which is the measure of all our strength—"Abide in Me, and I in you. As the branch cannot bear fruit of itself, except it abide in the vine, no more can ye, except ye abide in Me."

Again, this summons calls us to the faithful use of the power which, on condition of that communion, we have.

There is no doubt a temptation, in all times like the present, to look for some new and extraordinary forms of blessing, and to substitute such expectation for present work with our present strength. There is nothing new to look for. There is no need to wait for anything more than we possess. Remember the homely old proverb, "You never know what you can do till you try," and though we are conscious of much unfitness, and would sometimes gladly wait till our limbs are stronger, let us brace ourselves for the work, assured that in it strength will be given to us that equals our desire. There is a wonderful power in honest work to develop latent energies and reveal a man to himself. I suppose, in most cases, nobody is half so much surprised at a great man's greatest deeds as he is himself. They say that there is dormant electric energy enough to make a thunderstorm in a few raindrops, and there is dormant spiritual force enough in the weakest of us to flash into beneficent light, and peal notes of awaking into many a deaf ear. The effort to serve your Lord will *reveal* to you strength that you know not.

And it will *increase* the strength which it brings into play, as the used muscles grow like whipcord, and the practised fingers become deft at their task, and every faculty employed is increased, and every gift wrapped in a napkin melts like ice folded in a cloth, according to that solemn law, "To him that hath shall be given, and from him that hath not shall be taken away even that which he hath."

Then be sure that to its last particle you are using the strength you have, ere you complain of not having enough for your tasks. Take heed of the vagrant expectations that wait for they know not what, and the apparent prayers that are really substitutes for possible service. "Why liest thou on thy face? Speak unto the children of Israel that they go forward."

The Church's resources are sufficient for the Church's work, if the resources were used. We are tempted to doubt it, by reason of our experience of failure and our consciousness of weakness. We are more than ever tempted to doubt it to-day, when so many wise men are telling us that our Christ is a phantom, our God a stream of tendency, our Gospel a decaying error, our hope for the world a dream, and our work in the world done. We stand before our Master with doubtful hearts, and, as we look along the ranks sitting there on the green grass, and then at the poor provisions which make all our store, we are sometimes tempted almost to think that He errs when He says with that strange calmness of His, "They need not depart, give ye them to eat."

But go out among the crowds and give confidently what you have, and you will find that you have enough and to spare. If ever our stores seem inadequate, it is because they are reckoned up by sense, which takes cognizance of the visible, instead of faith which beholds the real. Certainly five loaves and two small fishes are not enough, but are not five loaves and two small fishes and a miracle-working hand behind them, enough ? It is poor calculation that leaves out Christ from the estimate of our forces. The weakest man and Jesus to back him are more than all antagonism, more than sufficient for all duty. Be not seduced into doubt of your power, or of your success, by others' sneers, or by your own faint-heartedness. The confidence of ability is ability. "Screw your courage to the sticking place, and you will *not* fail"—and see to it that you use the resources you have, as good stewards of the manifold grace of God. "Put on *thy* strength, O Zion."

So, dear brethren, to gather all up in a sentence, let us confidently look for times of blessing, penitently acknowledge that our own faithlessness has hindered the arm of the Lord, earnestly beseech Him to come in His rejoicing strength, and, drawing ever fresh power from constant communion with our dear Lord, use it to its last drop for Him.

Then, like the mortal leader of Israel, as he pondered doubtingly with sunken eyes on the hard task before his untrained host, we shall look up and be aware of the presence of the sworded angel, the immortal Captain of the host of the Lord standing ready to save, " putting on righteousness as a breastplate, an helmet of salvation on His head, and clad with zeal as a cloak." From his lips, which give what they command, comes the call, " Take unto you the whole armour of God, that ye may be able to withstand in the evil day, and having done all, to stand." Hearkening to His voice, the city of the strong ones shall be made an heap before our wondering ranks, and the land open to our conquering march.

Wheresoever *we* lift up the cry, "Awake, awake, put on strength, O arm of the Lord," there follows, swift as the thunderclap on the lightning flash, the rousing summons, "Awake, awake, put on thy strength, O Zion; put on thy beautiful garments, O Jerusalem!" Wheresoever it is obeyed there will follow in due time the joyful chorus, as in this context, "Sing together, ye waste places of Jerusalem; the Lord hath made bare His holy arm in the eyes of all the nations, and all the ends of the earth have seen the salvation of our God."

SERMON IV.

"TIME FOR THEE TO WORK."*

Psalm cxix. 126-8.

It is time for Thee, Lord, to work: for they have made void Thy Law. Therefore I love Thy commandments above gold; yea, above fine gold. Therefore I esteem all Thy precepts concerning all things to be right; and I hate every false way.

IF much that we hear be true, a society to circulate Bibles is a most irrational and wasteful expenditure of energy and money. We cannot ignore the extent and severity of the opposition to the very idea of Revelation even if we would; we should not if we could. We are told with some exaggeration—the wish being father to the thought —that the educated mind of the country has broken with Christianity,—a statement which is equally remarkable for its accuracy and for its modesty. But it has a basis of truth in the widespread disbelief diffused through the literary and so-called cultivated classes. There is no need to spend your time in referring at length to facts which are only too familiar to most of us. Every sphere of knowledge, every form of literature, is enlisted

* Preached before the National Bible Society of Scotland.

in the crusade. Periodicals that lie on all our tables, works of imagination that your daughters read, newspapers that go everywhere, are full of it. Poetry, forgetting her lineage and her sweetness, strains *her* voice in rhapsodies of hostility. Science, leaping the hedge beyond which *she* at all events is a trespasser,—or, in finer language, " prolonging its gaze backwards beyond the boundary of experimental evidence,"—or, in still plainer terms, *guessing*, —affirms that she discerns in matter the promise and potency of every form of life; or presently, in a devouter mood, looking on the budding glories of the spring, declines to *profess* the creed of Atheism. Learned criticism demonstrates the impossibility of supernatural religion. The leader of an influential school leaves behind him a voice hollow and sad, as from the great darkness, in which we seem to hear the echoes of a life baffled in the attempt to harmonize the logical and the spiritual elements of a large soul : " There may be a God. The evidence is insufficient for proof. It only amounts to one of the lower degrees of probability. He may have given a revelation of His will. There are grounds sufficient to remove all antecedent improbability. The question is wholly one of evidence ; but the evidence required has not been, and cannot be, forthcoming. There is room to hope for a future life, but there is no assurance whatever. Therefore cultivate in the region of the imagination merely those hopes which can never become certainties, for they are infinitely precious to mankind."

Ah, brethren, do we not hear in these dreary words the cry of the immortal hunger of the soul for God, for the living God? The concessions they make to Christian apologists are noteworthy, but that unconscious confession of need is the most noteworthy. Surely, as the eye prophesies light, so the longing of the soul and the capacity for forming such ideals is the token that He is for whom heart and flesh do thus yearn. And how blessed is it to set over against these dreary ghosts that call themselves hopes, and that pathetic vain attempt to find refuge in the green fields of the imagination from the choking dust of the logical arena, the old faithful words: "This is the record, that God hath given to us eternal life, and that this life is in His Son"!

But my object in referring to these forms of opinion was merely to prepare the way for my subsequent observations; I have no intention of dealing with any of them by way of criticism or refutation. This is not the place nor the audience, nor am I the person, for that task. But I have thought that it might not be inappropriate to this occasion if I were to ask you to consider with me, from these words, the attitude of mind and heart to God's word which becomes Christian in times of opposition.

The Psalmist was surrounded, as would appear, by widespread defection from God's law. But instead of trembling as if the sun were about to expire, he turns himself to God, and in fellowship with Him sees in all the antagonism but the premonition that He is about to act for the vindication of His own work. That confidence finds expression in the sublime invocation of our text. Then, with another movement of thought, the contemplation of the departures makes him tighten his own hold on the law of the Lord, and the contempt of the gainsayers quicken his love: " *Therefore* I love," etc. And, as must needs be the case, that love is the measure of his abhorrence of the opposite: and because God's commandments are so dear to him, therefore he recoils with healthy hatred from false ways. So, I think, we have a fourfold representation here of our true attitude in the face of existing antagonism,—calm confidence in God's work for His law; earnest prayer, which secures the forth-putting of the divine energy: an increased intensity of cleaving to the word; and a decisive opposition to the ways which make it void.

I ask your attention to some remarks on each of these in their order. So, then, we have—

I. *Calm confidence that times of antagonism evoke God's work for His word.*

Now I daresay that some of you feel that is not the first thought that should be excited by the opposition around us. "We have no sort of doubt," you may say, "that God will take care of His own word, if there be such a thing; but the question that presses is, Have we it in this book? Answer that for us, and we will thank you; but platitudes about God watching over His truth are naught. The first thing to do is to meet these arguments and establish the origin of Scripture. Then it will follow of itself that it will not perish."

But I take leave to think we, as Christians, are not bound to revise the foundation belief of our lives at the call of every new antagonist. Life is too short for that.

There is too much work waiting, to suspend our activity till we have answered each denier. We do not hold our faith in the word of God, as the winners at a match do their cups and belts, on condition of wrestling for them with any challenger. It is a perfectly legitimate position to say, We hold a ground of certitude, from which none of this strife of tongues is able to dislodge us. We have heard Him ourselves, and know that this is the Christ. The Scriptures which we have received, not without knowledge of the grounds on which controversialists defend them, have proved themselves to us by their own witness. The light is its own proof. We have the experience of Christ and His law. He has saved our souls; He has changed our lives. We know in whom we have believed; and we are neither irrational nor obstinate when we avow that we will not pretend to suspend these convictions on the issue of any debate. We decline to dig up the piles of the bridge that carries us over the abyss because voices tell us that is rotten. It is shorter and perfectly reasonable to answer: "Rotten, did you say? Well, we have tried it, and it bears;" which, being translated into less simple language, is just the assertion of certitude built on facts and experience which leaves no place for doubt. All the opposition will be broken into spray against that rock bulwark: "Thy words were found, and I did eat them, and they are the joy and rejoicing of my heart."

So I venture to think that, speaking to Christian men and women, I have a right to speak on the basis of our common belief, and to encourage them to cherish it notwithstanding gainsayers. I am not counselling stolid indifference to the course of modern thought, nor desertion of the duty of defence. We are not to say, "God will interfere; I need do nothing." But the task of controversy is not for all Christians, nor the duty of following the flow of opinion. There is plenty of more profitable work than that for most of us. The temper which our text enjoins *is* for us all; and this calm confidence, that at the right time God will work for His word, is its first element.

This confidence rests upon our belief in a divine Providence that governs the world, and on the observed laws of its working. It is ever His method to send His succour *after* the evil has been developed, and *before* it has triumphed. Had it come sooner, the priceless benefits of struggle, the new perceptions won in controversy of the many-sided meaning and value of His truth, the vigour from conflict, the wholesome sense of our weakness, had all been lost. Had it come later, it had come too late. So He times His help, in order that we may derive the greatest possible benefit from both the trial and the aid. We have all been dealt with so in our personal histories, whereof the very motto might be, "When I said my foot slippeth, Thy mercy, O Lord, held me up." The same law works on the wider platform. The enemy shall be allowed to pass through the breadth of the land, to spread dread and sorrow through village and hamlet, to draw his ranks round Jerusalem, as a man closes his hand on some insect he would crush. *To-morrow*, and the assault will be made; but *to-night* "the angel of the Lord went forth and smote the camp; and when they arose in the morning," expecting to hear the wild war-cry of the conquerors as they stormed across the undefended walls, "they were all dead corpses." Then, as it would appear, a psalmist, moved by that mighty victory, cast it into words, which remain for all generations the law of the divine aid, and imply all that I am urging now: "The Lord is in the midst of her, she shall not be moved; the Lord shall help her at the dawning of the morning." True, we are no judges of the time. Our impatience is ever outrunning His calm deliberation. An illusion besets us all that *our* conflicts with unbelief are the severest the world has ever seen; and there is a great deal of exaggeration on both sides at present as to the real extent and importance of existing antagonism to God's revelation. A widespread literature provides so many—I would not say empty—spaces for any voice to reverberate in, that both the shouters and the listeners are apt to fancy the assailants are an army, when they are only a handful, armed mainly with trumpets and pitchers. There have been darker days of antagonism than these. He that believeth shall not make haste. This confidence in the punctual wisdom of His working involves the other belief, that if He does not "work," it is because the time is not yet ripe; the negations and contradictions have still an office to fulfil, and no hurt that cannot be repaired has been done to the faith of the Church or the power of the word.

Nor can we forecast the manner of His working. He can call forth from the solitary sheepfolds the defenders of His word, as has ever been His wont, raising the man when the hour had come, even as He sent His Son in the fulness of time. He can lead science on to deeper truth; He can quicken His Church into new life; He can guide the spirit of an age. We believe that the history of the world is the unfolding of His will, and the course of opinion guided in its channel by the Voice which the depths have obeyed from of old. Therefore we wait for His working, expecting no miracle, prescribing no time, hurried by no impatience, avoiding no task of defence or confession; but knowing that, unhasting and unresting He will arise when the storm is loudest, and somehow will say, " Peace! be still. " Then they who had not cast away their confidence for any fashion of unbelief that passeth away will rejoice as they sing, " Lo! this is our God; we have waited for Him, and He will save us."

This confidence is confirmed by the *history of all the past assaults* on Scripture.

The whole history of the origin, collection, preservation, transmission, diffusion, and present influence of the Bible involves so much that is surprising and unique, as to amount to at least a strong presumption of a divine care. Among all the remarkable things about the Book, nothing is more remarkable than that there it is, after all that has happened. When we think of the gaps and losses in ancient literature, and the long stormy centuries that lie between us and its earlier pages, we can faintly estimate the chances against their preservation. It is strange that the Jewish race should have so jealously preserved books which certainly did not flatter national pride, which put a mortifying explanation on national disasters, which painted them and their fathers in dark colours, which proclaimed truths they never loved, and breathed a spirit they never caught. It is stranger still, that in the long years of dispersion the very vices and limitations of the people subserved the same end, and that stiff pedantry and laborious trifling—the poorest form of intellectual activity—should have guarded the letter of the word, as the coral insects painfully build up their walls round some fair island of the Southern Sea. When one thinks of the great gulf of language between the Old and New Testaments, of the variety of authors, periods, subjects, literary form, the animosities of Christian and Jew, it *is* strange that we have the Book here *one*, and that all these parts should blend into unity, unless the source and theme were one, and One Hand had shaped each, and cared for the gathering together of all.

It has been demonstrated over and over again to have no pretensions to a divine revelation; and yet here it is, believed by millions, and rooted so firmly in European language and thought, that no revolution short of a return to barbarism can abolish it. It has been proved to be a careless, unauthenticated collection of works of different periods, styles, and schools of thought, having no unity but what is given by the bookbinder: and lo! here it is still, not disintegrated, much less dissolved. Each age brings its own destructive criticism to play on it, confessing thereby that its predecessors have effected nothing; for, as the Bible says about sacrifices, so we may say about assaults on Scripture, "If they had done their work, would they not have ceased to be offered?" And the effect of the heaviest artillery that can be brought into position is as transient as the boom of their report and the puff of their smoke. Why, who knows anything about the world's wonders of books that a hundred years ago made good men's hearts tremble for the ark of God? You may find them in dusty rows on the top shelves of great libraries. But if their names had not occurred in the pages of Christian apologists, flies in amber, nobody in this generation would ever have heard of them. And still more conspicuously is it so with earlier examples of the same kind. Their work is as hopelessly dead as they. And the Book seems none the worse for all the shot—like the rock that a ship fired at all night, taking it for an enemy, and could not provoke to answer nor succeed in sinking. Surely some dim suspicion of the hopelessness of the attempt might creep into the hearts of men who know what *has* been. Surely the signal failure and swift fading away of all former efforts to dethrone the Bible might lead to the question, "Does it not lay its deep foundations in the heart of man and the purpose of God, too deep to be reached by the short tools of mere criticism, too massive to be overthrown by all the weight of materialistic science?" It is with the Bible as it was with the apostle, on whose hand, as he crouched over the newly-lit flame, the viper fastened, "and he shook off the beast into the fire, and felt no harm." The barbarous people, who changed their minds after they had looked a great while and saw no harm come to him, were not altogether wrong, and might teach a lesson to some modern wise men, if, among the other facts which they deal with, they would try to estimate this fact of the continued existence and influence of Scripture, and the failure thus far of all attempts to shake its throne or break the sweet influences of its bands.

Brethren, we, at all events, should learn the lesson of historical experience. The gospel, and the Book which is its record, have met with eager, eloquent, learned antagonists before to-day, and they have passed. Little more than a generation has sufficed to sweep them to oblivion. So it will be again. The forms of opinion, the tendencies of thought, which now seem to some of its enemies so certain to conquer, will follow these forgotten precursors into the dim land. May we not see them—these ancient discrowned kings that ruled over men and rebelled against Christ, these beliefs that no man now believes—rising from their shadowy thrones in the underworld to meet the now living and ruling unbelief, when it, too, shall have gone down to them? "All they shall speak and say unto thee, Art thou also become weak as we? art thou become like unto us?" Yes, each in its turn "becomes but a noise" when he "passes the time appointed"—the time when God arises to do His act and vindicate His word.

We have here, secondly, *Earnest prayer which brings that divine energy.*

The confidence that God *will* work underlies and gives energy to the prayer that God *would* work. The belief that a given thing is in the line of the divine purpose is not a reason for saying, "We need not pray; God means to do it," but is a reason for saying on the contrary, "God means to do it; let us pray for it." And this prayer, based upon the confidence that it is His will, is the best service that any of us can render to the gospel in troublous times.

I shall have a word to say presently on the *sort* of outflow of the divine energy which we should principally expect and desire; but let me first remind you, very briefly, how the prayers of Christian men do condition—I had almost said regulate—that outflow.

I need not put this matter on its abstract and metaphysical side. Two facts are enough for my present purpose —one, a truth of faith, that the actual power wherewith God works for His word remains ever the same; one, a truth of observation and experience, that there are variations in the intensity of its operations and effects in the world. Wherefore? Surely because of the variations in the human recipients and organs of the power. Here at one end is the great fountain, ever brimming. Draw from it ever so much, it sinks not one hair's-breadth in its pure basin. Here, on the other side, is an intermittent flow, sometimes in scanty driblets, sometimes in painful drops, sometimes more full and free on the pastures of the wilderness. Wherefore these jerks and spasms? It must be something stopping the pipe. Yes, of course. God's might is ever the same, but our capacity of receiving and transmitting that might varies, and with it varies the energy with which that unchanging power is exerted in the world. Our faith, our earnestness of desire, our ardour and confidence of prayer, our faithfulness of stewardship and strenuousness of use, measure the amount of the unmeasured grace which we can receive. So long as our vessels are brought, the golden oil does not cease to flow. When they are full, it stays. The principle of the variation in actual manifestation of the unvarying might of God is found in the Lord's words: "According to your faith be it unto you." So, then, we may expect periods of quickened energy in the forth-putting of the divine power. And these will correspond to, and be consequent on, the faithful prayers of Christian men. See to it, brethren, that you keep the channels clear, that the flow may continue full and increase. Let no mud and ooze of the world, no big blocks of sin nor subtler accumulations of small negligences, choke them again. Above all, by simple, earnest prayer keep your hearts, as it were wide open to the Sun, and His light will shine on you, and His grace fructify through you, and His Spirit will work in you mightily.

The tenor of these remarks presupposes a point on which I wish to make one or two observations now, viz. that the manner of the divine working which we should most earnestly desire in a time of diffused unbelief is the elevation of Christian souls to a higher spiritual life.

I do not wish to exclude other things, but I believe that the true antidote to a widespread scepticism is a quickened Church. We may indeed desire that in other ways the enemy should be met. We ought to pray that God would work by sending forth defenders of the truth, by establishing His Church in the firm faith of disputed verities, and by all the multitude of ways in which He can sway the thoughts and tendencies of men. But I honestly confess that I, for my part, attach but secondary importance to controversial defences of the faith. No doubt they have their office: they may confirm a waverer; they may establish a believer; they may show onlookers that the Christian position is tenable; they may, in some rare cases of transcendent power, prevent a heresy from spreading and from descending to another generation. But oftenest they are barren of result; and where they do their work, it is not to be forgotten there may remain as true a making void of God's law by an evil heart of unbelief as by an understanding cased in the mail of denial. You may hammer ice on an anvil, or bray it in a mortar. What then? It is pounded ice still, except for the little portion melted by heat of percussion, and it will soon all congeal again. Melt it in the sun, and it flows down in sweet water, which mirrors that light which loosed its bonds of cold. So hammer away at unbelief with your logical sledge-hammers, and you will change its shape, perhaps; but it is none the less unbelief because you have ground it to powder. It is a mightier agent that must melt it,—the fire of God's love, brought close by a will itself ablaze with the sacred glow.

Therefore, while giving all due honour to other forms of Christian opposition to the prevailing unbelief, I urge the cultivation of a quickened spiritual life as by far the most potent. Does not history bear me out in that view? What, for instance, was it that finished the infidelity of last century? Whether had Butler's " Analogy " or Charles

Wesley's hymns, Paley's "Evidences" or Whitefield's sermons, most to do with it? A languid Church breeds unbelief as surely as a decaying oak fungus. In a condition of depressed vitality, the seeds of disease, which a full vigour would shake off, are fatal. Raise the temperature, and you kill the insect germs. A warmer tone of spiritual life would change the atmosphere which unbelief needs for its growth. It belongs to the fauna of the glacial epoch, and when the rigours of that wintry time begin to melt, and warmer days to set in, the creatures of the ice have to retreat to arctic wildernesses, and leave a land no longer suited for their life. A diffused unbelief, such as we see around us to-day, does not really arise from the logical basis on which it seems to repose. It comes from something much deeper,—a certain habit and set of mind which gives these arguments their force. For want of a better name, we call it the spirit of the age. It is the result of very subtle and complicated forces, which I do not pretend to analyze. It spreads through society, and forms the congenial soil in which these seeds of evil, as we believe them to be, take root. Does anybody suppose that the growth of popular unbelief is owing to the logical force of certain arguments? It is in the air; a wave of it is passing over us. We are in a condition in which it becomes epidemic. That is a doctrine which one influential school of modern disbelievers, at all events, cannot but admit. What then? Why, this—that to change the opinions you must change the atmosphere; or, in other words, the true antagonist of a diffused scepticism is a quickened Christian life.

Brethren, if we had been what we ought, would such an environment have ever been possible as that which produces this modern unbelief? Even now, depend upon it, we shall do more for Christ by catching and exhibiting more of His spirit than by many arguments—more by words of prayer to God than by words of reasoning to men. A higher tone of spiritual life would prove that the gospel was mighty to mould and ennoble character. If our own souls were gleaming with the glory of God, men would believe that we had met more than the shadow of our own personality in the secret place. If the fire of faith were bright in us, it would communicate itself to others, for nothing is so contagious as earnestness. If we believed, and therefore spoke, the accent of conviction in our tones would carry them deep into some hearts. If we would trust Christ's cross to stand firm without our stays, and, arguing less about it, would seldomer try to *prop* it, and oftener to *point* to it, it would draw men to it. When the power and reality of Scripture as the revelation of God are questioned, the best answer in the long-run will be a Church which can adduce itself as the witness, and can say to the gainsayers: "Why, herein is a marvellous thing, that ye know not from whence He is, and yet He hath opened mine eyes." Brethren, do you see to it that your life be thus a witness that you have heard His voice; and make it your contribution to the warfare of this day, that if you do not bear a weapon, you lift your hands and heart to God. Moses on the mount helped the struggling ranks below in their hand-to-hand combat with Amalek. Hezekiah's prayer, when he spread the letter of the invader before the Lord, was more to the purpose than all his munitions of war. Let your voice rise to heaven like a fountain. Blessings will fall on earth. "Arise, O Lord, plead Thine own cause. The tumult of those that rise up against Thee increaseth continually."

III. We have here, thirdly, as the fitting attitude in times of widespread unbelief, *a love to God's word made more fervid by antagonism.*

There may be a question what reason for the Psalmist's love is pointed at in this "therefore." We shall hardly be satisfied with the slovenly and not very reverent explanation, that the word is introduced, without any particular meaning, because it begins with the initial letter proper to this section; nor does it seem enough to suppose a mere general reference to the excellences of the law of the Lord, which are the theme of the whole psalm. Such an interpretation blunts the sharp edge of the thought, and has nothing in its favour but the general want of connection between the separate verses. There are, however, one or two other instances where a thought is pursued through more than one verse, and the usual mere juxtaposition gives place to an interlocking, so that the construction is not unexampled. It is most natural to take the plain meaning of the words, and to suppose that when the Psalmist said, " They have made void Thy law, therefore I love Thy commandments," he meant, " The prevailing opposition is the reason why I, for my part, grasp Thy law more strongly." The hostility of others evokes my warmer love. The thought, so understood, is definite, true, and important, and so I venture to construe it, and enforce it as containing a lesson for the day.

And here I would first observe, that I desire not to be understood as urging the substitution of feeling for reason, nor as trying to enlist passion in a crusade against the opponent's logic. Still less do I desire to counsel the exaggeration of opinions because they are denied—that besetting danger of all controversy.

But, surely, the emotions have a place and an office, if not indeed in the search for, and the submission to, the truth of God, yet in the defence and adherence to that truth when found. The heart may not be the organ for the investigation and apprehension of truth, though it has a part to play even there; but the tenacity with which I cleave to it, when apprehended, is far more an affair of the will than of the understanding—it is the heart's love steadying the mind, and holding it fixed to the rock. And love has a place in the defence of the truth. It gives weight to blows, and wings to the arrows. It makes arguments to be wrought in fire rather than in frost. It lights the enthusiasm which cannot despair, the diligence that will not weary, the fervour that often goes farther to sway other minds than the sharpest dialectics of a passionless understanding. There *are* causes in which an unimpassioned advocacy is worse than silence; and this is one of them. The word of the living God, which has saved our souls and brought to us all that makes our natures rich and strong, and all that peoples the great darkness with fair hopes solid as certainties, demands and deserves fervour in its soldiers, and loyal love in its subjects.

And while it is weakness to over-emphasise our beliefs *merely* because they are denied, and one of the saddest issues of controversy, that both sides are apt to be hurried into exaggerated statements which calmer thoughts would repudiate; on the other hand, there *is* a legitimate prominence which ought to be given to a truth *precisely* because it is denied. The time to underline and accentuate strongly our convictions is, when society is slipping away from them, provided it be done without petulance, passion, or the falsehood of extremes.

If ever there was a period when such general considerations as these had a practical application, this is the time. Would that all such as my voice reaches now would take these grand words for theirs: " They make void Thy law, therefore I love Thy commandments above gold; yea, above fine gold!"

Such increase of affection because of gainsayers is the *natural instinct of loyal and chivalrous love.* If your mother's name were defiled, would not your heart bound to her defence? When a prince is a dethroned exile, his throne is fixed deeper in the hearts of his adherents " though his back be at the wall" and common souls become heroes because their devotion has been heightened to sublimity of self-sacrifice by a nation's rebellion. And when so many voices are proclaiming that God has never spoken to men, that our thoughts of His Book are dreams, and its long empire over men's spirits a waning tyranny, does cool indifference become us? Will not fervour be sobriety, and the glowing emotion of our whole nature our reasonable service?

Such increase of affection because of gainsayers is the *fitting end and main blessing* of the controversy which is being waged. We never fully hold our treasures till we have grasped them hard, lest they should be plucked from us. No truth is established till it has been denied and has survived. Antagonism to the word of God should have, and will have, to those who use it rightly, a blessing in its train, in bringing out yet more of the preciousness and manyfoldness, the all-sufficiency and the universality of the Book. "The more 'tis shook, the more it shines." The fiercer the blast, the firmer our confidence in the inexpugnable solidity of that tower of strength that stands four square to every wind that blows. "The word of the Lord is tried, therefore Thy servant loveth it."

Such increase of attachment to the word of God because of gainsayers, is *the instinct of self-preservation.* The sight of so many making void the law makes a man bethink himself of what his own standing is. We, as they, are the children of the age. The tendencies to which they have yielded operate on us, too, and our only strength is, "Hold Thou me up, and I shall be safe." The present condition of opinion remands us all to our foundations, and should teach us that nothing but firm adherence to God revealed in His word, and to the word which reveals God, will prevent us, too, from drifting away to shoreless, solitary seas of doubt, barren as the foam, and changeful as the crumbling, restless wave.

Such strength of affection in the presence of diffused doubt is not to be won without an effort. All our Churches afford us but too many examples of men and women who have lost the warmth of their first love, if not their love itself, for no better reason than because so many others have lost it. The effect of popular unbelief stretches far beyond those who are directly affected by its arguments, or avowedly adopt its conclusions. It is hard to hold by a creed which so many influential voices tell you it is a sign of folly, and being behind the age to believe. The consciousness that Christian truth is denied, makes some of you falter in its profession, and fancy that it is less certain simply because it is gainsaid. The mist wraps you in its folds, and it is difficult to keep warm in it, or to believe that love and sunshine are above it all the same. " Because iniquity shall abound, the love of many shall wax cold."

Therefore, brethren, do you consciously endeavour that the tempest shall make you tighten your hold on Christ and His word. He appeals to us, too, with that most pathetic question, in which yearning for our love and sorrow over the departed disciples blend so wondrously, as if He cast Himself on our loyalty: " Will ye also go away?" Let us answer, not with the self-confidence that was so signally put to shame: "Though all should forsake Thee, yet will not I"; but with the resolve that draws its firmness from His fulness and from our knowledge of the power of His truth: "Lord, to whom shall we go? Thou hast the words of eternal life."

IV. And, lastly, we have here, as the final trait in the temper which becomes such times, *healthy opposition to the ways which make void the word of the Lord.*

That is the Psalmist's last movement of feeling, and you see that it comes second, not first, in the order of his emotions. It is the consequence of his love, the recoil of his heart from the practices and theories which contradicted God's law.

Now, far be it from me to say a word which should fan the embers of the *odium theologicum* into a blaze against either men or opinions. But there is a truth involved which seems to be in danger of being forgotten at present, and that to the detriment of large interests as well as of the forgetters. The correlative of a hearty love for any principle or belief is—we may as well use the obnoxious word—a healthy hatred for its denial and contradiction. They are but two aspects of one thing, like that pillar of old which, in its single substance, was a cloud and darkness to the foes, and gave light by night to the friends, of Him who dwelt in it. Nay, they are but two names for the very same thing viewed in the very same motion, which is love as it yearns towards and cleaves to its treasure; and hatred, as by the identical same act it recoils and withdraws from the opposite: "He will hold to the one, and therefore and therein despise the other."

Much popular teaching as to Christian truth seems to me to ignore this plain principle, and to be working harm, especially among our younger cultivated men and women, whom it charms by an appearance of liberality, which, in their view, contrasts very favourably with the narrowness of us sectarians. I am free to admit that in our zeal about small matters (and in a certain "provincialism," so to speak, which characterised the type of English Christianity till within a recent period) we needed, and still need, the lesson, and I will thankfully accept the rebuke that reminds me of what I ever tend to forget, that the golden rod, wherewith the divine Builder measures from jewel to jewel in the walls of the New Jerusalem, takes in wider spaces than we have meted with our lines. But that is a very different matter from the tone which vitiates and weakens so much modern adherence to Christ's Gospel and Christ's Church. The old principle, "in essential unity, in non-essential liberty," made no attempt to determine what belonged to these two classes, and in practice their bounds may often have been wrongly set, so as to include many of the latter among the former; but it at all events recognised the distinction as the basis of its next clause, "in all things charity." But now-a-days, to listen to some liberal teachers, one would think that nothing was necessary, except the great sacred principle, that nothing is necessary; and that charity could not exist, unless that distinction were effaced.

I pray you, and if I may venture so far, I would especially pray my younger hearers, to take note, that however fair this way of looking at varying forms of Christian opinion may be, it really reposes on a basis which they will surely think twice before accepting, the denial that there is such a thing as intellectual certitude in religion which can be cast into definite propositions. If there be any truth at all, to confess *it* is to deny its opposite, to cleave to *this* is to reject that, to love the one is to hate the other. I fear, I know, that there are many minds among us who began with simply catching this tone of tolerance, and who have been insensibly borne along to an enfeebled belief that there is such a thing as religious truth at all, and that that truth lies in the word of God. Dear friends, let me beseech you to take heed lest, while you are only conscious of your hearts expanding with the genial glow of liberality, by little and little you lose your power of discerning between things that differ, your sense of the worth of the Scripture as the depository of divine truth, and from your slack hand the hem of the vesture in which is healing should fall away.

As broad a liberality as you please within the limits that are laid down by the very nature of the case. "These things are written that ye might believe that Jesus is the Christ, the Son of God, and that believing ye might have life through His name." Wheresoever that record is accepted, that divine name confessed, that faith exercised, and that life possessed, there, with all diversities, own a brother. Wheresoever these things are not, loyalty to your Lord demands that the strength of your love for His word should be manifested in the strength of your recoil from that which makes it void. "I love Thy commandments, and I hate every false way."

I am much mistaken if times are not rapidly coming on us when a decisive election of His side will be forced on every man. The old antagonists will be face to face once more. Compromises and hesitations will not serve. The country between the opposing forces will be stript of every spot that might serve as cover for neutrals. On the one side a mighty host, its right the Pharisees of ecclesiasticism and ritual, with their banner of authority, making void the law of God by their tradition; its left, and never far away from their opposites on the right, with whom they are strangely leagued, working into each other's hands, the Sadducees denying angel and spirit, with their war-cry of unfettered freedom and scientific evidence; and in the centre, far rolling, innumerable, the dusky hosts of mere animalism, and worldliness, and self, making void the law by their sheer godlessness. And on the other side, " He was clothed with a vesture dipped in blood, and His name is called The Word of God, and they that were with Him were called, and chosen, and faithful." The issue is certain from of old. Do you see to it that you are of those who were valiant for the truth upon the earth.

Let not the contradiction of many move you from your faith; let it lift your eyes to the hills from whence cometh our help. Let it open your desires in prayer to Him who keeps His own word, that it may keep His Church and bless the world. Let it kindle into fervent enthusiasm, which is calm sobriety, your love for that word. Let it make decisive your rejection of all that opposes. Driftwood may swim with the stream; the ship that holds to her anchor swings the other way. Send that word far and wide. It is its own best evidence. It will correct all the misrepresentation of its foes, and supplement the inadequate defences of its friends. Amid all the changes of attacks that have their day and cease to be, amid all the changes of our representations of its endless fulness, it will live. Schools of thought that assail and defend it pass, but it abides. Of both enemy and friend it is true, "The grass withereth, and the flower thereof passeth away." How antique and ineffectual the pages of the past generations of either are, compared with the ever-fresh youth of the Bible, which, like the angels, is the youngest and is the oldest of books. The world can never lose it; and notwithstanding all assaults, we may rest upon *His* assurance, whose command is prophecy, when He says, "Write it before them in a table, and note it in a book, that it may be *for the time to come for ever and ever.*"

SERMON V.

THE EXHORTATION OF BARNABAS.*

Acts xi. 23.

Who, when he came, and had seen the grace of God, was glad, and exhorted them all, that with purpose of heart they would cleave unto the Lord.

BEFORE coming to the mere immediate consideration of these words, I may be allowed a brief reference to the innovation on the customary arrangements of your meetings, which gives me the honour of addressing you here. This is, I believe, the first occasion on which a member of another communion has preached before the Congregational Union. And though I unfeignedly wish that the task had fallen to some more worthy representative of other Churches, I rejoice that you have set us all the example of thus recognising, in your most denominational gatherings, your nearest ecclesiastical kindred. In our several localities and labour side by side, and on the whole, shoulder to shoulder, why should we ignore one another in our respective theories, conferences, and

* Preached before the Congregational Union of England and Wales.

general assemblies, even if for the present we may not add "convocations," to the list? May your example be imitated! It does not become me to speak here of my own sense of the honour which you have done me, or of the extreme gratification with which I accept the responsible duty of addressing an audience, including many from whom I would more gladly learn—a gratification shaded only by the feeling of my inability to speak words level with the occasion. And, now, let me turn to my text. The first purely heathen converts had been brought into the Church by the nameless men of Cyprus and Cyrene, private persons with no office or commission to preach, who, in simple obedience to the instincts of a Christian heart, leaped the barrier which seemed impassable to the Church in Jerusalem, and solved the problem over which apostles were hesitating. Barnabas is sent down to see into this surprising new phenomenon, and his mission, though, probably, not hostile, was, at all events, one of inquiry and doubt. But like a true man, he yielded to fact, and widened his theory to suit them. He saw the token of Christian life in these Gentile converts, and that compelled him to admit that the Church was wider than some of his friends in Jerusalem thought. A pregnant lesson for modern theorists who, on one ground or another of doctrine or of orders, narrow the great conception of Christ's Church! Can you see "the grace of God in the people"? Then they are in the Church, whatever becomes of your theories, and the sooner you let them out so as to fit the facts, the better for you and for them.

Satisfied as to their true Christian character, he sets

himself to help them to grow. Now, remember how recently they had been converted; how, from their Gentile origin, they can have had next to no systematic instruction, how the taint of heathen morals, such as were common in that luxurious corrupt Antioch, must have clung to them; how unformed must have been their loose Church organisation—and remembering all this, think of this one exhortation as summing up all what Barnabas had to say to them. He does not say, Do this, or Believe that, or Organise the other; but he says, Stick to Jesus Christ the Lord. On this commandment hangs all the law; it is the one all-inclusive summary of the duties of the Christian life.

So, brethren and fathers, I venture to take these words now, as containing large lessons for us all, appropriate at all times, and especially in a sermon on such an occasion as the present.

We may deal with the thoughts suggested by these words very simply, just looking at the points as they lie —what he *saw*, what he *felt*, what he *said*.

I. *What He saw.*

The grace of God here has very probably the specific meaning of the miracle-working gift of the Holy Spirit. That is rendered probable by the analogy of other instances recorded in the Acts of the Apostles, such as Peter's experience at Caesarea, where all his hesitations and reluctance were swept away when "the Holy Ghost fell on them as on us at the beginning, and they spake with tongues." So, what convinced Barnabas that these uncircumcised Gentiles were Christians like himself, may have been their equal possession of the visible and audible effects of that gift of God. But the language does not compel this interpretation; and the absence of all distinct reference to these extraordinary powers as existing, there, among the new converts at Antioch may be intended to mark a difference in the nature of the evidence. At any rate, the possibly intentional generality of the expression is significant and fairly points to an extension of the principle involved much beyond the limits of miraculous powers. There are other ways by which the grace of God may be seen and heard, thank God! than by speaking with tongues and working miracles; and the first lesson of our text is that wherever that grace is made visible by its appropriate manifestations there we are to recognise a brother.

Augustine said, "where Christ is there is the Church," and that is true, but vague; for the question still remains, "and where *is* Christ?" The only satisfying answer is, Christ is wherever Christlike men manifest a life drawn from, and kindred with, His life. And so the true form of the dictum for practical purposes comes to be : Where the grace of Christ is visible, there is the Church.

That great truth is sinned against and denied in many ways. Most chiefly, perhaps, by the successors in modern garb of the more Jewish portion of that Church at Jerusalem who sent Barnabas to Antioch. They had no objection to Gentiles entering the Church, but they must come in by the way of circumcision; they quite believed that it was Christ who saved, and His grace which sanctified, but they thought that His grace would only flow in a given channel; and so their modern representatives, who exalt sacraments, and consequently priests, to the same place as the Judaizers in the early Church did the rite of the old Covenant. Such teachers have much to say about the notes of the Church, and have elaborated a complicated system of identification by which you may know the genuine article, and unmask impostors. The attempt is about as wise as to try to measure a network fine enough to keep back a stream. The water will flow through the closest meshes, and when Christ pours out the Spirit He is apt to do it in utter disregard of notes of the Church, and of channels of sacramental grace.

We Congregationalists, who have no orders, no sacraments, no apostolic succession; who in order not to break loose from Christ and conscience have had to break loose from "Catholic tradition," and have been driven to separation by the true schismatics, who have insisted on another bond of Church unity than union to Christ, are denied now-a-days a place in His Church.

The true answers to all that arrogant assumption and narrow pedantry which confines the free flow of the water of life to the conduits of sacraments and orders, and will only allow the wind that bloweth where it listeth to make music in the pipes of their organs, is simply the homely one which shivered a corresponding theory to atone in the fair open mind of Barnabas.

The Spirit of Christ at work in men's hearts, making them pure and gentle, simple and unworldly, refining their characters, elevating their aims, toning their whole being into accord with the music of His life, is the true proof that men are Christians, and that communities of such men are Churches of His. Mysterious efficacy is claimed for Christian ordinances. Well, the question is a fair one. Is the type of Christian character produced within these sacred limits which we are hopelessly outside conspicuously higher and more manifestly Christlike than that nourished by no sacraments, and grown not under glass, but in the unsheltered open? Has not God set His seal on these communities, to which we belong? With many faults for which we have to be, and are, humble before Him, we can point to the lineaments of the family likeness, and say "Are they Hebrews? so are we. Are they Israelites? so are we. Are they the seed of Abraham? so are we."

Once get that truth wrought into men's minds that the true test of Christianity is the visible presence of a grace in character which is evidently God's, and whole mountains of prejudice and error melt away. We are just as much in danger of narrowing the Church in accordance with our narrowness as any "sacramentarian" of them all. We are tempted to think that no good thing can grow up under the baleful shadow of that tree, a sacerdotal Christianity. We are tempted to think that all the good people are dissenters, just as Churchmen are to think that nobody can be a Christian who prays without a prayer-book. Our own type of denominational character—and there is such a thing—comes to be accepted by us as the all but exclusive ideal of a devout man; and we have not imagination enough to conceive, nor charity enough to believe in, the goodness which does not speak our dialect, nor see with our eyes. Dogmatical narrowness has built as high walls as ceremonial Christianity round the fold of Christ. And the one deliverance for us all from the transformed selfishness, which has so much to do with shaping all these wretched narrow theories of the Church, is to do as this man did—open our eyes with sympathetic eagerness to see God's grace in many an unexpected place, and square our theories with His dealings.

It used to be an axiom that there was no life in the sea beyond a certain limit of a few hundred feet. It was learnedly and conclusively demonstrated that pressure and absence of light, and I know not what beside, made life at greater depths impossible. It was proved that in such conditions creatures could not live. And then when that was settled, "The Challenger" put down her dredge five miles, and brought up healthy and good-sized living things, with eyes in their heads, from that enormous depth. So, then, the savant had to ask, *how* can there be life? instead of asserting there cannot be; and, no doubt, the answer will be forthcoming some day.

We have all been too much accustomed to draw arbitrary limits to the diffusion of the life of Christ among men. Let us rather rejoice when we see forms of beauty, which bear the mark of His hand, drawn from depths that we deemed waste, and thankfully confess that the bounds of our expectation, and the framework of our institutions, do not confine the breadth of His working, nor the sweep of His grace.

II. *What he felt—he " was glad."*

It was a triumph of Christian principle to recognise the grace of God under new forms, and in so strange a place. It was a still greater triumph to hail it with rejoicing. One need not have wondered if the acknowledgement of a fact, dead in the teeth of all his prejudices, and seemingly destructive of some profound convictions, had been somewhat grudging. Even a good, true man might have been bewildered and reluctant to let go so much as was involved in the admission—" Then hath God granted to the Gentiles also repentance unto life,"—and might have been pardoned if he had not been able to do more than acquiesce and hold his peace. We are scarcely just to these early Jewish Christians when we wonder at their hesitation on this matter, and are apt to forget the enormous strength of the prejudices and sacred conviction which they had to overcome. Hence the context seems to consider that the quick recognition of their Christian character on the part of Barnabas, and his gladness at the discovery, need explanation, and so it adds, with special reference to these, as it would seem, "for he was a good man full of the Holy Ghost and of faith," as if nothing short of such characteristics could have sufficiently emancipated him from the narrowness that would have refused to discern the good, or the bitterness that would have been offended at it.

So, dear brethren, we may well test ourselves with this

question: Does the discovery of the working of the grace of God outside the limits of our own Churches and communions excite a quick spontaneous emotion of gladness in *our* hearts? It may upset some of our theories; it may teach us that things which we thought very important, distinctive principles and the like, are not altogether as precious as we thought them; it may require us to give up some pleasant ideas of our superiority, and of the necessary conformity of all good people to our type. Are we willing to let them all go, and without a twinge of envy or a hanging back from prejudice, to welcome the discovery that God fulfils Himself in many ways? Have we schooled ourselves to say honestly, "Therein I do rejoice, yea, and will rejoice"?

There is much to overcome if we would know this Christlike gladness. The good and the bad in us may both oppose it. The natural deeper interest in the well-being of the Churches of our own faith and order, the legitimate ties which unite us with these, our conscientious convictions, our friendships, the *esprit de corps* born of fighting shoulder to shoulder, will, of course, make our sympathies flow most quickly and deeply in denominational channels. And then come in abundance of less worthy motives, some altogether bad and some the exaggeration of what is good, and we get swallowed up in our own individual work, or in that of our "denomination," and have but a very tepid joy in anybody else's prosperity.

In almost every town of England, your Churches, and those to which I belong, with Presbyterians and Wesleyans, stand side by side. The conditions of our work make some rivalry inevitable, and none of us, I suppose, object to that. It helps to keep us all diligent: a sturdy adherence to our several "distinctive principles," and an occasional hard blow in fair fight on their behalf we shall all insist upon. Our brotherhood is all the more real for frank speech, and "the animated no" is an essential in all intercourse which is not stagnant or mawkish. There is much true fellowship and much good feeling among all these. But we want far more of an honest rejoicing in each other's success, a quicker and truer manly sympathy with each other's work, a fuller consciousness of our solidarity in Christ, and a clearer exhibition of it before the world.

And on a wider view, as our eyes travel over the wide field of Christendom, and our memories go back over the long ages of the story of the Church, let gladness, and not wonder or reluctance, be the temper with which we see the graces of Christian character lifting their meek blossoms in corners strange to us, and breathing their fragrance over the pastures of the wilderness. In many a cloister, in many a hermit's cell, from amidst the smoke of incense, through the dust of controversies, we should see, and be glad to see, faces bright with the radiance caught from Christ. Let us set a jealous watch over our hearts that self-absorption, or denominationalism, or envy do not make the sight a pain instead of a joy; and let us remember that the eye salve which will purge our dim sight to behold the grace of God in all its forms is that grace itself, which ever recognises its own kindred, and lives in the gladness of charity, and the joy of beholding a brother's good. If we are to have eyes to know the grace of God when we see it, and a heart to rejoice when we know it, we must get them as Barnabas got his, and be good men, because we are full of the Holy Ghost, and full of the Holy Ghost because we are full of faith.

III. *What he said: he exhorted them all, that with purpose of heart they would cleave unto the Lord.*

The first thing that strikes one about this all-sufficient directory for Christian life is the emphasis with which it sets forth "the Lord" as the one object to be grasped and held. The sum of all objective Religion is Christ— the sum of all subjective Religion is cleaving to Him. A living person to be laid hold of, and a personal relation to that person, such is the conception of Religion, whether considered as revelation or as inward life, which underlies this exhortation. Whether we listen to His own words about Himself, and mark the altogether unprecedented way in which He was His own theme, and the unique decisiveness and plainness with which He puts His own personality before us as the Incarnate Truth, the pattern for all human conduct, the refuge and the rest for the world of weary ones; or whether we give ear to the teaching of His apostles; from whatever point of view we approach Christianity, it all resolves itself into the person of Jesus Christ. He is the *Revelation* of God; theology properly so called is but the formulating of the facts which He gives us; and for the modern world the alternative is, Christ the manifested God, or no God at all, other than the shadow of a name. He is the perfect *exemplar* of humanity! The law of life and the power to fulfil the law are both in Him; and the superiority of Christian morality consists not in this or that isolated precept, but in the embodiment of all goodness in His life, and in the new motive which He supplies for keeping the commandment. Wrenched away from Him, Christian morality has no being. He is the *sacrifice for the world*, the salvation of which flows from what He does, and not merely from what He taught, or was. His personality is the foundation of His work, and the gospel of forgiveness and reconciliation is all contained in the name of Jesus.

There is a constant tendency to separate the results of Christ's life and death, whether considered as revelation, ethics, or atonement, from Him, and unconsciously to make *these* the sum of our Religion, and the object of our faith. Especially is this the case in times of restless thought and eager canvassing of the very foundations of religious belief like the present. Therefore it is wholesome for us all to be brought back to the pregnant simplicity of the thought which underlies this text, and to mark how vividly these early Christians apprehended a living Lord as the sum and substance of all which they had to grasp.

There is a whole world between the man to whom God's revelation consists in certain doctrines given to us by Jesus Christ, and the man to whom it consists in that Christ Himself. Grasping a living person is not the same as accepting a proposition. True, the propositions are about Him, and we do not know Him without them. But equally true, we need to be reminded that *He* is our Saviour and not *they*, and that God has revealed Himself to us not in words and sentences but in a life.

For, alas! the doctrinal element has overborne the personal among all Churches and all schools of thought, and in the necessary process of formulating and systematising the riches which are in Jesus, we are all apt to confound the creeds with the Christ, and so to manipulate Christianity until, instead of being the revelation of a person and a gospel, it has become a system of divinity. Simple, devout souls have to complain that they cannot find even a dead Christ, to say nothing of a living one, for the theologians have taken away their Lord, and they know not where they have laid Him.

It is, therefore, to be reckoned as a distinct gain that one result of the course of the more recent thought, both among friends and foes, has been to make all men feel more than before, that all revelation is contained in the living person of Jesus Christ. So did the Church believe before creeds were. So it is coming to feel again with a consciousness enriched and defined by the whole body of doctrine, which has flowed from Him during all the ages. That solemn, gracious figure rises day by day more clearly before men, whether they love Him or no, as the vital centre of this great whole of doctrines, laws, institutions, which we call Christianity. Round the story of His life the final struggle is to be waged. The foe feels that, so long as that remains, all other victories count for nothing. We feel that if that goes, there is nothing to keep. The principles and the precepts will perish alike, as the fair palace of the old legend, that crumbled to dust when its builder died. But so long as He stands before mankind as He is painted in the Gospel, it will endure. If all else were annihilated, Churches, creeds and all, leave us these four gospels, and all else would be evolved again. The world knows now, and the Church has always known, though it has not always been true to the significance of the fact, that Jesus Christ is Christianity, and that because He lives, it will live also.

And consequently the sum of all personal religion is this simple act described here as *cleaving to Him*.

Need I do more than refer to the rich variety of symbols and forms of expression under which that thought is put alike by the Master and by His servants? Deepest of all are His own great words, of which our text is but a feeble echo, "Abide in Me, and I in you." Fairest of all is this lovely emblem of the vine, setting forth the sweet mystery of our union with Him. Far as it is from the outmost pliant tendril to the root, one life passes to the very extremities, and every cluster swells and reddens and mellows because of its mysterious flow. So also is Christ. We remember how often the invitation flowed from His lips, *Come* unto Me; how He was wont to beckon men away from self and the world with the great command, *Follow* Me; how He explained the secret of all true life to consist in *eating* Him. We may recall, too, the emphasis and perpetual reiteration with which Paul speaks of being "in Jesus" as the condition of all blessedness, power, and righteousness; and the emblems which he so often employs of the *building* bound into a whole on the foundation from which it derives its stability, of the *body* compacted and organised into a whole by the head from which it derives its life.

We begin to be Christians, as this context tells us, when we "*turn* to the Lord." We continue to be Christians, as Barnabas reminded these ignorant beginners, by "cleaving to the Lord." Seeing, then, that our great task is to preserve that which we have as the very foundation of our Christian life, clearly the truest method of so keeping it will be the constant repetition of the act by which we got it at first. In other words, faith joined us to Christ, and continuously reiterated acts of faith keep us united to Him. So, if I may venture, fathers and brethren, to cast *my* words into the form of exhortation, even to such an audience as the present, I would earnestly say, *Let us cleave to Christ by continual renewal of our first faith in Him.*

The longest line may be conceived of as produced simply by the motion of its initial point. So should our lives be, our progress not consisting in leaving our early acts of faith behind us, but in repeating them over and over again till the points coalesce in one unbroken line which goes straight to the Throne and Heart of Jesus. True, the repetition should be accompanied with fuller knowledge, with calmer certitude, and should come from a heart ennobled and encircled by a Christ-possessing past. As in some great symphony the theme which was given out in low notes on one poor instrument recurs over and over again embroidered with varying harmonies, and unfolding a richer music till it swells into all the grandeur of the triumphant close, so our lives should be bound into a unity, and in their unity bound to Christ by the constant renewal of our early faith, and the fathers come round again to the place which they occupied when as children they first knew Him that is from the Beginning to the End one and the same. Such constant reiteration is needed, too, because yesterday's trust has no more power to secure to-day's union than the shreds of cloth and nails which hold last year's growth to the wall will fasten this year's shoots. Each moment must be united to Christ by its own act of faith, or it will be separated from Him. So living *in the Lord* we shall be strong and wise, happy and holy. So dying *in the Lord* we shall be of the dead who are blessed. So sleeping *in Jesus*, we shall at the last be found *in Him* at that day, and shall be raised up together, and made to sit together in heavenly places *in Christ Jesus*.

But more specially let us cleave to Christ *by habitual contemplation*. There can be no real continuous closeness of intercourse with Him, except by thought ever recurring to Him amidst all the tumult of our busy days. I do not mean professional thinking, or controversial thinking, of which we ministers have more than enough.

There is another mood of mind in which to approach our Lord than these, a mood sadly unfamiliar, I am afraid, in these days: when poor Mary has hardly a chance of a reputation for "usefulness" by the side of busy bustling Martha—that still contemplation of the truth which we possess, not with the view of discovering its foundations, or investigating its applications, or even of increasing our knowledge of its contents, but of bringing our own souls more completely under its influence, and saturating our being with its fragrance. The Church has forgotten how to meditate. We are all so occupied arguing and deducing and elaborating, that we have no time for retired still contemplation and, therefore, lose the finest aroma of the truth we profess to believe. Many of us are so busy thinking about Christianity that we have lost our hold of Christ. Sure I am that there are few things more needed by our modern Religion than the old exhortation, " Come, My people, enter into thy chambers and shut thy doors about thee." Cleave to the Lord by habitual play of meditative thought on the treasures hidden in His name, and waiting like gold in the quartz, to be the prize of our patient sifting and close gaze.

And when the great truths embodied in Him stand clear before us, then let us remember that we have not done with them when we have *seen* them. Next must come into exercise the moral side of faith, the voluntary act of trust, the casting ourselves on Him whom we behold, the making our own of the blessings which He holds out to us. Flee to Christ as to our strong habitation to which we may continually resort. Hold tightly by Christ with a grasp which nothing can slacken (that whitens your very knuckles as you clutch Him), lean on Christ all your weight and all your burdens. Cleave to the Lord with full purpose of heart.

Let us cleave to the Lord *by constant outgoings of our love to Him.* That is the bond which unites human spirits together in the only real union, and Scripture teaches us to see in the sweetest sacredest closest tie that men and women can know, a real though faint shadow of the far deeper and truer union between Christ and us. The same love which is the bond of perfectness between man and man, is the bond between us and Christ. In no dreamy semi-pantheistic fusion of the believer with His Lord do we find the true conception of the unity of Christ and His Church, but in a union which preserves the individualities lest it should slay the love. Faith knits us to Christ, and faith is the mother of love, which maintains the blessed union. So let us not be ashamed of the *emotional* side of our religion, nor deem that we can cleave to Christ unless our hearts twine their tendrils round Him, and our love pours its odorous treasures on His sacred feet, not without weeping nor embraces. Cold natures may carp, but Love is justified of her children, and Christ accepts the homage that has a heart in it. Cleaving to the Lord is not merely love, but it is impossible without it. The order is Faith, Love, Obedience, that threefold cord knits men to Christ, and Christ to men. For the understanding a continuous grasp of Him as the object of thought. For the heart a continuous out-going to Him as the object of our love. For the will a continuous submission to Him as the Lord of our Obedience. For the whole nature a continuous cleaving to Him as the object of our faith and worship.

Such is the true discipline of the Christian life. Such is the all-sufficient command; as for the newest convert from heathenism, with little knowledge and the taint of his old vices in his soul, so for the saint fullest of wisdom and nearest the Light.

It *is* all-sufficient. If Barnabas had been like some of us, he would have had a very different style of exhortation. He would have said, This irregular work has been well done, but there are no authorised teachers here, and no provision has been made for the due administration of the sacraments of the Church. The very first thing of all is to give these people the blessing of bishops and priests. Some of us would have said, A good work has been done, but these good people are terribly ignorant. The best thing would be to get ready as soon as possible some manual of Christian doctrine, and in the meantime provide for their systematic instruction in at least the elements of the faith. Some of us would have said, No doubt they have been converted, but we fear there has been too much of the emotional in the preaching. The moral side of Christianity has not been pressed home, and what they chiefly need is to be taught that it is not feeling but righteousness. Plain practical instruction in Christian duty is the one thing they want.

Barnabas knew better. He did not despise organisation, nor orthodoxy, nor practical righteousness, but he knew that all three, and everything else that any man needed for his perfecting, would come, if only they kept near to Christ, and that nothing else was of any use if they did not. That same conviction should for us settle the relative importance which we attach to these subordinate and derivative things, and to the primary and primitive duty. Obedience to it will secure them. They, without it, are not worth securing.

We spend much pains and effort now-a-days in perfecting our organisations and consolidating our resources; and I have not a word to say against that. But heavier machinery needs more power in the engine, and that means greater capacity in your boilers and more *fire* in your furnace. The more complete our organisation, the more do we need a firm hold of Christ, or we shall be overweighted by it, shall be in danger of burning incense to our own net, shall be tempted to trust in drill rather than in courage, in mechanism rather than in the life drawn from Christ. On the other hand, putting as our first care the preservation of the closeness of our union with Christ, that life will shape a body for itself, and to every seed its own body.

True *conceptions* of Him, and a definite *theology*, are good and needful. Let us cleave to Him with mind and heart, and we shall receive all the knowledge we need, and be guided into the deep things of God. In Him are hid all the treasures of wisdom and knowledge, and the basis of all theology is the personal possession of Him who is the wisdom of God, and the light of the world. Every one that loveth is born of God and knoweth God. *Pectus facit Theologum.*

Plain straightforward morality, and every-day righteousness are better than all emotion and all dogmatism and all churchism, says the world, and Christianity says much the same; but plain straightforward righteousness and every-day morality come most surely when a man is keeping close to Christ. In a word, everything that can adorn the character with beauty, and clothe the Church with glorious apparel, whatsoever things are lovely and of good report, all that the world or God call virtue and crown with praise, they are all in their fulness in Him, and all are most surely derived from Him by keeping fast hold of His hand, and preserving the channels clear through which His manifold grace may flow into our souls. The same life is strength in the arm, pliancy in the fingers, swiftness in the foot, light in the eye, music on the lips; so the same grace is Protean in its forms, and to His servants who trust Him Christ ever says, "What would ye that I should do unto you? Be it even as thou wilt." The same mysterious power lives in the swaying branch, and in the veined leaf, and in the blushing clusters. With like wondrous transformations of the one grace, the Lord pours Himself into our spirits, filling all needs and fitting for all circumstances. Therefore for us all, individuals and Churches, this remains the prime command, With purpose of heart cleave unto the Lord. Dear brethren, in the ministry how sorely we need this exhortation! Our very professional occupation with Christ and His truth is full of danger for us, we are so accustomed to handle these sacred themes as a means of instructing or impressing others that we get to regard them as our weapons, even if we do not degrade them still further by thinking of them as our stock-in-trade and means of oratorical effect. We must keep very firm hold of Christ for ourselves by much solitary communion, and so retranslating into the nutriment of our own souls the message we bring to men, else when we have preached to others we ourselves may be cast away. All the ordinary tendencies which draw men from Him work on us, and a host of others peculiar to ourselves, and all around us run strong currents of thought which threaten to sweep many away. Let us tighten our grasp of Him in the face of modern doubt; and take heed to ourselves that neither vanity, nor worldliness, nor sloth; neither the gravitation earthward common to all, nor the temptations proper to *our* office; neither unbelieving voices without nor voices within seduce us from His side. There only is our peace, there our wisdom, there our power.

Subtly and silently the separating forces are ever at work upon us, and all unconsciously to ourselves our hold may relax, and the flow of this grace into our spirits may cease, while yet we mechanically keep up the round of outward service, nor even suspect that our strength is departed from us. Many a stately elm that seems full of vigorous life, for all its spreading boughs and clouds of dancing leaves is hollow at the heart, and when the storm comes goes down with a crash, and men wonder as they look at the ruin, how such a mere shell of life with a core of corruption could stand so long. It rotted within, and fell at last because its roots did not go deep down to the rich soil, where they would have found nourishment, but ran along near the surface among gravel and stones. If we would stand firm, be sound within, and bring forth much fruit, we must strike our roots deep in Him Who is the anchorage of our souls, and the nourisher of all our being.

Hearken, beloved brethren, in this great work of the ministry, not to the exhortation of the servant, but to the solemn command of the Master, "Abide in Me, and I in you. As the branch cannot bear fruit of itself, except it abide in the vine, no more can ye, except ye abide in Me." And let us, knowing our own weakness, take heed of the self-confidence that answers, "Though all should forsake Thee, yet will not I," and turn the vows, which spring to our lips into the lowly prayer "My soul cleaveth unto the dust, quicken Thou me according to Thy word." Then, thinking rather of His cleaving to us, than of ours cleaving to Him, let us, resolutely, take as the motto of our lives the grand words: "I follow after it that I may lay hold of that, for which also I am laid hold of by Christ Jesus."

SERMON VI.

MEASURELESS POWER AND ENDLESS GLORY.

Ephesians iii. 20, 21.

Now unto Him that is able to do exceeding abundantly above all that we ask or think, according to the power that worketh in us, Unto Him be glory in the Church by Christ Jesus throughout all ages, world without end. Amen.

ONE purpose and blessing of faithful prayer is to enlarge the desires which it expresses, and to make us think more loftily of the grace to which we appeal. So the apostle, in the wonderful series of supplications which precedes the text, has found his thought of what he may hope for his brethren at Ephesus grow greater with every clause. His prayer rises like some songbird, in ever widening sweeps, each higher in the blue, and nearer the throne; and at each a sweeter, fuller note.

"Strengthened with might by His Spirit"; "that Christ may dwell in your hearts by faith"; "that ye may be able to know the love of Christ"; "that ye might be filled with all the fulness of God." Here he touches the very throne. Beyond that nothing can be conceived. But though that sublime petition may be the end of thought, it is not the end of faith. Though God can give us nothing more than it is, He can give us more than we think it to be, and more than we ask, when we ask this. Therefore the grand doxology of our text crowns and surpasses even this great prayer. The higher true prayer climbs, the wider is its view; and the wider is its view, the more conscious is it that the horizon of its vision is far within the borders of the goodly land. And as we gaze into what we can discern of the fulness of God, prayer will melt into thanksgiving and the doxology for the swift answer will follow close upon the last words of supplication. So is it here : so it may be always.

The form of our text, then, marks the confidence of Paul's prayer. The exuberant fervour of his faith, as well as his natural impetuosity and ardour, comes out in the heaped-up words expressive of immensity and duration. He is like some archer watching, with parted lips, the flight of his arrow to the mark. He is gazing on God confident that he has not asked in vain. Let us look with him, that we, too, may be heartened to expect great things of God. Notice, then—

I. *The Measure of the Power* to which we trust.

This Epistle is remarkable for its frequent references to the Divine rule, or standard, or measure, in accordance with which the great facts of redemption take place. The "things on the earth"—the historical processes by which salvation is brought to men and works in men —are ever traced up to the "things in heaven;" the Divine counsels from which they have come forth. That phrase, "according to," is perpetually occurring in this connection in the Epistle. It is applied mainly in two directions. It serves sometimes to bring into view the ground, or reason, of the redemptive facts, as, for instance, in the expression that these take place "according to His good pleasure which He hath purposed in Himself. It serves sometimes to bring into view the measure by which the working of these redemptive facts is determined; as in our text, and in many other places.

Now there are three main forms under which this standard, or measure, of the Redeeming Power is set forth in this Epistle, and it will help us to grasp the greatness of the apostle's thought if we consider these.

Take, then, first, that clause in the earlier portion of the preceding prayer, "that He would grant you *according to the riches of His glory.*" The measure, then, of the gift that we may hope to receive is the measure of God's own fulness. The "riches of His glory" can be nothing less than the whole uncounted abundance of that majestic and far-shining Nature, as it pours itself forth in the dazzling perfectnesses of its own Self-manifestation. And nothing less than this great treasure is to be the limit and standard of His gift to us. We are the sons of the King, and the allowance which He makes us even before we come to our inheritance is proportionate to our Father's wealth. The same stupendous thought is given us in that prayer, heavy with the blessed weight of unspeakable gifts, "that ye might be filled with all the fulness of God"; this, then, is the measure of the grace that we may possess. This limitless limit alone bounds the possibilities for every man, the certainties for every Christian.

The effect must be proportioned to the cause. And what effect will be adequate as the outcome of such a cause as "the riches of His glory"? Nothing short of absolute perfectness, the full transmutation of our dark, cold being into the reflected image of His own burning brightness, the ceaseless replenishing of our own spirits with all graces and gladnesses akin to His, the eternal growth of the soul upward and Godward. Perfection is the sign-manual of God in all His works, just as imperfection and the falling below our thought and wish is our "token in every Epistle" and deed of ours. Take the finest needle, and put it below a microscope, and it will be all ragged and irregular, the fine, tapering lines will be broken by many a bulge and bend, and the point blunt and clumsy. Put the blade of grass to the same test, and see how true its outline, how delicate and true the spear-head of its point. God's work is perfect, man's is clumsy and incomplete. God does not leave off till He has finished. When He rests, it is because, looking on His work, He sees it all "very good." His Sabbath is the Sabbath of an achieved purpose, of a fulfilled counsel. The palaces which we build are ever like that in the story, where one window remains dark and unjewelled, while the rest blaze in beauty. But when God builds, none can say, "He was not able to finish." In His great palace He makes her "windows of agates" and *all* her "borders of pleasant stones."

So we have a right to enlarge our desires and stretch

our confidence of what we may possess and become to this, His boundless bound : " The riches of glory."

But another form in which the standard, or measure, is stated in this letter is : " The working of His mighty Power, which He wrought in Christ, when He raised Him from the dead" (i. 19, 20); or, as it is put with a modification, " grace according to the measure of the gift of Christ" (iv. 7). That is to say, we have not only the whole riches of the Divine glory as the measure to which we may lift our hopes, but lest that celestial brightness should seem too high above us, and too far from us, we have Christ in His Human-Divine manifestation, and especially in the great fact of the resurrection, set before us, that by Him we may learn what God wills we should become. The former phase of the standard may sound abstract, cloudy, hard to connect with any definite anticipations; and so this form of it is concrete, historical, and gives human features to the fair ideal. His resurrection is the high-water-mark of the Divine power, and to the same level it will rise again in regard to every Christian. That Lord, in the glory of His risen life, and in the riches of the gifts which He received when He ascended up on high, is the pattern for us, and the power which fulfils its own pattern. In Him we see what man may become, and what His followers must become. The limits of that power will not be reached until every Christian soul is perfectly assimilated to that likeness, and bears all its beauty in his face, nor till every Christian soul is raised to participation in Christ's dignity and sits on His throne. Then, and not till then, shall the purpose of God be fulfilled and the gift which is measured by the riches of the Father's glory, and the fulness of the Son's grace, be possessed or conceived in its measureless measure.

But there is a third form in which this same standard is represented. That is the form which is found in our text, and in other places of the Epistle : "*According to the Power that worketh in us.*"

What power is that but the power of the Spirit of God dwelling in us? And thus we have the measure, or standard, set forth in terms respectively applying to the Father, the Son, and the Holy Ghost. For the first, the riches of His glory; for the second, His resurrection and ascension; for the third, His energy working in Christian souls. The first, carries us up into the mysteries of God, where the air is almost too subtle for our gross lungs; the second draws nearer to earth and points us to an historical fact that happened in this every-day world; the third, comes still nearer to us, and bids us look within, and see whether what we are conscious of there, if we interpret it by the light of these other measures, will not yield results as great as theirs, and open before us the same fair prospect of perfect holiness and conformity to the Divine nature.

There is already a Power at work within us, if we be Christians, of whose workings we may be aware, and from them forecast the measure of the gifts which it can bestow upon us. We may estimate what will be by what we know has been, and by what we feel is. That is to say, in other words, the effects already produced, and the experiences we have already had, carry in them the pledge of completeness.

I suppose that if the mediæval dream had ever come true, and an alchemist had ever turned a grain of lead into gold, he could have turned all the lead in the world in time, and with crucibles and furnaces enough. The first step is all the difficulty, and if you and I have been changed from enemies into sons, and had one spark of love to God kindled in our hearts, that is a mightier change than any that remains to be effected in order to make us perfect. One grain has been changed, the whole mass will be in due time.

The present operations of that power carry in them the pledge of their own completion. The strange mingling of good and evil in our present nature, our aspirations so crossed and contradicted, our resolution so broken and falsified, the gleams of light, and the eclipses that follow —all these, in their opposition to each other, are plainly transitory, and the workings of that Power within us, though they be often overborne, are as plainly the stronger in their nature, and meant to conquer and to endure. Like some half-hewn block, such as travellers find in long abandoned quarries whence Egyptian temples, that were destined never to be completed, were built, our spirits are but partly "polished after the similitude of a palace," while much remains in the rough. The builders of these temples have mouldered away, and their unfinished handiwork will lie as it was when the last chisel touched it centuries ago, till the crack of doom; but stones for God's temple will be wrought to completeness and set in their places. The whole threefold Divine cause of our salvation supplies the measure, and lays the foundation for our hopes, in the glory of the Father, the grace of the Son, the power of the Holy Ghost. Let us lift up our cry: "Perfect that which concerneth me, forsake not the works of Thine own hands," and we shall have for answer the ancient word, fresh as when it sounded long ago from among the stars to the sleeper at the ladder's foot," I will not leave thee, until I have done that which I have spoken to thee of."

II. Notice the *relation of the Divine Working to our thoughts and desires.*

The apostle in his fervid way strains language to express how far the possibility of the Divine working extends. He is able, not only to do all things, but " beyond all things "—a vehement way of putting the boundless reach of that gracious power. And what he means by this "beyond all things" is more fully expressed in the next words, in which he labours by accumulating synonyms to convey his sense of the transcendent energy which waits to bless : " exceeding abundantly above what we ask." And as, alas! our desires are but shrunken and narrow beside our thoughts, he sweeps a wider orbit when he adds "above what we *think.*" He has been asking wonderful things, and yet even his farthest-reaching petitions fall far on this side of the greatness of God's power. One might think that even it could go no further than filling us "with all the fulness of God." Nor can it; but it may far transcend our conceptions of what that is, and astonish us by its surpassing our thoughts, no less than it shames us by exceeding our práyers.

Of course, all this is true, and is meant to apply, only about the inward gifts of God's grace. I need not remind you that, in the outer world of Providence and earthly gifts, prayers and wishes often surpass the answers; that there a deeper wisdom often contradicts our thoughts and a truer kindness refuses our petitions, and that so the rapturous words of our text are only true in a very modified and partial sense about God's working *for* us in the world. It is His work *in* us concerning which they are absolutely true.

Of course, we know that in all regions of His working He is *able* to surpass our poor human conceptions, and that, properly speaking, the most familiar, and, as we insolently call them, "smallest" of His works holds in it a mystery—were it none other than the mystery of Being—against which Thought has been breaking its teeth ever since men began to think at all.

But as regards the working of God on our spiritual lives, this passing beyond the bounds of thought and desire is but the necessary result of the fact already dealt with, that the only measure of the power is God Himself, in that Threefold Being. That being so, no plummet of our making can reach to the bottom of the abyss, no strong-winged thought can fly to the outermost bound of the encircling heaven. Widely as we stretch our reverent conceptions, there is ever something beyond. After we have resolved many a dim white cloud in the starry sky, and found it all ablaze with suns and worlds, there will still hang, faint and far before us, hazy magnificences which we have not apprehended. Confidently and boldly as we may offer our prayers and largely as we may expect, the answer is ever more than the petition. For indeed, in every act of His quickening grace, in every God-given increase of our knowledge of God, in every bestowment of His fulness, there is always more bestowed than we receive, more than we know even while we possess it. Like some gift given in the dark, its true preciousness is not discerned when it is first received. The gleam of the gold does not strike our eye all at once. There is ever an unknown margin felt by us to be over after our capacity of receiving is exhausted. "And they took up of the fragments that remained, twelve baskets full."

So, then, let us remember that while our thoughts and prayers can never reach to the full perception, or reception either, of the gift, the exuberant amplitude with which it reaches far beyond both is meant to draw both after it. And let us not forget either that, while the grace which we receive has no limit or measure but the fulness of God, the working limit, which determines what we receive of the grace, is these very thoughts and wishes which it surpasses. We may have as much of God as we can hold, as much as we wish. All Niagara may roar past a man's door, but only as much as he diverts through his own sluice will drive his mill, or quench his thirst. That grace is like the figures in the Eastern tales, that will creep into a narrow room no bigger than a nutshell, or will tower heaven high. Our spirits are like the magic tent whose walls expanded or contracted at the owner's wish—we may enlarge them to enclose far more of the grace than we have ever possessed. We are not straitened in God, but in ourselves. He is "able to do exceeding abundantly above what we ask or think." Therefore let us stretch desires and thoughts to their utmost, remembering that while they can never reach the measure of His grace in itself, they make the practical measure of our possession of it. "According to thy faith," is a real measure of the gift received, even though "according to the riches of His glory" be the measure of the gift bestowed. Note, again.

III. *The Glory that springs from the Divine Work.*

"The glory of God" is the lustre of His own perfect character the bright sum total of all the blended brilliancies that compose His name. When that light is welcomed and adored by men, they are said to "give glory to God" and this doxology is at once a prophecy that the working of God's power on His redeemed children will issue in setting forth the radiance of His name yet more, and a prayer that it may. So we have here the great thought expressed in many places of Scripture, that the highest exhibition of the Divine character for the reverence and love—of the whole universe, shall we say?—lies in His work on Christian souls, and the effect produced thereby on them. God takes His stand, so to speak, on this great fact in His dealings, and will have His creatures estimate Him by it. He reckons it His highest praise that He has redeemed men, and by His dwelling in them, fills them with His own fulness. And this chiefest praise and brightest glory accrues to Him "in the Church in Christ Jesus." The weakening of the latter words into "by Christ Jesus," as in the English version, is to be regretted, as substituting another thought, Scriptural no doubt and precious, for the precise shade of meaning in the apostle's mind here. As has been well said, "the first words denote the outward province; the second, the inward and spiritual sphere in which God was to be praised." His glory is to shine in the Church, the theatre of His power, the standing demonstration of the might of redeeming love. By this He will be judged, and this He will point to if any ask what is His Divinest work, which bears the clearest imprint of His Divinest self. His glory is to be set forth by men on condition that they are "in Christ," living and moving in Him, in that mysterious but most real union without which no fruit grows on the dead branches, nor any music of praise breaks from dead lips.

So, then, think of that wonder that God sets His glory in His dealings with us. Amid all the majesty of His works and all the blaze of His creation, this is what He presents as the highest specimen of His power—the Church of Jesus Christ, the company of poor men, wearied and conscious of many evils, who follow afar off the footsteps of their Lord. How dusty and toil-worn the little group of Christians that landed at Puteoli must have looked as they toiled along the Appian Way and entered Rome! How contemptuously emperor and philosopher and priest and patrician would have curled their lips, if they had been told that in that little knot of Jewish prisoners lay a power before which theirs would cower and finally fade! Even so is it still. Among all the splendours of this great universe, and the mere obtrusive tawdrinesses of earth, men look upon us Christians as poor enough; and yet it is to His redeemed children that God has entrusted His praise, and in their hands He has lodged the sacred deposit of His own glory.

Think loftily of that office and honour, lowly of yourselves who have it laid upon you as a crown. His honour is in our hands. We are the "secretaries of His praise." This is the highest function that any creature can discharge. The Rabbis have a beautiful bit of teaching buried among their rubbish about angels. They say that there are two kinds of angels: the angels of service and the angels of praise, of which two orders the latter is the higher, and that no angel in it praises God twice, but having once lifted up his voice in the psalm of heaven, then perishes and ceases to be. He has perfected his being, he has reached the height of his greatness, he has done what he was made for, let him fade away. The garb of legend is mean enough, but the thought it embodies is that ever true and solemn one, without which life is nought: "Man's chief end is to glorify God."

And we can only fulfil that high purpose in the measure of our union with Christ. "In Him" abiding, we manifest God's glory, for in Him abiding we receive God's grace. So long as we are joined to Him, we partake of His life, and our lives become music and praise. The electric current flows from Him through all souls that are "in Him," and they glow with fair colours which they owe to their contact with Jesus. Interrupt the communication, and all is darkness. So, brethren, let us seek to abide in Him, severed from Whom we are nothing. Then shall we fulfil the purpose of His love, Who "hath shined in our hearts," that we might give to others "the light of the knowledge of the glory of God in the face of Jesus Christ." Notice, lastly,

IV. *The Eternity of the Work and of the Praise.*

As in the former clauses, the idea of the transcendent greatness of the power of God was expressed by accumulated synonyms, so here the kindred thought of its eternity, and consequently of the ceaseless duration of the resulting glory, is sought to be set forth by a similar aggregation. The language creaks and labours, as it were, under the weight of the great conception. Literally rendered, the words are—"to all generations of the age of the ages"—a remarkable fusing together of two expressions for unbounded duration, which are scarcely congruous. We can understand "to all generations" as expressive of duration as long as birth and death shall last. We can understand "the age of the ages" as pointing to that endless epoch whose moments are "ages"; but the blending of the two is but an unconscious acknowledgment that the speech of earth, saturated, as it is, with the colouring of time, breaks down in the attempt to express the thought of eternity. Undoubtedly that solemn conception is the one intended by this strange phrase.

The work is to go on for ever and ever, and with it the praise. As the ages which are the beats of the pendulum of eternity come and go, more and more of God's power will flow out to us, and more and more of God's glory will be manifested in us. It must be so. For God's gift is infinite, and man's capacity of reception is indefinitely capable of increase. Therefore eternity will be needful in order that redeemed souls may absorb all of God which He can give or they can take. The process has no limits, for there is no bound to be set to the possible approaches of the human spirit to the Divine, and none to the exuberant abundance of the beauty and glory which God will give to His child. Therefore we shall live for ever: and for ever show forth His praise and blaze out like the sun with the irradiation of His glory. We cannot die till we have exhausted God. Till we comprehend all His nature in our thoughts, and reflect all His beauty in our character; till we have attained all the bliss that we can think, and received all the good that we can ask; till Hope has nothing before her to reach towards, and God is left behind: we "shall not die, but live, and declare the works of the Lord."

Let His grace work on you, and yield yourselves to Him, that His fulness may fill your emptiness. So on earth we shall be delivered from hopes which mock, and wishes that are never fulfilled. So in heaven, after "ages of ages" of growing glory, we shall have to say, as each new wave of the shoreless, sunlit sea bears us onward, "It doth not yet appear what we shall be."

SERMON VII.

LOVE'S TRIUMPH.

ROMANS viii. 38, 39.

Neither death, nor life, nor angels, nor principalities, nor powers, nor things present, nor things to come, nor height, nor depth, nor any other creature, shall be able to separate us from the love of God.

THESE rapturous words are the climax of the apostle's long demonstration that the Gospel is the revelation of "the righteousness of God from faith to faith," and is thereby "the power of God unto salvation." What a contrast there is between the beginning and the end of his argument! It started with sombre, sad words about man's sinfulness and aversion from the knowledge of God. It closes with this sunny outburst of triumph; like some stream rising among black and barren cliffs, or melancholy moorlands, and foaming through narrow rifts in gloomy ravines, it reaches at last fertile lands, and flows calm, the sunlight dancing on its broad surface, till it loses itself at last in the unfathomable ocean of the love of God.

We are told that the Biblical view of human nature is too dark. Well, the important question is not whether it be dark, but whether it be true. But, apart from that, the doctrine of Scripture about man's moral condition is not dark, if you will take the whole of it together. Certainly, a part of it is very dark. The picture, for instance, of what men are, painted at the beginning of this Epistle, is black like a canvas of Rembrandt's. The Bible is "Nature's sternest painter but her best." But to get the whole doctrine of Scripture on the subject, we have to take its confidence as to what men may become, as well as its portrait of what they are—and then who will say that the anthropology of Scripture is gloomy? To me it seems that the unrelieved blackness of the view which, because it admits no fall, can imagine no rise, which sees in all man's sins and sorrows no token of the dominion of an alien power, and has, therefore, no reason to believe that they can be separated from humanity, is the true "Gospel of despair," and that the system which looks steadily at all the misery and all the wickedness, and calmly proposes to cast it all out, is really the only doctrine of human nature which throws any gleam of light on the darkness. Christianity begins indeed with, "There is none that doeth good, no, not one," but it ends with this victorious pæan of our text.

And what a majestic close it is to the great words that have gone before, fitly crowning even their lofty height! One might well shrink from presuming to take such words as a text, with any idea of exhausting or of enhancing them. My object is very much more humble. I simply wish to bring out the remarkable order, in which Paul here marshals, in his passionate, rhetorical amplification, all the enemies that can be supposed to seek to wrench us away from the love of God; and triumphs over them all. We shall best measure the fulness of the words by simply taking these clauses as they stand in the text.

I. The love of God is *unaffected by the extremest changes of our condition.*

The apostle begins his fervid catalogue of vanquished foes by a pair of opposites which might seem to cover the whole ground—" neither death nor life." What more can be said? Surely, these two include everything. From one point of view they do. But yet, as we shall see, there is more to be said. And the special reason for beginning with this pair of possible enemies is probably to be found by remembering that they are a pair, that between them they do cover the whole ground, and represent the *extremes* of change which can befall us. The one stands at the one pole, the other at the other. If these two stations, so far from each other, are equally near to God's love, then no intermediate point can be far from it. If the most violent change which we can experience does not in the least matter to the grasp which the love of God has on us, or to the grasp which we may have on it, then no less violent a change can be of any consequence. It is the same thought in a somewhat modified form, as we find in another word of Paul's "Whether we live, we live unto the Lord; and whether we die, we die unto the Lord." Our subordination to Him is the same, and our consecration should be the same in all varieties of condition, even in that greatest of all variations. His love to us makes no account of that mightiest of changes. How should it be affected by slighter ones?

The distance of a star is measured by the apparent change in its position, as seen from different points of the earth's surface or orbit. But this great Light stands steadfast in our heaven, nor moves a hair's breadth, nor pours a feebler ray on us, whether we look up to it from the midsummer day of busy life, or from the midwinter of death. These opposites are parted by a distance to which the millions of miles of the world's path among the stars are but a point, and yet the love of God streams down on them alike.

Of course, the confidence of immortality is implied in this thought. Death does not, in the slightest degree, affect the essential vitality of the soul; so it does not, in the slightest degree, affect the outflow of God's love to that soul. It is a change of condition and circumstance, and no more. He does not lose us in the dust of death. The withered leaves on the pathway are trampled into mud, and indistinguishable to human eyes; but He sees them even as when they hung green and sunlit on the mystic tree of life.

How beautifully this thought contrasts with the saddest aspect of the power of death in our human experience! He is Death the Separater, who unclasps our hands from the closest, dearest grasp, and divides asunder joints and marrow, and parts soul and body, and withdraws us from all our habitude and associations and occupations, and loosens every bond of society and concord, and hales us away into a lonely land. But there is one bond which his "abhorred shears" cannot cut. Their edge is turned on *it*. One Hand holds us in a grasp which the fleshless fingers of Death in vain strive to loosen. The separater becomes the uniter; he rends us apart from the world that he may "bring us to God." The love filtered by drops on us in life is poured upon us in a flood in death; "for I am persuaded, that neither death nor life shall be able to separate us from the love of God."

II. The love of God is *undiverted from us by any other order of beings*.

"Nor angels, nor principalities, nor powers," says Paul. Here we pass from conditions affecting ourselves to living beings beyond ourselves. Now, it is important for understanding the precise thought of the apostle to observe that this expression, when used without any qualifying adjective, seems uniformly to mean good angels, the hierarchy of blessed spirits before the throne. So that there is no reference to "spiritual wickedness in high places" striving to draw men away from God. The supposition which the apostle makes is, indeed, an impossible one, that these ministering spirits, who are sent forth to minister to them who shall be heirs of salvation, should so forget their mission and contradict their nature as to seek to bar us out from the love which it is their chiefest joy to bring to us. He knows it to be an impossible supposition, and its very impossibility gives energy to his conclusion, just as when in the same fashion he makes the other equally impossible supposition about an angel from heaven preaching another gospel than that which he had preached to them.

So we may turn the general thought of this second category of impotent efforts in two different ways, and suggest, first, that it implies the utter powerlessness of any third party in regard to the relations between our souls and God.

We alone have to do with Him alone. The awful fact of individuality, that solemn mystery of our personal Being, has its most blessed or its most dread manifestation in our relation to God. There no other Being has any power. Counsel and stimulus, suggestion or temptation, instruction or lies, which may tend to lead us nearer to Him or away from Him, they may indeed give us; but after they have done their best or their worst, all depends on the personal act of our own innermost being. Man nor angel can affect that, but from without. The old mystics called prayer "the flight of the lonely soul to the only God." It is the name for all religion. These two, God and the soul, have to "transact," as our Puritan forefathers used to say, as if there were no other beings in the universe but only they two. Angels and principalities and powers may stand beholding with sympathetic joy; they may minister blessing and guardianship in many ways; but the decisive act of union between God and the soul they can neither effect nor prevent.

And as for them, so for men around us; the limits of their power to harm us are soon set. They may shut us out from human love by calumnies, and dig deep gulfs of alienation between us and dear ones; they may hurt and annoy us in a thousand ways with slanderous tongues, and arrows dipped in poisonous hatred. But one thing they cannot do. They may build a wall around us, and imprison us from many a joy and many a fair prospect. But they cannot put a roof on it to keep out the sweet influences from above, or hinder us from looking up to the heavens. Nobody can come between us and God but ourselves.

Or, we may turn this general thought in another direction, and say, These blessed spirits around the throne do not absorb and intercept His love. They gather about its steps in their "solemn troops and sweet societies;" but close as are their ranks, and innumerable as is their multitude, they do not prevent that love from passing beyond them to us on the outskirts of the crowd. The planet nearest the sun is drenched and saturated with fiery brightness, but the rays from the centre of life pass on to each of the sister spheres in its turn, and travel away outwards to where the remotest of them all rolls in its far-off orbit, unknown for millenniums to dwellers closer to the sun, but through all the ages visited by warmth and light according to its needs. Like that poor sickly woman who could lay her wasted fingers on the hem of Christ's garment, notwithstanding the thronging multitude, we can reach our hands through all the crowd, or rather He reaches His strong hand to us and heals and blesses us. All the guests are fed full at that great table. One's gain is not another's loss. The multitudes sit on the green grass, and the last man of the last fifty gets as much as the first: "They did all eat, and were filled"; and more remains than fed them all.

So all beings are "nourished from the King's country," and none jostle others out of their share. This healing fountain is not exhausted of its curative power by the early comers. "I will give unto this last, even as unto thee." "Nor angels, nor principalities, nor powers, shall be able to separate us from the love of God."

III. The love of God is *raised above the power of Time.*

"Nor things present, nor things to come," is the apostle's next class of powers impotent to disunite us from the love of God. The rhythmical arrangement of the text deserves to be noticed, as bearing not only on its music and rhetorical flow, but as affecting its force. We had first a pair of opposites, and then a triplet; "death and life: angels, principalities, and powers." We have again a pair of opposites; "things present, things to come," again followed by a triplet, "height nor depth, nor any other creature." The effect of this is to divide the whole into two, and to throw the first and second classes more closely together, as also the third and fourth. Time and Space, these two mysterious ideas, which work so fatally on all human love, are powerless here.

The great Revelation of God, on which the whole of Judaism was built, was that made to Moses of the name "I Am that I Am." And parallel to the verbal revelation was that symbol of the Bush, burning and unconsumed, which is so often misunderstood. It appears wholly contrary to the usage of Scriptural visions, which are ever wont to express in material form the same truth which accompanies them in words, that the meaning of that vision should be, as it frequently taken as being, the continuance of Israel, unharmed by the fiery furnace of persecution. Not the continuance of Israel, but the eternity of Israel's God is the teaching of that flaming wonder. The burning Bush and the Name of the Lord proclaimed the same great truth of self-derived, self-determined, timeless, undecaying Being. And what better symbol than the bush burning, and yet not burning out, could be found of that God in Whose life there is no tendency to death, Whose work digs no pit of weariness into which it falls, Who gives and is none the poorer, Who fears no exhaustion in His spending, no extinction in His continual shining?

And this eternity of Being is no mere metaphysical abstraction. It is eternity of love, for God is love. That great stream, the pouring out of His own very inmost Being, knows no pause, nor does the deep fountain from which it flows ever sink one hair's breadth in its pure basin.

We know of earthly loves which cannot die. They have entered so deeply into the very fabric of the soul, that like some cloth dyed in grain, as long as two threads hold together they will retain the tint. We have to thank God for such instances of love stronger than death, which make it easier for us to believe in the unchanging duration of His. But we know, too, of love that can change, and we know that all love must part. Few of us have reached middle life, who do not, looking back, see our track strewed with the gaunt skeletons of dead friendships, and dotted with "oaks of weeping," waving green and mournful over graves, and saddened by footprints striking away from the line of march, and leaving us the more solitary for their departure.

How blessed then to know of a love which cannot change or die! The past, the present and the future are all the same to Him, to Whom "a thousand years," that can corrode so much of earthly love, are in their power to change "as one day," and "one day," which can hold so few of the expressions of our love, may be "as a thousand years" in the multitude and richness of the gifts which it can be expanded to contain. The whole of what He has been to any past, He is to us to-day. "The God of Jacob is our refuge." All these old-world stories of loving care and guidance may be repeated in our lives.

So we may bring the blessedness of all the past into the present, and calmly face the misty future, sure that it cannot rob us of His love.

"Do whate'er thou wilt, swift-footed Time,
To this wide world and all her fading sweets,"

it matters not, if only our hearts are stayed on His love, which neither things present, nor things to come, can alter or remove. Looking on all the flow of ceaseless change, the waste and fading, the alienation and cooling, the decrepitude and decay of earthly affection, we can lift up with gladness, heightened by the contrast, the triumphant song of the ancient Church: "Oh, give thanks unto the Lord: for He is good: because *His mercy endureth for ever!*"

IV. The love of God is *present everywhere.*

The apostle ends his catalogue with a singular trio of antagonists; "nor height, nor depth, nor any other creature," as if he had got impatient of the enumeration of impotencies, and having named the outside boundaries in space of the created universe, flings, as it were, with one rapid toss, into that large room the whole that it can contain, and triumphs over it all.

As the former clause proclaimed the powerlessness of Time, so this proclaims the powerlessness of that other great mystery of creatural life which we call Space. Height or depth, it matters not. That diffusive love diffuses itself equally in all directions. Up or down, it is all the same. The distance from the centre is equal to Zenith or to Nadir.

Here, we have the same process applied to that idea of Omnipresence as was applied in the former clause to the idea of Eternity. That thought, so hard to grasp with vividness, and not altogether a glad one to a sinful soul, is all softened and glorified, as some solemn Alpine cliff of bare rock is when the tender morning light glows on it, when it is thought of as the Omnipresence of Love. "Thou, God, seest me," may be a stern word, if the God Who sees be but a mighty Maker or a righteous Judge. As reasonably might we expect a prisoner in his solitary cell to be glad when he thinks that the jailer's eye is on him from some unseen spy-hole in the wall, as expect any thought of God but one to make a man read that grand one hundred and thirty-ninth Psalm with joy: "If

I ascend into heaven, Thou art there; if I make my bed in Sheol, behold, Thou art there." So may a man say shudderingly to himself, and tremble as he asks in vain, "Whither shall I flee from Thy Presence?" But how different it all is when we can cast over the marble whiteness of that solemn thought the warm hue of life, and change the form of our words into this of our text: "Nor height, nor depth, shall be able to separate us from the love of God."

In that great ocean of the Divine love we live and move and have our being, floating in it like some sea flower which spreads its filmy beauty and waves its long tresses in the depths of mid-ocean. The sound of its waters is ever in our ears, and above, beneath, around us, its mighty currents run evermore. We need not cower before the fixed gaze of some stony god, looking on us unmoved like those Egyptian deities that sit pitiless with idle hands on their laps, and wide-open lidless eyes gazing out across the sands. We need not fear the Omnipresence of Love, nor the Omniscience which knows us altogether, and loves us even as it knows. Rather we shall be glad that we are ever in His Presence, and desire, as the height of all felicity and the power for all goodness, to walk all the day long in the light of His countenance, till the day come when we shall receive the crown of our perfecting in that we shall be "ever with the Lord."

The recognition of this triumphant sovereignty of love over all these real and supposed antagonists makes us, too, lords over them, and delivers us from the temptations which some of them present us to separate ourselves from the love of God. They all become our servants and helpers, uniting us to that love. So we are set free from the dread of death and from the distractions incident to life. So we are delivered from superstitious dread of an unseen world, and from craven fear of men. So we are emancipated from absorption in the present and from careful thought for the future. So we are at home everywhere, and every corner of the universe is to us one of the many mansions of our Father's house. "All things are yours, . . . and ye are Christ's; and Christ is God's."

I do not forget the closing words of this great text. I have not ventured to include them in our present subject, because they would have introduced another wide region of thought to be laid down on our already too narrow canvas.

But remember, I beseech you, that this love of God is explained by our apostle to be "in Christ Jesus our Lord." Love illimitable, all-pervasive, eternal; yes, but a love which has a channel and a course; love which has a method and a process by which it pours itself over the world. It is not, as some representations would make it, a vague, nebulous light diffused through space as in a chaotic, half-made universe, but all gathered in that great Light which rules the day—even in Him Who said: "I am the Light of the World." In Christ the love of God is all centred and embodied, that it may be imparted to all sinful and hungry hearts, even as burning coals are gathered on a hearth that they may give warmth to all that are in the house. "God *so* loved the world" —not merely *so much*, but in *such a fashion*—"that"— that what? Many people would leap at once from the first to the last clause of the verse, and regard eternal life for all and sundry as the only adequate expression of the universal love of God. Not so does Christ speak. Between that universal love and its ultimate purpose and desire for every man He inserts two conditions, one on God's part, one on man's. God's love reaches its end, namely, the bestowal of eternal life, by means of a Divine act and a human response. "God *so* loved the world, that He *gave* His only-begotten Son, that whosoever *believeth* in Him should not perish, but have everlasting life." So all the universal love of God for you and me and for all our brethren is " in Christ Jesus our Lord," and faith in Him unites us to it by bonds which no foe can break, no shock of change can snap, no time can rot, no distance can stretch to breaking. " For I am persuaded, that neither death, nor life, nor angels, nor principalities, nor powers, nor things present, nor things to come, nor height, nor depth, nor any other creature, shall be able to separate us from the love of God, which is in Christ Jesus our Lord."

SERMON VIII.

THE GRAVE OF THE DEAD JOHN AND THE GRAVE OF THE LIVING JESUS.

St. Matthew xiv. 12.

And John's disciples came, and took up the body, and buried it, and went and told Jesus.

St. Matthew xxviii. 8.

And they departed quickly from the sepulchre with fear and great joy.

THERE is a remarkable parallel and still more remarkable contrast between these two groups of disciples at the graves of their respective masters. John the Baptist's followers venture into the very jaws of the lion to rescue the headless corse of their martyred teacher from a prison grave. They bear it away and lay it reverently in its unknown sepulchre, and when they have done these last offices of love they feel that all is over. They have no longer a centre, and they disintegrate. There was nothing to hold them together any more. The shepherd had been smitten, and the flock were scattered. As a "school" or a distinct community they cease to be, and are mostly absorbed into the ranks of

Christ's followers. That sorrowful little company that turned from John's grave, perhaps amidst the grim rocks of Moab, perhaps in his native city amongst the hills of Judah, parted, then, to meet no more, and to bear away only a common sorrow that time would comfort, and a common memory that time would dim.

The other group laid their martyred Master in his grave with as tender hands and as little hope as did John's disciples. The bond that held them together was gone too, and the disintegrating process began at once. We see them breaking up into little knots, and soon they, too, will be scattered. The women come to the grave to perform the woman's office of anointing, and they are left to go alone. Other slight hints are given which show how much the ties of companionship had been relaxed, even in a day, and how certainly and quickly they would have fallen asunder. But all at once a new element comes in, all is changed. The earliest visitors to the sepulchre leave it, not with the lingering sorrow of those who have no more that they can do, but with the quick buoyant step of people charged with great and glad tidings. They come to it wrapped in grief—they leave it with great joy. They come to it, feeling that all was over, and their union with the rest who had loved Him was little more than a remembrance. They go away feeling that they are bound together more closely than ever.

The grave of John was the end of a "school." The grave of Jesus was the beginning of a Church. Why? The only answer is the message which the women brought back from the empty sepulchre on that Easter day: "The Lord is risen." The whole history of the Christian Church, and even its very existence, is unintelligible, except on the supposition of the resurrection. But for that, the fate of John's disciples would have been the fate of Christ's—they would have melted away into the mass of the nation, and at most there would have been one more petty Galilean sect, that would have lived on for a generation and died out when the last of his companions died.

So from these two contrasted groups we may fairly gather some thoughts as to the Resurrection of Christ, as attested by the very existence of a Christian Church, and as to the joy of that resurrection.

I. Now the first point to be considered is, That the conduct of Christ's disciples after His death was exactly the opposite of what might have been expected.

They held together. The natural thing for them to do would have been to disband; for the one bond was gone; and if they had acted according to the ordinary laws of human conduct they would have said to themselves, Let us go back to our fishing-boats and our tax-gathering, and seek safety in separation, and nurse our sorrow apart. A few lingering days might have been given to weep together at His grave, and to assuage the first bitterness of grief and disappointment; but when these were over, nothing could have prevented Christianity and the Church from being buried in the same sepulchre as Jesus. As certainly as the stopping up of the fountain would empty the river's bed, so surely would Christ's death have scattered His disciples. And that strange fact, that it did not scatter them, needs to be looked well into and fairly accounted for in some plausible manner. The end of John's school gives a parallel which brings the singularity of the fact into stronger relief; and looking at these two groups as they stand before us in these two texts, the question is irresistibly suggested, Why did not the one fall away into its separate elements, as the other did? The keystone of the arch was in both cases withdrawn —why did the one structure topple into ruin while the other stood firm?

Not only did the disciples of Christ keep united, but their conceptions of Jesus underwent a remarkable change, on His death. We might have expected indeed that, when memory began to work, and the disturbing influence of daily association was withdrawn, the same idealising process would have begun on their image of Him, which reveals and ennobles the characters of our dear ones who have gone away from us. Most men have to die before their true beauty is discerned. But no process of that sort will suffice to account for the change and heightening of the disciples' thoughts about their dead Lord. It was not merely that, as they remembered, they said, Did not our hearts burn within us by the way while He talked with us?—but that His death wrought exactly the opposite effect from what it might have been expected to do. It ought to have ended their hope that He was the Messiah, and we know that within forty-eight hours it was beginning to do so, as we learn from the plaintive words of disappointed and fading hope: "We trusted that it had been He which should have redeemed Israel." If, so early, the cold conviction was stealing over their hearts that their dearest expectation was proved by His death to have been a dream, what could have prevented its entire dominion over them, as the days grew into months and years? But somehow or other that process was arrested, and the opposite one set in. The death that should have shattered Messianic dreams confirmed them. The death that should have cast a deeper shadow of incomprehensibleness over His strange and lofty claims poured a new light upon them, which made them all plain and clear. The very parts of His teaching which His death would have made those who loved Him wish to forget, became the centre of His followers' faith. His cross became His throne. Whilst He lived with them they knew not what He said in His deepest words, but, by a strange paradox, His death convinced them that He was the Son of God, and that that which they had seen with their eyes, and their hands had handled, was the Eternal Life. The cross alone could never have done that. Something else there must have been, if the men were sane, to account for this paradox.

Nor is this all. Another equally unlikely sequel of the death of Jesus is the unmistakable moral transformation effected on the disciples. Timorous and tremulous before, something or other touched them into altogether new boldness and self-possession. Dependent on His presence before, and helpless when He was away from them for an hour, they become all at once strong and calm; they stand before the fury of a Jewish mob and the threatenings of the Sanhedrim, unmoved and victorious. And these brave confessors and saintly heroes are the men who, a few weeks before, had been petulant, self-willed, jealous, cowardly. What had lifted them suddenly so far above themselves? Their Master's death? That would more naturally have taken any heart or courage out of them, and left them indeed as sheep in the midst of wolves. Why, then, do they thus strangely blaze up into grandeur and heroism? Can any reasonable account be given of these paradoxes? Surely it is not too much to ask of people who profess to explain Christianity on naturalistic principles, that they shall make the process clear to us by which, Christ being dead and buried, His disciples were kept together, learned to think more loftily of Him and sprang at once to a new grandeur of character. Why did not they do as John's disciples did, and disappear? Why was not the stream lost in the sand, when the head-waters were cut off.

II. Notice then, next, that the disciples' immediate belief in the Resurrection furnishes a reasonable, and the only reasonable, explanation of the facts. There is no better historical evidence of a fact than the existence of an institution built upon it, and coeval with it. The Christian Church is such evidence for the fact of the resurrection; or, to put the conclusion in the most moderate fashion, for the belief in the resurrection. For, as we have shown, the natural effect of our Lord's death would have been to shatter the whole fabric: and if that effect were not produced, the only reasonable account of the force that hindered it is, that His followers believed that He rose again. Since that was their faith, one can understand how they were banded more closely together than ever. One can understand how their eyes were opened to know Him who was "declared to be the Son of God with power by the resurrection from the dead." One can understand how, in the enthusiasm of these new thoughts of their Lord, and in the strength of His victory over death, they put aside their old fears and littlenesses and clothed themselves in armour of light. "The Lord is risen indeed" was the belief which made the continuous existence of the Church possible. Any other explanation of that great outstanding fact is lame and hopelessly insufficient.

We know that that belief was the belief of the early Church. Even if one waived all reference to the gospels we have the means of demonstrating that in Paul's undisputed epistles. Nobody has questioned that he wrote the First Epistle to the Corinthians. The date most generally assumed to that letter brings it within about five-and-twenty years of the crucifixion. In that letter, in addition to a multitude of incidental references to the Lord as risen, we have the great passage in the fifteenth chapter, where the apostle not only declares that the Resurrection was one of the two facts which made his "gospel," but solemnly enumerates the witnesses of the risen Lord, and alleges that this gospel of the resurrection was common to him and to all the Church. He tells us of Christ's appearance to himself at his conversion, which must have taken place within six or seven years of the crucifixion, and assures us that at that early period he found the whole Church believing and preaching Christ's resurrection. Their belief rested on their alleged intercourse with Him a few days after his death, and it is inconceivable that within so short a period such a belief should have sprung up and been universally received if it had not begun when and as they said it did.

But we are not left even to inferences of this kind to show that from the beginning the Church witnessed to the resurrection of Jesus. Its own existence is the great witness to its faith. And it is important to observe that, even if we had not the documentary evidence of the Pauline epistles as the earliest records of the gospels, and of the Acts of the Apostles, we should still have sufficient proof that the belief in the resurrection is as old as the Church. For the continuance of the Church cannot be explained without it. If that faith had not dawned on their slow sad hearts on that Easter morning, a few weeks would have seen them scattered : and if once they had been scattered, as they inevitably would have been, no power could have reunited them, any more than a diamond once shattered can be pieced together again. There would have been no motive and no actors to frame a story of resurrection when once the little company had melted away. The existence of the Church depended on their belief that the Lord was risen. In the nature of the case that belief must have followed immediately on his death. It, and it only, reasonably accounts for the facts. And so, over and above apostles, and gospels, and epistles, the Church is the great witness, by its very being, to its own immediate and continuous belief in the resurrection of our Lord.

III. Again, we may remark that such a belief could not have originated or maintained itself unless it had been true.

Our previous remarks have gone no farther than to establish the belief in the resurrection of Christ, as the basis of primitive Christianity. It is vehemently alleged, and we may freely admit, that the step is a long one from subjective belief to objective reality. But still it is surely perfectly fair to argue that a given belief is of such a nature that it cannot be supposed to rest on anything less solid than a fact; and this is eminently the case in regard to the belief in Christ's resurrection. There have been many attempts on the part of those who reject that belief to account for its existence, and each of them in succession has "had its day, and ceased to be." Unbelief devours its own children remorselessly, and the succession to the throne of anti-christian scepticism is won, as in some barbarous tribes, by slaying the reigning sovereign. The armies of the aliens turn their weapons against one another, and each new assailant of the historical veracity of the gospels commences operations by showing that all previous assailants have been wrong, and that none of their explanations will hold water.

For instance, we hear nothing now of the coarse old explanation that the story of the resurrection was a lie, and became current through the conscious imposture of the leaders of the Church. And it was high time that such a solution should be laid aside. Who, with half an eye for character, could study the deeds and the writings of the apostles, and not feel that, whatever else they were, they were profoundly honest, and as convinced as of their own existence, that they had seen Christ " alive after His passion, by many infallible proofs"? If Paul and Peter and John were conspirators in a trick, then their lives and their words were the most astounding anomaly. Who, either, that had the faintest perception of the forces that sway opinion and frame systems, could believe that the fair fabric of Christian morality was built on the sand of a lie, and cemented by the slime of deceit bubbling up from the very pit of hell? Do men gather grapes of thorns, or figs of thistles? That insolent hypothesis has had its day.

Then when it was discredited, we were told the mythical tendency would explain everything. It showed us how good men could tell lies without knowing it, and how the religious value of an alleged fact in an alleged historical revelation did not in the least depend on its being a fact. And that great discovery, which first converted solid historical Christianity into a gaseous condition, and then caught the fumes in some kind of retort, and professed to hand us them back again improved by the sublimation, has pretty well gone the way of all hypotheses. Myths are not made in three days, or in three years, and no more time can be allowed for the formation of the myth of the resurrection. What was the Church to feed on while the myth was growing? It would have been starved to death long before.

Then, the last new explanation which is gravely put forward, and is the prevailing one now, sustains itself by reference to undeniable facts in the history of religious movements, and of such abnormal attitudes of the mind as modern spiritualism. On the strength of which analogy we are invited to see in the faith of the early Christians in the resurrection of the Lord a gigantic instance of "hallucination." No doubt there have been, and still are, extraordinary instances of its power, especially in minds excited by religious ideas. But we have only to consider the details of the facts in hand to feel that they cannot be accounted for on such a ground. Do hallucinations lay hold on five hundred people at once? Does a hallucination last for a long country walk, and give rise to protracted conversation? Does hallucination explain the story of Christ eating and drinking before His disciples? The uncertain twilight of the garden might have begotten such an airy phantom in the brain of a single sobbing woman; but the appearances to be explained are so numerous, so varied in character, embrace so many details, appeal to so many of the senses—to the ear and hand as well as to the eye—were spread over so long a period, and were simultaneously shared by so large a number, that no theory of such a sort can account for them, unless by impugning the veracity of the records. And then we are back again on the old abandoned ground of deceit and imposture. It sounds plausible to say, Hallucination is a proved cause of many a supposed supernatural event—why not of this? But the plausibility of the solution ceases as soon as you try it on the actual facts in their variety and completeness. It has to be eked out with a length of the fox's skin of deceit before it covers them; and we may confidently assert that such a belief as the belief of the early Church in the resurrection of the Lord was never the product either of deceit or of illusion, or of any amalgam of the two.

What new solutions the fertility of unbelief may yet bring forth, and the credulity of unbelief may yet accept, we know not : but we may firmly hold by the faith which breathed new hope and strange joy into that sad band on the first Easter morning, and rejoice with them in the glad wonderful fact that He is risen from the dead.

IV. For that message is a message to us as truly as to the heavy-hearted unbelieving men that first received it. We may think for a moment of the joy with which *we* should return from the sepulchre of the risen Saviour.

How little these women knew that, as they went back from the grave in the morning twilight, they were the bearers of "great joy which should be to all people!" To them and to the first hearers of their message there would be little clear in the rush of glad surprise, beyond the blessed thought, Then He is not gone from us altogether. Sweet visions of the resumption of happy companionship would fill their minds, and it would not be until calmer moments that the stupendous significance of the fact would reveal itself.

Mary's rapturous gesture to clasp Him by the feet,

when the certainty that it was in very deed He, flooded her soul with dazzling light, reveals her first emotion, which no doubt was also the first with them all, "Then we shall have Him with us again, and all the old joy of companionship will be ours once more." Nor were they wrong in thinking so, however little they as yet understood the future manner of their fellowship, or anticipated His leaving them so soon. Nor are we without a share even in that phase of their joy; for the resurrection of Jesus Christ gives us a living Lord for our love, an ever present Companion and Brother for our hearts to hold, even if our hands cannot clasp Him by the feet. A dead Christ might have been the object of faint historical admiration, and the fair statue might have stood amidst others in the halls of the world; but the risen, living Christ can love and be loved, and we too may be glad with the joy of those who have found a heart to rest their hearts upon, and a companionship that can never fail.

As the early disciples learned to reflect upon the fact of Christ's resurrection, its riches unfolded themselves by degrees, and the earliest aspect of its "power" was the lihgt it shed on His person and work. Taught by it, as we have seen, they recognised Him for the Messiah whom they had long expected, and for something more —the Incarnate Son of God. That phase of their joy belongs to us too. If Christ, who made such avowals of His nature as we know He did, and hazarded such assertions of His claims, His personality and His office, as fill the gospels, were really laid in the grave and saw corruption, then the assertions are disproved, the claims unwarranted, the office a figment of His imagination. He may still remain a great teacher, with a tremendous deduction to be made from the worth of His teaching. But all that is deepest in His own words about Himself, and His relation to men, must be sorrowfully put on one side. But if He, after such assertions and claims, rose from the dead, and rising, dieth no more, then for the last time, and in the mightiest tones, the voice that rent the heavens at His baptism and His transfiguration proclaims: "This is My beloved Son; hear ye Him." Our joy in His resurrection is the joy of those to whom He is therein declared to be the Son of God, and who see in Christ risen their accepted Sacrifice, and their ever-living Redeemer.

Such was the earliest effect of the resurrection of Jesus, if we trust the records of apostolic preaching. Then by degrees the joyful thought took shape in the Church's consciousness that their Shepherd had gone before them into the dark pen where Death pastured his flocks, and had taken it for His own, for the quiet resting-place where He would make them lie down by still waters, and whence He would lead them out to the lofty mountains where His fold should be. The power of Christ's resurrection as the pattern and pledge of ours is the final source of the joy which may fill our hearts as we turn away from that empty sepulchre.

The world has guessed and feared, or guessed and hoped, but always guessed and doubted the life beyond. Analogies, poetic adumbrations, probabilities drawn from consciousness and from conscience, from intuition and from anticipation, are but poor foundations on which to build a solid faith. But to those to whom the resurrection of Christ is a fact their own future life is a fact. Here we have a solid certainty, and here alone. The heart says as we lay our dear ones in the grave, "Surely we part not for ever." The conscience says, as it points us to our own evil deeds, "After death the judgment." A deep indestructible instinct prophesies in every breast of a future. But all is vague and doubtful. The one proof of a life beyond the grave is the resurrection of Jesus Christ. Therefore let us be glad with the gladness of men plucked from a dark abyss of doubt and uncertainty, and planted on the rock of solid certainty; and let us rejoice with joy unspeakable, and laden with a prophetic weight of glory, as we ring out the ancient Easter morning's greeting, " The Lord is risen indeed !"

SERMON IX.

THE TRANSLATION OF ELIJAH AND THE ASCENSION OF CHRIST.

2 KINGS ii. 11.

And it came to pass, as they still went on, and talked, that, behold, there appeared a chariot of fire, and horses of fire, and parted them both asunder; and Elijah went up by a whirlwind into heaven.

ST. LUKE xxiv. 51.

And it came to pass, while he blessed them, he was parted from them, and carried up into heaven.

THESE two events, the Translation of Elijah and the Ascension of our Lord, have sometimes been put side by side in order to show that the latter narrative is nothing but a "variant" of the former. See, it is said, the source of your New Testament story is only the old legend shaped anew by the wistful regrets of the early disciples. But to me it seems that the simple comparison of the two narratives is sufficient to bring out such fundamental difference in the ideas which they respectively embody as amount to opposition, and make any such theory of the origin of the later absurdly improbable. I could wish no better foil for the history of the ascension than the history of Elijah's rapture. The comparison brings out contrasts at every step, and there is no readier way of throwing into strong relief the meaning and purpose of the former, than holding up beside it the story of the latter. The real parallel makes the divergences the more remarkable, for likeness sharpens our perception of unlikeness, and no contrast is so forcible as the contrast of things that correspond. I am much mistaken if we shall not find almost every truth of importance connected with our Lord's ascension emphasised for us by the comparison to which we now proceed.

I. The first point which may be mentioned is the contrast between the *manner* of Elijah's translation, and that of our Lord's ascension.

It is perhaps not without significance that the place of the one event was on the uplands or in some of the rocky gorges beyond Jordan, and that of the other, the slopes of Olivet above Bethany. The lonely prophet, who had burst like a meteor on Israel from the solitudes of Gilead, whose fervour had ever and again been rekindled by return to the wilderness, whose whole career had isolated him from men, found the fitting place for that last wonder amidst the stern silence where he had so often sought asylum and inspiration. He was close to the scenes of mighty events in the past. There, on that overhanging peak, the lawgiver whose work he was continuing and with whom he was to be so strangely associated on the Mount of Transfiguration, had made him ready for his lonely grave. Here at his feet, the river had parted for the victorious march of Israel. Away down on his horizon the sunshine gleamed on the waters of the Dead Sea; and thus, on his native soil, surrounded by memorials of the Law which he laboured to restore, and of the victories which he would fain have brought back, and of the judgments which he saw again impending over Israel, the stern solitary ascetic, the prophet of righteousness, whose single arm stayed the downward course of a nation, passed from his toil and his warfare.

What a different set of associations cluster round the place of Christ's ascension—"Bethany," or, as it is more particularly specified in the Acts, "Olivet!" In the very heart of the land, close by and yet out of sight of the great city, in no wild solitude, but perhaps in some dimple of the hill, neither shunning nor courting spectators, with the quiet home where he had rested so often in the little village at their feet there, and Gethsemane a few furlongs off, in such scenes did the Christ whose delights were with the sons of men, and His life lived in closest companionship with His brethren, choose the place whence He should ascend to their Father and His Father. Nor perhaps was it without a meaning that the Mount which received the last print of His ascending footstep was that which a mysterious prophecy designated as destined to receive the first print of the footstep of the Lord coming to end the long warfare with evil at a future day.

But more important than the localities is the contrasted manner of the two ascents. The prophet's end was like the man. It was fitting that he should be swept up the skies in tempest and fire. The impetuosity of his nature, and the stormy energy of his career had already been symbolised in the mighty and strong wind which rent the rocks, and in the fire that followed the earthquake; and similarly nothing could be more appropriate than that sudden rapture in storm and whirlwind, escorted by the flaming chivalry of heaven.

Nor is it only as appropriate to the character of the prophet and his work that this tempestuous translation is noteworthy. It also suggests very plainly that Elijah was lifted to the skies by power acting on him from without. He did not ascend; he was carried up; the earthly frame and the human nature had no power to rise. "No man hath ascended into heaven." The two men of whom the Old Testament speaks were alike in this, that "God *took* them." The tempest and the fiery chariot tell us how great was the exercise of Divine power which bore the gross mortality thither, and how unfamiliar the sphere into which it passed.

How full of the very spirit of Christ's whole life is the contrasted manner of His ascension! The silent gentleness, which did not strive nor cry nor cause His voice to be heard in the streets, marks Him even in that hour of lofty and transcendent triumph. There is no outward sign to accompany His slow upward movement through the quiet air. No blaze of fiery chariots, nor agitation of tempest is needed to bear Him heavenwards. The out-stretched hands drop the dew of His benediction on the little company, and so He floats upward, His own will and indwelling power the royal chariot which bears him, and calmly "leaves the world and goes unto the

Father." The slow continuous movement of ascent is emphatically made prominent in the brief narratives, both by the phrase in Luke, "He was carried up," which expresses the continuous leisurely motion, and by the picture in the Acts, of the disciples gazing into heaven "as He went up," in which latter word is brought out, not only the slowness of the movement, but its origin in His own will and its carrying out by His own power.

Nor is this absence of any vehicle or external agency destroyed by the fact that " a cloud " received Him out of their sight, for its purpose was not to raise Him heavenward, but to hide Him from the gazers' eyes, that He might not seem to them to dwindle into distance, but that their last look and memory might be of His clearly discerned and loving face. Possibly too, we may be intended to remember the cloud which guided Israel, the glory which dwelt between the cherubim, the cloud which overshadowed the Mount of Transfiguration, and to see in this a symbol of the Divine Presence welcoming to itself, His battle fought, the Son of His love.

Be that as it may, the manner of our Lord's ascension by His own inherent power is brought into boldest relief when contrasted with Elijah's rapture, and is evidently the fitting expression, as it is the consequence, of His sole and singular Divine nature. It accords with His own manner of reference to the ascension, while He was on earth, which ever represents Him not as *being taken*, but as *going:* "I leave the world and go to the Father." "I ascend to my Father and their Father." The highest hope of the devoutest souls before Him had been, "Thou wilt afterwards take me to glory." The highest hope of devout souls since Him has been, "We shall be caught up to meet the Lord." But this man ever speaks of Himself as able when He will, by His own power, to rise where no man hath ascended. His Divine nature and pre-existence shine clearly forth, and as we stand gazing at Him blessing the world as He rises into the heavens, we know that we are looking on no mere mysterious elevation of a mortal to the skies, but are beholding the return of the Incarnate Lord, that willed to tarry among our earthly tabernacles for a time, to the glory where He was before, "His own calm home, His habitation from eternity."

II. Another striking point of contrast embraces the relation which these two events respectively bear to *the life's work which had preceded them.*

The falling mantle of Elijah has become a symbol known to all the world, for the transference of unfinished tasks and the appointment of successors to departed greatness. Elisha asked that he might have a double portion of his master's spirit, not meaning twice as much as his master had had, but the eldest son's share of the father's possessions, the double of the other children's portion. And, though his master had no power to bestow the gift, and had to reply as one who has nothing that he has not received, and cannot dispose of the grace that dwells in him, the prayer was answered, and the feebler nature of Elisha was fitted for the continuance of the work which Elijah left undone.

The mantle that passed from one to the other was the symbol of office and authority transferred; the functions were the same, whilst the holders had changed. The sons of the prophets bow before the new master; "the spirit of Elijah doth rest on Elisha."

So the world goes on. Man after man serves his generation by the will of God, and is gathered to his fathers; and a new arm grasps the mantle to smite Jordan, and a new voice speaks from his empty place, and men recognise the successor, and forget the predecessor.

We turn to Christ's ascension, and there we meet with nothing analogous to this transference of office. No mantle falling from His shoulders lights on any of that group, none are hailed as His successors. What He has done bears and needs no repetition whilst time shall roll, whilst eternity shall last. His work is one: "the help that is done on earth, He doeth it all Himself." His ascension completed the witness of heaven begun at His resurrection that "He has offered one sacrifice for sins, for ever." He has left no unfinished work which another may perfect. He has done no work which another may do again for new generations. He has spoken all truth, and none may add to His words. He has fulfilled all righteousness, and none may better His pattern. He has borne all the world's sin, and no time can waste the power of that sacrifice, nor any man add to its absolute sufficiency. This king of men wears a crown to which there is no heir. This priest has a priesthood which passes to no other. This "prophet" does "live for ever." The world sees all other guides and helpers pass away, and every man's work is caught up by other hands and carried on where he drops it, and the short memories and shorter gratitudes of men turn to the rising sun ; but one name remains undimmed by distance, and one work remains unapproached and unapproachable, and one man remains whose office none other can hold, whose bow none but He can bend, whose mantle none can wear. Christ has ascended up on high and left a finished work for all men to trust, for no man to continue.

III. Whilst our Lord's ascension is thus marked as the seal of a work in which He has no successor, it is also emphatically set forth, by contrast with Elijah's translation, as *the transition to a continuous energy* for and in the world.

Clearly the other narrative derives all its pathos from the thought that Elijah's work is done. His task is over, and nothing more is to be hoped for from him. But that same absence from the history of Christ's ascension, of any hint of a successor, to which we have referred in the previous remarks, has an obvious bearing on His present relation to the world as well as on the completeness of His unique past work.

When He ascended up on high, He relinquished nothing of His activity for us, but only cast it into a new form, which in some sense is yet higher than that which it took on earth. His work for the world is in one aspect completed on the cross, but in another it will never be completed until all the blessings which that cross has lodged in the midst of humanity, have reached their widest possible diffusion and their highest possible development. Long ages ago He cried, "It is finished," but we may be far yet from the time when He shall say, "It is done;" and for all the slow years between His own word gives us the law of his activity, "My father worketh hitherto, and I work."

That ascension is no withdrawal of the Captain of our salvation from the field where we are left to fight, nor has He gone up to the mountain, leaving us alone to tug at the oar, and shiver in the cold night air. True, there may seem a strange contrast between the present condition of the Lord who "was received up into heaven, and sat on the right hand of God," and that of the servants wandering through the world on *His* business; but the contrast is harmonised by the next words, "the Lord also worketh with them." Yes, He has gone up to sit at the right hand of God. That session at God's right hand to which the ascension is chiefly of importance as the transition, means the repose of a perfected redemption, the communion of Divine worship, the exercise of all the omnipotence of God, the administration of the world's history. He has ascended that He might fill all things, that He might pour out His spirit upon us, that the path to God may be trodden by our lame feet, that the whole resources of the Divine nature may be wielded by the hands that were nailed to the cross, and for the furtherance of the same mighty purpose of salvation.

Elijah knew not whether his spirit could descend upon his follower. But Christ, though as we have said, He left no legacy of falling mantle to any, left His spirit to His people. What Elisha gained, Elijah lost. What Elisha desired, Elijah could not give nor guarantee. How firm and assured beside Elijah's dubious "Thou hast asked a hard thing," and his "If thou see me, it shall be so" is Christ's "It is expedient for you that I go away. For if I go not away the Comforter will not come, but if I depart, I will send him unto you."

So manifold are the forms of that new and continuous activity of Christ into which He had passed when He left the earth: and as we contrast these with the utter helplessness any longer to counsel, rebuke or save, to which death reduces those who love us best, and to which even his glorious rapture into the heavens brought the strong prophet of fire, we can take up, with a new depth of meaning, the ancient words that tell of Christ's exclusive prerogative of succouring and inspiring from within the veil: "Thou hast ascended on high; thou hast led captivity captive; thou hast received gifts for men."

IV. The ascension of Christ is still further set forth, in its very circumstances, by contrast with Elijah's translation, as bearing on the *hopes of humanity for the future.*

The prophet is caught up to the glory and the rest for himself alone, and the sole share which the gazing follower or the sons of the prophets, straining their eyes there at Jericho, had in his triumph, was a deepened conviction of this prophet's mission, and perhaps some clearer faith in a future life. Their wonder and sorrow,

Elisha's immediate grasping of his new power, the prophets' immediate transference of their allegiance to their new head, show that on both sides it was felt they had no interest in the event beyond that of awe-struck beholders. No light streamed from it on their own future. The path they had to tread was still the common road into the great darkness, as solitary and unknown as before. The chariot of fire parted their master from the common experience of humanity as from their fellowship, making him an exception to the sad rule of death, which frowned the grimmer and more inexorable by contrast with his radiant translation.

The very reverse is true of Christ's ascension. In Him our nature is taken up to the throne of God. His resurrection assures us that "them which sleep in Jesus will God bring with him." His passage to the heavens assures us that "they who are alive and remain shall be caught up together with them," and that all of both companies shall with Him live and reign, sharing His dominion, and moulded to His image.

If we would know of what our manhood is capable, if we would rise to the height of the hopes which God means that we should cherish, if we would gain a living grasp of the power that fulfils them, we have to stand there gazing on the piled cloud that sails slowly upwards, the pure floor for our Brother's feet. As we watch it rising with a motion which is rest, we have the right to think, "Thither the forerunner is for us entered." We see there what man is meant for, what men who love Him attain. True, the world is still full of death and sorrow, man's dominion seems a futile dream and a hope that mocks, but we see Jesus, ascended up on high, and in Him we too are made to sit together in heavenly places. " The breaker is gone up before them. Their king shall pass before them, and the Lord at the head of them."

There is yet another aspect in which our Lord's ascension bears on our hopes for the future, namely, as connected with His coming again.

There, too, the contrast of Elijah's translation may serve for emphasis. Prophecy, indeed, in its latest voice, spoke of sending Elijah the prophet before the coming of the day of the Lord, and rabbinical legends delighted to tell how he had been carried to the Garden of Eden, whence he would come again, in Israel's sorest need. But the prophecy had no thought of a personal reappearance, and the dreams are only dreams such as we find in the legendary history of many nations. As Elisha recrossed the Jordan, he bore with him only a mantle and a memory, not a hope.

" Ye men of Galilee, why stand ye gazing up into heaven? This same Jesus, which is taken up from you into heaven, shall so come in like manner as ye have seen him go into heaven." How grand is the use in these mighty words of the name Jesus, the name that speaks of His true humanity, with all its weakness, limitations, and sorrow, with all its tenderness and brotherhood! The man who died and rose again, has gone up on high. " He will so come as He has gone." " So "—that is to say, personally, corporeally, visibly, on clouds, perhaps to that very spot, " and his feet shall stand in that day upon the Mount of Olives." Thus Scripture teaches us ever to associate together the departure and the coming of the Lord, and always when we meditate on His ascension to prepare a place for us, to think of His real presence with us through the ages, and of His coming again to receive us to Himself.

That parting on Olivet cannot be the end. Such a leave-taking is the prophecy of happy greetings and an inseparable reunion. The king has gone to receive a kingdom, and to return. Memory and hope coalesce, as we think of Him who is passed into the heavens, and the heart of the church has to cherish at once the glad thought that its Head and helper has entered within the veil, and the still more joyous one, which lightens the days of separation and widowhood, that the Lord will come again.

So let us take our share in the great joy with which the disciples returned to Jerusalem, left like sheep in the midst of wolves as they were, and "let us set our affections on things above, where Christ is, sitting at the right hand of God."

SERMON X.

CAN WE MAKE SURE OF TO-MORROW?

A NEW YEAR'S SERMON.

ISAIAH lvi. 12.

To-morrow shall be as this day, and much more abundant.

THESE words, as they stand, are the call of boon companions to new revelry. They are part of the prophet's picture of a corrupt age when the men of influence and position had thrown away their sense of duty, and had given themselves over, as aristocracies and plutocracies are ever tempted to do, to mere luxury and good living. They are summoning one another to their coarse orgies. The roystering speaker says, "Do not be afraid to drink; the cellar will hold out. To-day's carouse will not empty it; there will be enough for to-morrow." He forgets to-morrow's headaches; he forgets that on some to-morrow the wine will be finished; he forgets that the fingers of a hand may write the doom of the rioters on the very walls of the banqueting chamber.

What have such words, the very motto of insolent presumption and short-sighted animalism, to do with New Year's thoughts? Only this, that base and foolish as they are on such lips, it is possible to lift them from the mud, and take them as the utterance of a lofty and calm hope which will not be disappointed, and of a firm and lowly resolve which may ennoble life. Like a great many other sayings, they may fit the mouth either of a sot or of a saint. All depends on what the things are which we are thinking about when we use them. There are things about which it is absurd and worse than absurd to say this, and there are things about which it is the soberest truth to say it. So looking forward into the merciful darkness of another year, we may look at these words as either the expressions of hopes which it is folly to cherish, or of hopes that it is reasonable to entertain.

I. This expectation, if directed to any outward things, is an illusion and a dream.

These coarse revellers into whose lips our text is put only meant by it to brave the future and defy to-morrow in the riot of their drunkenness. They show us the vulgarest, lowest form which the expectation can take, a form which I need say nothing about now.

But I may just note in passing that to look forward principally to anticipate pleasure or enjoyment is a very poor and unworthy thing. It is weakening and lowering every day, to use our faculty of hope mainly to paint the future as a scene of delights and satisfactions. We spoil to-day by thinking how we can turn it to the account of pleasure. We spoil to-morrow before it comes, and hurt ourselves, if we are more engaged with fancying how it will minister to our joy, than how we can make it minister to our duty. It is base and foolish to be forecasting our pleasures, the true temper is to be forecasting our work.

But, leaving that consideration, let us notice how useless such anticipation, and how mad such confidence, as that expressed in the text is, if directed to anything short of God.

We are so constituted as that we grow into a persuasion that what has been will be, and yet we can give no sufficient reason to ourselves of why we expect it.

"The uniformity of the course of nature" is the cornerstone, not only of physical science, but, in a more homely form, of the wisdom which grows with experience. We all believe that the sun will rise to-morrow because it rose to-day, and for all the yesterdays. But there was a to-day which had no yesterday, and there will be a to-day which will have no to-morrow. The sun will rise for the last time. The uniformity had a beginning and will have an end.

So, even as an axiom of thought, the anticipation that things will continue as they have been because they have been, seems to rest on an insufficient basis. How much more so, as to our own little lives and their surroundings! There the only thing which we may be quite sure of about to-morrow is that it will not be "as this day." Even for those of us who may have reached, for example, the level plateau of middle life, where our position and tasks are pretty well fixed, and we have little more to expect than the monotonous repetition of the same duties recurring at the same hour every day—even for such each day has its own distinctive character. Like a flock of sheep they seem all alike, but each, on closer inspection, reveals a physiognomy of its own. There will be so many small changes that even the same duties or enjoyments will not be quite the same, and even if the outward things remained absolutely unaltered, we who meet them are not the same. Little variations in mood and tone, diminished zest here, weakened power there, other thoughts breaking in, and over and above all the slow silent change wrought on us by growing years, make the perfect reproduction of any part impossible. So, however familiar may be the road we have to traverse, however uneventfully the same our days may sometimes for long spaces in our lives seem to be, though to ourselves often our day's work may appear a mill-horse round, yet in deepest truth, if we take into account the whole sum of the minute changes in it and in us, it may be said of each step of our journey, "Ye have not passed this way heretofore."

But, besides all this, we know that these breathing-times when "we have no changes," are but pauses in the storm, landing-places in the ascent, the interspaces between the shocks. However hope may tempt us to dream that the future is like the present, a deeper wisdom lies in all our souls which says No. Drunken bravery may front that darkness with such words as these of our text, but the least serious spirit, in its most joyous moods, never quite succeeds in forgetting the solemn probabilities, possibilities, and certainties which lodge in the unknown future. So to a wise man it is ever a sobering exercise to look forward, and we shall be nearest the truth if we take due account, as we do so to-day, of the undoubted fact that the only thing certain about to-morrow is that it will not be as this day.

There are the great changes which come to some one every day, which may come to any of us any day, which will come to all of us some day. Some of us will die this year; on a day in our new diaries some of us will make no entry, for we shall be gone. Some of us will be smitten down by illness; some of us will lose our dearest; some of us will lose fortune. Which of us it is to be, and where within these twelve months the blow is to fall, is mercifully hidden. The only thing that we certainly know is that these arrows will fly. The thing we do not know is whose heart they will pierce. This makes the gaze into the darkness grave and solemn. There is ever something of dread in Hope's blue eyes. True, the ministry of change is blessed and helpful; true, the darkness which hides the future is merciful, and needful if the present is not to be marred. But helpful and merciful as they are, they invest the unknown to-morrow with a solemn power which it is good, though sobering, for us to feel, and they silence on every lip but that of riot and foolhardy debauchery the presumptuous words, "To-morrow shall be as this day, and much more abundant."

II. But yet there is a possibility of so using the words as to make them the utterance of a sober certainty which will not be put to shame.

So long as our hope and anticipations creep along the low levels of earth, and are concerned with external and creatural good, their language can never rise beyond, "To-morrow *may* be as this day." Oftenest it reaches only to the height of the wistful wish, "May it be as this day!" But there is no need for our being tortured with such slippery possibilities. We may send out our hope like Noah's dove, not to hover restlessly over a heaving ocean of change, but to light on firm, solid, certainty, and fold its wearied wings there. Forecasting is ever close by foreboding. Hope is interwoven with fear, the golden threads of the weft crossing the dark ones of the warp, and the whole texture gleaming bright or glooming black according to the angle at which it is seen.

So is it always until we turn our hope away from earth to God, and fill the future with the light of His presence and the certainty of His truth. Then the mists and doubts roll away; we get above the region of "perhapses" into that of "surelys;" the future is as certain as the past: hope as assured of its facts as memory, prophecy as veracious as history.

Looking forward then, let us not occupy ourselves with visions which we know may or may not come true. Let us not feed ourselves with illusions which may make the reality, when it comes to shatter them, yet harder to bear. But let us make God in Christ our hope, and pass from peradventures to certitudes; from "To-morrow may be as this day—would that it might," to "It shall be, it shall be, for God is my expectation and my hope."

We have an unchanging and an inexhaustible God, and He is the true guarantee of the future for us. The more we accustom ourselves to think of Him as shaping all that is contingent and changeful in the nearest and in the remotest to-morrow, and as being Himself the immutable portion of our souls, the calmer will be our outlook into the darkness, and the more bright will be the clear light of certainty which burns for us in it.

To-day's wealth may be to-morrow's poverty, to-day's health to-morrow's sickness, to-day's happy companionship of love to-morrow's aching solitude of heart, but to-day's God will be to-morrow's God, to-day's Christ will be to-morrow's Christ. Other fountains may dry up in heat or freeze in winter, but this knows no change, " in summer and winter it shall be." Other fountains may sink low in their basins after much drawing, but this is ever full, and after a thousand generations have drawn from it its stream is broad and deep as ever. Other fountains may be left behind on the march, and the wells and palm-trees of each Elim on our road be succeeded by a dry and thirsty land where no water is, but this spring follows us all through the wilderness, and makes music and spreads freshness ever by our path. We can forecast nothing beside. We can be sure of this, that God will be with us in all the days that lie before us. What may be round the next headland we know not; but this we know, that the same sunshine will make a broadening path across the waters right to where we rock on the unknown sea, and the same unmoving mighty star will burn for our guidance. So we may let the waves and currents roll as they list—or rather as He wills, and be little concerned about the incidents or the companions of our voyage, since He is with us. We can front the unknown to-morrow, even when we most keenly feel how solemn and sad are the things it may bring.

> "It can bring with it nothing
> But He will bear us through."

If only our hearts be fixed on God and we are feeding our minds and wills on Him, His truth and His will, then we may be quite certain that, whatever goes, our truest riches will abide, and whoever leaves our little company of loved ones, our best Friend will not go away. Therefore, lifting our hopes beyond the low levels of earth, and making our anticipations of the future the reflection of the brightness of God thrown on that else blank curtain, we may turn into the worthy utterance of sober and saintly faith, the folly of the riotous sensualist when he said, "To-morrow shall be as this day."

The past is the mirror of the future for the Christian; we look back on all the great deeds of old by which God has redeemed and helped souls that cried to Him, and we find in them the eternal laws of His working. They are all true for to-day as they were at first; they remain true for ever. The whole history of the past belongs to us, and avails for our present and for our future. "As we have heard, so have we seen in the city of our God." To-day's experience runs on the same lines as the stories of the "years of old," which are "the years of the right hand of the Most High." Experience is ever the parent of hope, and the latter can only build with the bricks which the former gives. So the Christian has to lay hold on all that God's mercy has done to the ages that are gone by, and because He is a "faithful Creator" to transmute history into prophecy, and triumph in that "the God of Jacob is our refuge."

Nor only does the record of what He has been to others come in to bring material for our forecast of the future, but also the remembrance of what He has been to ourselves. Has He been with us in six troubles? We may be sure He will not abandon us at the seventh. He is not in the way of beginning to build and leaving His work unfinished. Remember what He has been to you, and rejoice that there has been one thing in your lives which, you may be sure, will always be there. Feed your certain hopes for to-morrow on thankful remembrances of many a yesterday. "Forget not the works of God," that you may "set your hopes on God." Let our anticipations base themselves on memory, and utter themselves in the prayer, "Thou hast been my help; leave me not, neither forsake me, O God of my salvation." Then the assurance that He whom we know to be good and wise and strong will shape the future, and Himself be the future for us, will take all the fear out of that forward gaze, will condense our light and unsubstantial hopes into solid realities, and set before us an endless line of days, in each of which we may gain more of Him, whose face has brightened the past and will brighten the future, till days shall end and time shall open into eternity.

III. Looked at in another aspect, these words may be taken as the vow of a firm and lowly resolve.

There is a future which we can but very slightly influence, and the less we look at that the better every way. But there is also a future which we can mould as we wish — the future of our own characters, the only future which is really ours at all—and the more clearly we set it before ourselves, and make up our minds as to whither we wish it to be tending the better. In that region, it is eminently true that "to-morrow shall be as this day, and much more abundant." The law of continuity shapes our moral and spiritual characters. What I am to-day, I shall increasingly be to morrow. The awful power of habit solidifies actions into customs, and prolongs the reverberation of every note once sounded, along the vaulted roof of the chamber where we live. To-day is the child of yesterday and the parent of to-morrow.

That solemn certainty of the continuance and increase of moral and spiritual characteristics works in both good and bad, but with a difference. To secure its full blessing in the gradual development of the germs of good there must be constant effort and tenacious resolution. So many foes beset the springing of the good seed in our hearts—what with the flying flocks of light-winged fugitive thoughts ever ready to swoop down as soon as the sower's back is turned and snatch it away, what with the hardness of the rock which the roots soon encounter, what with the thick-sown and quick-springing thorns—that if we trust to the natural laws of growth and neglect our careful tending, we may sow much but we shall gather little. But to inherit the full consequences of that same law working in the growth and development of the evil in us nothing is needed but carelessness. Leave it alone for a year or two and the "fruitful field will be a forest," a jungle of matted weeds, with a struggling blossom where cultivation had once been.

But if humbly we resolve and earnestly toil, looking for His help, we may venture to hope that our characters will grow in goodness and in likeness to our dear Lord, that we shall not cast away our confidence, nor make shipwreck of our faith, that each new day shall find in us a deeper love, a perfecter consecration, a more joyful service, and that so, in all the beauties of the Christian soul and in all the blessings of the Christian life, "to-morrow shall be as this day, and much more abundant." "To him that hath shall be given." "The path of the just is as the shining light, that shineth more and more until the noon tide of the day."

So we may look forward undismayed, and while we recognise the darkness that wraps to-morrow in regard to all mundane affairs, may feed our fortitude and fasten our confidence on the double certainties that we shall have God and more of God for our treasure, that we shall have likeness to Him and more of likeness in our characters. Fleeting moments may come and go. The uncertain days may exercise their various ministry of giving and taking away, but whether they plant or root up our earthly props, whether they build or destroy our earthly houses, they will increase our riches in the heavens, and give us fuller possession of deeper draughts from the inexhaustible fountain of living waters.

How dreadfully that same law of the continuity and development of character works in some men there is no need now to dwell upon. By slow, imperceptible, certain degrees the evil gains upon them. Yesterday's sin smooths the path for to-day's. The temptation once yielded to gains power. The crack in the embankment which lets a drop or two ooze through is soon a hole which lets out a flood. It is easier to find a man who has done a wrong thing than to find a man who has done it only once. Peter denied his Lord thrice, and each time more easily than the time before. So, before we know it, the thin gossamer threads of single actions are twisted into a rope of habit, and we are "tied with the cords of our sins." Let no man say, "Just for once I may venture on evil; so far I will go and no farther." Nay, "to-morrow shall be as this day, and much more abundant."

How important, then, the smallest acts become when we think of them as thus influencing character! · The microscopic creatures, thousands of which will go into a square inch, make the great white cliffs that beetle over the wildest sea and front the storm. So, permanent and solid character is built up out of trivial actions, and this is the solemn aspect of our passing days, that they are making *us*.

We might well tremble before such a thought, which would be dreadful to the best of us, if it were not for pardoning mercy and renewing grace. The law of reaping what we have sown, or of continuing as we have begun, may be modified as far as our sins and failures are concerned. The entail may be cut off, and to-morrow need not inherit to-day's guilt, nor to-day's habits. The past may be all blotted out through the mercy of God in Christ. No debt need be carried forward to another page of the book of our lives, for Christ has given Himself for us, and He speaks to us all—" Thy sins be forgiven thee." No evil habit need continue its dominion over us, nor are we obliged to carry on the bad tradition of wrong-doing into a future day, for Christ lives, and " if any man be in Christ, he is a new creature; old things are passed away, all things are become new."

So then, brethren, let us humbly take the confidence which these words may be used to express, and as we stand on the threshold of a new year and wait for the curtain to be drawn, let us print deep on our hearts the uncertainty of our hold of all things here, nor seek to build nor anchor on these, but lift our thoughts to Him, who will bless the future as He has blessed the past, and will even enlarge the gifts of his love and the help of his right hand. Let us hope for ourselves not the continuance or increase of outward good, but the growth of our souls in all things lovely and of good report, the daily advance in the love and likeness of our Lord.

So each day, each succeeding wave of the ocean of time shall cast up treasures for us as it breaks at our feet.

As we grow in years, we shall grow in the grace and knowledge of our Lord and Saviour Jesus Christ, until the day comes when we shall exchange earth for heaven. That will be the sublimest application of this text, when, dying, we can calmly be sure that though to-day be on this side and to-morrow on the other bank of the black river, there will be no break in the continuity, but only an infinite growth in our life, and heaven's to-morrow shall be as earth's to-day, and much more abundant.

SERMON XI.

THE SOLITARINESS OF CHRIST IN HIS TEMPTATIONS.

St. Luke xxii. 28.

Ye are they which have continued with me in my temptations.

WE wonder at the disciples when we read of the unseemly strife for precedence which jars on the tender solemnities of the Last Supper. We think them strangely unsympathetic and selfish; and so they were. But do not let us be too hard on them, nor forget that there was a very natural reason for the close connection which is found in the gospels between our Lord's announcements of His sufferings and this eager dispute as to who should be the greatest in the kingdom. They dimly understood what He meant, but they did understand this much, that His "sufferings" were immediately to precede His "glory"—and so it is not, after all, to be so much wondered at if the apparent approach of these made the settlement of their places in the impending kingdom seem to them a very pressing question. We should probably have thought so too, if we had been among them.

Perhaps, too, the immediate occasion of this strife who

should be accounted the greatest, which drew from Christ the words of our text, may have been the unwillingness of each to injure his possible claim to pre-eminence by doing the servant's tasks at the modest meal. May we not suppose that the basin and the towel were refused by one after another, with muttered words growing louder and angrier : " It is not my place," says Peter ; "you, Andrew, take it "—and so from hand to hand it goes, till the Master ends the strife and takes it Himself to wash their feet. Then, when He had sat down again, He may have spoken the words of which our text is part—in which He tells the wrangling disciples what is the true law of honour in His kingdom, namely, *service*, and points to Himself as the great example. With what emphasis the pathetic incident of the foot-washing invests the clause before our text : " I am among you as he that serveth." On that disclosure of the true law of pre-eminence in His kingdom there follows in this and following verses the assurance, that, unseemly as their strife, there was reward for them, and places of dignity there, because in all their selfishness and infirmity, they had still clung to their Master.

This being the original purpose of these words, I venture to use them for another. They give us, if I mistake not, a wonderful glimpse into the heart of Christ, and a most pathetic revelation of His thoughts and experiences, all the more precious because it is quite incidental and, we may say, unconscious.

I. See then, here, *the tempted Christ.*

In one sense, our Lord is His own perpetual theme. He is ever speaking of Himself, inasmuch as He is ever presenting what He is to us, and what He claims of us. In another sense, He scarcely ever speaks of Himself, inasmuch as deep silence, for the most part, lies over His own inward experiences. How precious, therefore, and how profoundly significant is that word here—"in My temptations"! So He summed up all his life. To feel the full force of the expression, it should be remembered that the temptation in the wilderness was past before His first disciple attached himself to Him, and that the conflict in Gethsemane had not yet come when these words were spoken. The period to which they refer, therefore, lies altogether within these limits, including neither. After the former, "Satan," we read, "departed from Him for a season." Before the latter, we read, "the prince of this world cometh." The space between, of which people are so apt to think as free from temptation, is the time of which our Lord is speaking now. The time when His followers "companied with Him" is to His consciousness the time of His "temptations."

That is not the point of view from which the Gospel narratives present it, for the plain reason that they are not autobiographies, and that Jesus said little about the continuous assaults to which He was exposed. It is not the point of view from which we often think of it. We are too apt to conceive of Christ's temptations as all gathered together—curdled and clotted, as it were, at the two ends of His life, leaving the space between free. But we cannot understand the meaning of that life, nor feel aright the love and help that breathe from it, unless we think of it as a field of continual and diversified temptations.

How remarkable is the choice of the expression! To Christ, His life, looking back on it, does not so much present itself in the aspect of sorrow, difficulty or pain, as in that of temptation. He looked upon all outward things mainly with regard to their power to help or to hinder His life's work. So for us, sorrow or joy should matter comparatively little. The evil in the evil should be felt to be sin, and the true cross and burden of life should be to us, as to our Master, the appeals it makes to us to abandon our tasks, and fling away our filial dependance and submission.

This is not the place to plunge into the thorny questions which surround the thought of the tempted Christ. However these may be solved, the great fact remains, that His temptations were most real and unceasing. It was no sham fight which He fought. The story of the wilderness is the story of a most real conflict; and that conflict is waged all through his life. True, the traces of it are few. The battle was fought on both sides in grim silence, as sometimes men wage a mortal struggle without a sound. But if there were no other witness of the sore conflict, the Victor's shout at the close would be enough. His last words, "I have overcome the world," sound the note of triumph, and tells how sharp had been the strife. So long and hard had it been that He cannot forget it even in heaven, and from the throne holdsforth to all the churches the hope of overcoming, "even as I also overcame." As on some battle-field whence all traces of the agony and fury have passed away, and harvests wave, and larks sing where blood ran and men groaned their lives out, some grey stone raised by the victors remains, and only the trophy tells of the forgotten fight, so that monumental word, " I have overcome" stands to all ages as the record of the silent, lifelong conflict.

It is not for us to know how the sinless Christ was tempted. There are depths beyond our reach. This we can understand, that a sinless manhood is not above the reach of temptation; and this besides, that, to such a nature, the temptations must be suggested from without, not presented from within. The desire for food is simply a physical craving, but another personality than His own uses it to incite the Son to abandon dependence for his physical life on God. The trust in God's protection is holy and good, and it may be truest wisdom and piety to incur danger in dependence on it, when God's service calls, but a mocking voice without suggests, under the cloak of it, a needless rushing into peril at no call of conscience, and for no end of mercy, which is not religion but self-will. The desire to have the world for His own lay in Christ's deepest heart, but the enemy of Christ and man, who thought the world his already, used it as giving occasion to suggest a smoother and shorter road to win all men unto Him than the "Via dolorosa" of the Cross. So the sinless Christ was tempted at the beginning, and so the sinless Christ was tempted, in various forms of these first temptations, throughout His life. The path which He had to tread was ever before Him, the shadow of the Cross was flung along His road from the first. The pain and sorrow, the shame and spitting, the contradiction of sinners against Himself, the easier path which needed but a wish to become His, the shrinking of flesh—all these made their appeal to Him, and every step of the path which He trod for us was trodden by the power of a fresh consecration of Himself to His task and a fresh victory over temptation.

Let us not seek to analyse. Let us be content to worship, as we look. Let us think of the tempted Christ, that our conceptions of His sinlessness may be increased. His was no untried and cloistered virtue, pure because never brought into contact with seducing evil, but a militant and victorious goodness, that was able to withstand in the evil day. Let us think of the tempted Christ that our thankful thoughts of what He bore for us may be warmer and more adequate, as we stand afar off and look on at the mystery of His battle with our enemies and His. Let us think of the tempted Christ to make the lighter burden of our cross, and our less terrible conflict easier to bear and to wage. So will He " continue with *us* in *our* temptations," and patience and victory flow to us from Him.

II. See here *the lonely Christ*.

There is no aspect of our Lord's life more pathetic than that of His profound loneliness. I suppose the most utterly solitary man that ever lived was Jesus Christ. I we think of the facts of His life, we see how His nearest kindred stood aloof from Him, how "there were none to praise, and very few to love;" and how, even in the small company of His friends, there were absolutely none who either understood Him or sympathised with Him. We hear a great deal about the solitude in which men of genius live, and how all great souls are necessarily lonely. That is true, and that solitude of great men is one of the compensations which run through all life, and make the lot of the many little, more enviable than that of the few great. "The little hills rejoice together on every side," but far above their smiling companionships, the alpine peak lifts itself into the cold air, and though it be "visited all night by troops of stars," is lonely amid the silence and the snow. Talk of the solitude of pure character amid evil, like Lot in Sodom, or of the loneliness of uncomprehended aims and unshared thoughts— who ever experienced that as keenly as Christ did? That perfect purity must needs have been hurt by the sin of men as none else have ever been. That loving heart yearning for the solace of an answering heart must needs have felt a sharper pang of unrequited love than ever pained another. That Spirit to which the things that are seen were shadows, and the Father and the Father's house the ever-present, only realities, must have felt itself parted from the men whose portion was in this life by a gulf broader than ever opened between any other two souls that shared together human life.

The more pure and lofty a nature, the more keen its sensitiveness, the more exquisite its delights, and the sharper its pains. The more loving and unselfish a heart the more its longing for companionship: and the more its aching in loneliness.

Very significant and pathetic are many points in the Gospel story bearing on this matter. The very choice of the twelve had for its first purpose, "that they should be with Him," as one of the evangelists tells us. We know how constantly He took the three who were nearest to Him along with Him, and that surely not merely that they might be "eyewitnesses of His majesty" on the holy mount, or of His agony in Gethsemane, but as having a real gladness and strength even in their companionship amid the mystery of glory as amid the power of darkness. We read of His being alone but twice in all the gospels, and both times for prayer. And surely the dullest ear can hear a note of pain in that prophetic word: "The hour cometh that ye shall be scattered, every man to his own, and shall leave Me alone;" while every heart must feel the pitiful pathos of the plea, "Tarry ye here, and watch with Me." Even in that supreme hour, He longs for human companionship, however uncomprehending, and stretches out His hands in the great darkness, to feel the touch of a hand of flesh and blood—and, alas, for poor feeble love!—He gropes for it in vain. Surely that horror of utter solitude is one of the elements of His passion grave and sorrowful enough to be named by the side of the other bitterness poured into that cup, even as it was pain enough to form a substantive feature of the great prophetic picture: "I looked for some to take pity, but there was none; and for comforters, but I found none."

So here, a deep pain in His loneliness is implied in these words of our text which put the disciples' participation in the glories of His throne as the issue of their loyal continuance with Him in the conflict of earth. These, and these only, had been by His side, and so much does He care for their companionship, that therefore they shall share His dominion.

That lonely Christ sympathises with all solitary hearts. If ever we feel ourselves misunderstood and thrown back upon ourselves; if ever our hearts' burden of love is rejected; if our outward lives be lonely and earth yields nothing to stay our longing for companionship; if our hearts have been filled with dear ones and are now empty, or but filled with tears, let us think of Him and say, "Yet I am not alone." He lived alone, alone He died, that no heart might ever be solitary any more. "Could *ye* not watch with *Me*?" was His gentle rebuke in Gethsemane. "Lo, *I* am with *you* always," is His mighty promise from the throne. In every step of life we may have Him for a companion, a friend closer than all others, nearer us than our very selves, if we may so say—and in the valley of the shadow of death we need fear no evil, for He will be with us.

III. See here *the grateful Christ.*

I almost hesitate to use the word, but there seems a distinct ring of thanks in the expression, and in the connection. And we need not wonder at that, if we rightly understand it. There is nothing in it inconsistent with our Lord's character and relations to His disciples.

Do you remember another instance in which one seems to hear the same tone, namely, in the marked warmth with which He acknowledges the beautiful service of Mary in breaking the fragrant casket of nard upon his head?

All true love is glad when it is met, glad to give, and glad to receive. Was it not a joy to Jesus to be waited on by the ministering woman? Would He not thank them because they served Him for love? I trow, yes. And if any one stumbles at the word "grateful" as applied to Him, we do not care about the word so long as it is seen that His heart was gladdened by loving friends, and that He recognised in their society a ministry of love.

Notice, too, the loving estimate of what these disciples had done. Their companionship had been imperfect enough at the best. They had given Him but blind affection, dashed with much selfishness. In an hour or two they would all have forsaken Him and fled. He knew all that was lacking in them, and the cowardly abandonment which was so near. But He has not a word to say of all this. He does not count jealously the flaws in our work, or reject it because it is incomplete. So here is the great truth clearly set forth, that where there is a loving heart, there is acceptable service. It is possible that our poor, imperfect deeds shall be an odour of a sweet smell, acceptable, well-pleasing to Him. Which of us that is a father is not glad at his children's gifts, even though they be purchased with his own money, and be of little use? They mean love, so they are precious. And Christ, in like manner, gladly accepts what we bring, even though it be love chilled by selfishness, and faith broken by doubt, and submission crossed by self-will. The living heart of the disciples' acceptable service was their love, far less intelligent and entire than ours may be. They were joined to their Lord, though with but partial sympathy and knowledge, in His temptations. It is possible for us to be joined to Jesus Christ more closely and more truly than they were during His earthly life. Union with Him here is union with Him hereafter. If we abide in Him amid the shows and shadows of earth, He will continue with us in our temptations, and so the fellowship begun on earth will be perfected in heaven : " If so be that we suffer with Him, that we may also be glorified together."

SERMON XII.

THE WELLS OF SALVATION.

Isaiah xii. 3.

With joy shall ye draw water out of the wells of salvation.

TWO events, separated from each other by fifteen hundred years, bear upon these words. One was the origin of the peculiar form of this prophecy, the other contains its interpretation and claims to be its fulfilment.

The wandering march of the children of Israel had brought them to Rephidim, where there was no water. Their parched lips opened to murmur and rebel against their unseen Leader and his visible lieutenant. At his wits' end, Moses cried to God, and the answer is the command to take with him the elders of Israel, and with his rod in his hand to go up to Horeb; and then come grand words, "Behold, I will stand before thee there upon the rock, and thou shalt smite the rock, and there shall come water out of it." It is not the rock, nor the rod, nor the uplifted hand, but it is the presence of God which makes the sparkling streams pour out. How the thirsty men would drink, how gladly they would fling themselves on the ground and glue their lips to the glancing blessing or dip their cups and skins into it, as it flashed along!

Many a psalm and prophecy refer to this old story, and clearly Isaiah has it in his mind here, for the whole context is full of allusions to the history of the Exodus, as a symbol of the better deliverance from a worse bondage, which the "Root of Jesse" was to effect. The lyric burst of praise, of which the text is part, carries on the same allusion. The joyful band of pilgrims returning from this captivity sing the "Song of Moses," chanted first by the banks of the Red Sea, "The Lord is my strength and song, and he is become my salvation." This distinct quotation, which immediately precedes our text, makes the reference in it which we have pointed out, most probable and natural.

The connection of these words with the story in the Exodus was recognised by the Jews at a very early period, as is plain from their use in the remarkable ritual of the Feast of Tabernacles. That festival was originally appointed to preserve the remembrance of Israel's nomad life in the wilderness. In the later days of the nation, a number of symbolical observances were added to those of the original institution. Daily, amidst loud jubilations, the priests wound in long procession down the slope from the Temple to the fountain of Siloam in the valley beneath, and there drew water in golden urns. They bore it back, the crowd surging around them, and then amidst the blast of trumpets and a tumult of rejoicing, they poured it on the altar, while thousands of voices chanted

Isaiah's words, "With joy shall ye draw water out of the wells of salvation."

So much for the occasion of the prophecy, now for its meaning and fulfilment. Nearly eight hundred years have passed. Again the festival has come round. For seven days the glad ceremonial had been performed. For the last time the priestly procession has gone down the rocky road; for the last time the vases have been filled at the cool fountain below; for the last time the bright water has been poured out sparkling in the sunlight; for the last time the shout of joy has risen and fallen, and as the words of the ancient chant were dying on the ear, a sudden stir began among the crowd, and from the midst of them, as they parted for his passage, came a young man, rustic in appearance, and there, before all the silence-stricken multitude, and priests with their empty urns, "In the last day, that great day of the feast, Jesus stood and cried, If any man thirst, let him come unto me," and drink. Surely such words, in such a connection, at such a time, from such lips, are meant to point the path to the true understanding of the text.

So then, consider what we have to understand by *the wells of salvation.*

We are not to be content with any shallow and narrow interpretation of either idea in that phrase. No doubt "salvation" in the Old Testament often means merely outward deliverance from material peril. But there is surely a perceptible deepening of the meaning of the word in the mouth of this prophet, to whom was granted a nearer approximation to the light of the gospel both in respect of the Saviour and of His salvation, than had previously been given. We shall not strain his meaning here, if we take salvation almost in the fully developed New Testament sense, as including negatively the deliverance from all evil, both evil of sin and evil of sorrow, and positively the endowment with all good, good both of holiness and happiness, which God can bestow or man receive.

Then if so, God himself is, in the deepest truth, the Well of Salvation. We need only remind you that the figure of our text does not point to a well so much as to a spring. It is a source, not a reservoir. So we have but to recall the deep and wonderful words of the psalmist: "With thee is the fountain of life," and others not less profound, of the prophet, "They have forsaken me, the fountain of living waters," in order to be led up to the essential meaning of this text. All the springs from which salvation, in any measure and in any form, flows to the thirsty lips of men are in God Himself. What grand truths that thought involves! It declares that salvation has its origin in the depths of God's own nature. It wells up as of itself, not drawn forth by anything in us, but pouring out as from an inner impulse in His own deep heart. God is His own motive, as His own end. As His Being, so His Love (which is His Being) is determined by nothing beyond Himself, but ever streams out by an energy from within, like the sunlight whose beams reach the limits of the system and travel on through dim dark distances, not because they are drawn by the planet, but because they are urged from the central light. Surely, too, if God be the fountain of salvation, the essence of salvation must be His communication of Himself. The water is the same in the fountain as in the pitcher. So, while salvation includes and gives rise to many another blessing both in this life and in the next, the very core and heart of it is, the possession of God Himself, filling our spirits and changing our whole nature into His own image.

But, God being the true fountain of salvation, notice that Jesus Christ plainly and decisively puts Himself in the place that belongs to God : " If any man thirst, let him come unto me, and drink." Think of the extraordinary claims involved in that invitation. Here is a man who plants Himself over against the whole of the human race, and professes that He can satisfy every thirst of every soul through all the ages. Every craving of heart and mind, all longings for love and wisdom, for purity and joy, for strength and guidance, He assumes to be able to slake by the gift of Himself.

Moses sinned when he said, " Must *we* fetch water out of this rock ? " and expiated that sin by death. But his presumption was modesty compared with the unheard-of assumptions of the " meek and lowly " Christ. There is but one hypothesis by which the character of Jesus can be saved, if He ever said anything like these words—and that is that He who speaks them is God manifest in the flesh, the everlasting Son of the Father.

One other remark may be made on this part of our subject. The first word of our text carries us back to something preceding, on which the drawing water with joy is founded. That something is expressed immediately before: " The Lord Jehovah is may strength and song: He also is become my salvation." These words are quoted from Moses' song at the Red Sea, and there point to the one definite act by which God had saved the people from their pursuers. In like manner, we have to look to a definite historical act by which the fountain of salvation has been opened for us, and our glad drawing therefrom has been made possible. The mission and work of Jesus Christ, His incarnation, passion and death, are the means by which the sealed fountain has been opened. In these, or more truly in this, as one great whole, God becomes to us what in the depths of his Being He always was. The living stream is brought near. For men, Jesus Christ is as the river which flows from the closed and land-locked sea of the infinite Divine nature. He is for us the only source, the inexhaustible source, the perennial source—like some spring never hot or muddy, never frozen, never walled in, never sinking one hair's-breadth in its basin, though armies drink, and ages pass. " They drank of that Rock which followed them, and that Rock was Christ." So all the files of this moving host of men find the same spring beside them, wheresoever they pitch, and the last of all the generations shall draw joy from the eternal fountain, Jesus Christ !

Consider, again, what is *the way of drawing* from the well of salvation.

It is not difficult to come to a right understanding of the act which answers to this part of the metaphor.

People have given many answers to the question, If God be the fountain of salvation, how are we to get the water? If I may say so, pumps of all sorts have been tried, and there has been much weary working of arms at the handles, and much jangling of buckets and nothing brought up. The old word is true, with a new application to all who try in any shape to procure salvation by any work of their own: "Thou hast nothing to draw with, and the well is deep." But there is no need for all this profitless work. It is as foolish as it would be to spend money and pains in sinking a well in some mountainous country, where every hill-side is seamed with watercourses, and all that is needed is to put one end of any kind of wooden spout into the "burn" and your vessels under the other. The well of salvation is an Artesian well that needs no machinery to raise the water, but only pitchers to receive it as it rises.

Christ has taught us what "drawing" is. To the Samaritan woman He said, "Thou wouldst have asked of him, and he would have given thee living water." So, then, Drawing is Asking. To the crowds in the Temple courts He said, "Let him come unto me and drink." So, then, Drawing is Coming. To the listeners by the Sea of Galilee He said, "He that cometh to me shall never hunger; and he that believeth on me shall never thirst." So Coming, Asking, Drawing, are all explained by Believing. To trust Christ is to come to Him. To trust Christ is to draw, and to trust Christ is to drink. Simple faith draws all God's goodness into the soul.

Now that faith which is thus powerful, must fix

and fasten on a definite historical act. The faith which draws from the fountain of salvation is not a vague faith in generalities about God's goodness and the like, but it grasps God as revealed and becoming our salvation in the person and work of Jesus Christ. Nor is it a vague faith which has regard to Christ in his lovely character and perfect purity only, but one which lays hold on that great miracle of love perfected on the Cross where He bore our sins. In that wonderful discourse in which Christ proclaims Himself the Bread of Life, it is very instructive to note that He advances from the more general statement that life comes from eating of that bread which is Himself, to the more special and defined one, "Whoso eateth my flesh and drinketh my blood hath eternal life." Not merely Christ, but Christ crucified, is the food of our souls, the water of life. So then the drawing is faith, and that a faith which grasps the great sacrifice which Christ has made, as the channel whereby God's salvation comes near to each thirsty lip and drooping soul.

The words preceding our text suggest another characteristic of the faith which really draws water from the fountain : " He is become my salvation." That is to say, this believing grasp of Christ manifested in a definite historical act is an intensely personal thing. We are not merely to say "He is the Saviour of the world," but " He is *my* Saviour, He loved *me*, and gave Himself for *me*." We must lay hold of that love as embracing ourselves, and make our very own the treasure which belongs to all. No general faith in Christ's mercy, or in the atoning power of His Cross, will suffice to make us glad and to bow our souls in quick and quickening love. It must be something a great deal more personal than that: even the faith that His heart has love in it for *me*, that I am not lost in the crowd, nor forgotten in that abstraction, "the world," but that I had a place in His thought when He died, that I have a place in His heart while He lives. Thus making our own "the common salvation," and filling our own vessel at the great fountain, we shall have our own joy in the common gladness.

Consider too, *the joy of the water drawers*.

The well is the meeting-place in these hot lands, where the solitary shepherds from the pastures and the maidens from the black camels' hair tents meet in the cool evening, and ringing laughter and cheery talk go round. Or the allusion may be rather to the joy, as of escape from death, with which some exhausted travellers press towards the palm trees on the horizon that tell of a spring in the desert, and when they have reached it, crowd to the fountain and drink greedily, no matter how hot and muddy it may be.

So jubilant is the heart of the man whose soul is filled and feasted with the God of his salvation, and the salvation of his God. True Christianity is a joyful thing, not indeed with foolish laughter like the crackling of thorns under a pot, but with a joy too deep to be loud, too pure to be transient. Such a man has all the sources and motives for joy which the heart can ask. Salvation unfolds into manifold gladnesses—rare and profound. There is in it forgiveness, which makes us "hear joy and gladness, that the bones which thou hast broken may rejoice." There is companionship with God and Christ, and such society makes "our hearts burn within us." There is obedience to His will, and then His statutes become the "joy of our hearts." There is a bright hope beyond, and "in that hope of the glory of God we can rejoice." We are independent of externals, possessing that which no change can affect and of which nothing can bereave us. So we can sing the old song: "Though the fig-tree shall not blossom, neither shall fruit be in the vines, yet I will rejoice in the Lord, I will joy in the God of my salvation." How different the false and fleeting joys of earth, when men resort to their broken cisterns that can hold no water. The grim words of the prophet are only too true about all other springs of gladness: "They came to the pits, and found no water; they returned with their vessels empty. They were ashamed and confounded, and covered their heads."

That great Lord and Lover of all our souls calls to each of us now, as He did to the men of His generation, when He was on earth. To them He stretched out His hospitable arms as He stood in the Temple court and cried, "If any man thirst, let him come unto me and drink." To us He speaks from heaven, in the great words which all but close the volume of revelation: "Let him that is athirst come, and whosoever will, let him take the water of life freely." May each of us answer, "Sir, give me this water, that I thirst not, neither come to earth's broken cisterns to draw."

SERMON XIII.

SEEKING THE FACE OF GOD.

PSALM xxvii. 8, 9.

When thou saidst, Seek ye my face; my heart said unto thee, Thy face, Lord, will I seek. Hide not Thy-face far from me.

THERE appears to be a good deal of autobiography in this psalm. The writer, whom we take to be David, travels back in thought to the past of his life, and his backward glance fixes on two distinct objects. At one time he thinks of the past as God's past, all illumined by the radiance of His favour, and helped by the might of His imparted strength; and at another, he thinks of it as his own past, wherein he strove to love and serve his keeper God; and from both of these aspects of the days that are gone he draws encouragement to hope that God will be the same, and humbly resolves that he, for his part, will continue the habit of trust and obedience. For instances of the remembrance of God's past, we may take the words which follow this text, "Thou hast been my help; leave me not, neither forsake me, O God of my salvation," and the other reference to the signal deliverance of his early years, which is often unnoticed by ordinary readers, "When the wicked, even mine enemies and my foes, came upon me to eat up my flesh, they stumbled and fell" (ver. 2). The expressions recall the braggart boast of Goliath, " I will give *thy flesh* unto the fowls of the air, and to the beasts of the field," and the vivid picture of the end of the fight, when the stones went crashing into the thick skull of the bully, "and he *fell* upon his face to the earth." As instance of his retrospect of the past as *his*, take such words as these, " One thing have I desired of the Lord, that will I seek after," or, " I had fainted, unless I had believed to see the goodness of the Lord in the land of the living." Here, in these words of our text, these two ways of looking at the past are woven into one strong cord, that the Psalmist may hang his confidence and his prayers thereon. What God has been saying to him in days that are no more, and what he has been saying to God, are planted like the two piers of an arch, that from them may rise heavenwards the prayer and the hope, " Hide not thy face far from me;"." Leave me not, neither forsake me, O God of my salvation." Happy they who can look back on years made fair by God's recognised gifts and their own loving obedience, and who can feel that what God has been to them, and what they have been to God, has stamped their lives with an impress to which all the future will be true ! Happy they if their forward look is a prayer offered in lowliness, and not a boast made in presumption ! We have here then God's voice to the heart, the heart's echo to that voice, and the heart's cry to God, founded on both the Divine voice and the human echo.

There is here, first, *God's voice to the heart.*

There may be some difficulties about the rendering of our text, which, however, need not concern us now. Our English version is sufficient for our present purpose, and, according to it, we have here, as it were, summed up in a kind of dialogue of two phrases, the whole speech of God to us men, and the inmost meaning of all that devout souls say to God. "Seek ye my face"—such is the essential meaning of all God's words and works. "Thy face, Lord, will I seek"—such is the essential meaning of all prayer, worship, and obedience.

But let us observe a little more closely what the Psalmist means by that phrase, "Seeking God's face." It needs to be translated into a more modern dialect, in order to convey much meaning to some of us. We may begin then by asking the significance of that expression, "the face of God."

It is one of those strong Scripture phrases which escape any danger of misconstruction by the very boldness of their corporeal metaphors. The highest and most spiritual conception of God is reached, not by a pedantic scrupulosity in avoiding material representations, but by an unhesitating use of these, and the remembrance that they *are* representations. The unsubstantial abstraction of the metaphysical God, described only in terms as far removed as may be from human analogies, for fear of being guilty of "anthropomorphism," never helped or gladdened any human soul. It is but a bit of mist through which you can see the stars shining. But the God whom men need and can know and love, the God who is a Spirit, comes near to us in descriptions cast in the mould of humanity, and loses none of His purely Spiritual essence, nor any of His Infinitude, because we have learned to speak of the eye, and arm, and the hand, and the heart, and the face of the Lord. The more unmistakably "gross" and "carnal" the representations, the more do they proclaim their true character, and the less danger of their being misunderstood. The eye of the Lord is His all-seeing knowledge; the arm and the hand of the Lord are substantially the same, though with certain shades of difference in the ideas which they suggest, and may be said to express the active energy of the Divine nature. The face of the Lord, we may say, is that aspect or side of the divine nature which is turned to man, and is perceptible by him. It is, roughly speaking, almost equivalent to "the name of the Lord." That expression has a much profounder meaning than is ordinarily felt to belong to it. It means the manifested character of God, the net result of all His self-revelation by word and work. And so these two phrases—*the face of the Lord* and *the name of the Lord*, come to nearly the same thing. Both of them are worth noting for one reason besides others—namely, that they bring out into clear prominence the twin facts, that there is that in God which may be known, and also that which cannot be. Whilst once or twice in the Old Testament "the face of God" is used to express the dazzling brightness of His essential being, which no man can look on, it more usually means the knowable part of the Divine nature, and, like the other phrase which we have compared with it, draws a broad distinction between that and the unknowable depths—the unspeakable in God. We see the radiant brightness of the full moon, but no eye has ever beheld the other side of that pure silver shield. So the simple expression of our text keeps us from the twin errors of supposing that we can know nothing of God, and of forgetting that we can know but an aspect and a side of His nature.

It may be further noticed that another idea is usually connected with the expression—namely that of light. The face of God is thought of as the sun, and so we read " Lift thou up the light of thy countenance upon us," and other similar passages, in which the two ideas of the rising of the sun on an else dark world, and the rising of the Divine countenance on else dark and wintry hearts are paralleled. All thoughts, then, of brightness, of clear illumination, of gladness and knowledge, of favour and warmth, cluster round the emblem; and of the Jehovah of the Old Testament, as of the glorified Christ of the New, it may be said, " His countenance was as the sun shineth in his strength."

If these things be true, then we may learn what it is to " seek His face." We do not need long and painful search, as for something lost in dim darkness, in order to find the sun. We do not need to seek the sun with lanterns; nor to grope after God if haply we may find Him. A man need only come out of his dark hiding-place to find it. If he will but turn his face to the light, the glory will brighten his features and make glad his eyes.

And in like manner, to seek God's face is no long, dubious search, nor is He hard to be found. We have only to desire to possess—and to act in harmony with the desire—and we shall walk all the day in the light of His countenance. Count the knowledge of God and the experience of His sunny favour as more than all other treasures of wisdom or delights of love or lower things. "There be many that say, Who will show us any good?" and the search is vain, even because it has no clear knowledge of what is good, and seeks to make up for the limitations of its possessions by their multitude. "Lord, lift thou up the light of thy countenance upon us." That is the one pearl of great price, for which all the fragmentary and partial preciousnesses of many goodly pearls are wisely exchanged. Endeavour to keep vivid the consciousness of that face as looking always in on you, like the solemn frescoes of the Christ which Angelico painted on the walls of his convent cells, that each poor brother might feel His Master ever with him. Make Him your companion, and then, though you may feel the awe of the thought, "Thou hast set our secret sins in the light of Thy countenance," you will find a joy deeper than the awe, and learn the blessedness of those, sinful though they may be, who walk in the full brightness of that face. Let Him be the object of your thoughts, and more and more of your whole nature. Let feeling and desire, affection and will, mind and work, all turn to Him, taking Him for motive and end, for strength and means, and turning all your being towards Him as the sunflower turns to follow the sun. Scrupulously avoid whatever might dim the vision of His face. An invisible vapour may hide a star, and we only know that the film is in the nightly sky because Jupiter, which was blazing a moment ago, has become dim or has disappeared. So fogs and vapours from the undrained swamps of our own selfish, worldly hearts may rob the thought of God of all its genial lustre, and make it an angry ball of fire, or may hide Him altogether from us; and we cannot be seeking Him and earthly things any more than we can serve God and Mammon.

If this be the meaning of seeking God's face, then note that this invitation is God's merciful voice to us all. Whether the Psalmist is thinking about any special time or way in which God so spoke to him does not appear. Rather, we may suppose that he is summing up the meaning of the whole of God's dealings with him in the past. However that may be, it is true that God thus speaks to each of us, and that we may even say He speaks thus only to us. By the revelation to us of His own beauty and wonderful fitness to satisfy the hunger of our souls, He is wooing us to seek His face. So infinitely fair and good is He, that to make Himself visible is to draw us to Himself. To know Him is to love Him, and the heart of all His self-revelation by speech and deed is the gracious call to come to His brightness and be at rest. By the very make of our spirits, which bear on them alike in their weakness and their strength the sign that they are His, and can only be at rest in Him, He says, "Seek ye my face." By all His providences of joy or sorrow, by disappointments and fulfilments, by hopes and fruitions, by losses and gains, by all the alternations which "toss us to His breast," He says, "Seek ye my face." In all that befalls us our purged ears may hear "the great voice saying, Come up thither." And most of all in Jesus Christ, the true "angel of His face," in whom all the lustre of His radiance is gathered, does He beckon us to Himself. The highest, most loving, most beseeching form of that wonderful invitation, "Seek ye my face," is the call of Him in whose face we see the glory of God as we see it nowhere besides: "Come unto me, all ye that labour and are heavy laden." So He speaks to the whole world. So He speaks to each of us. So He speaks to me by Christ, who is the dearest utterance of His love and the express image of His person.

II. We have here *the heart's echo to the voice of God*. "My heart said unto thee, Thy face, Lord, will I seek." Swift and immediate, as the thunder to the lightning, the answer follows the invitation. If the resolve to seek God's face be not made by us at the very moment when we become aware of His loving call, it is very unlikely to be made at all. The first notes of that low voice fall on the heart with more persuasive power than they retain after it has become familiar with them, even as the first-heard song of the thrush in spring-time, that breaks the long wintry silence, has a sweetness all its own. The echo answers as soon as the mother voice ceases. But how many of us hesitate and delay, and content ourselves with intentions to answer, and so by lapse of time lose our very consciousness that God is speaking to us at all.

Some of us are as dead to the perception of His gracious call, just because it has been sounding on uninterruptedly, 'as are the dwellers by the waterfall to its unremitting voice. And it is always dangerous to delay for one moment the uprising of the heart in any resolution which we know to ·be right. Any unnecessary interval interposed between the perception of duty and the doing of duty weakens the perception and the resolution as well, and lowers the whole tone of a man. So do not let us tolerate any lingering hesitation in ourselves in yielding to the Divine summons. The only safety, the only peace lies in prompt obedience and in an immediate answer.

There is also brought out here very plainly the *complete correspondence* between the Divine command and the devout man's resolve. Word for word the invitation is repeated in the answer. This man's obedience is no partial obedience. He does not take part of God's call and yield to that, leaving the rest to be dispersed in empty air, but all the breadth and depth of the message that comes to him from God is contained in his announcement of his purpose. Like the sailor at the tiller, he answers his captain's directions by repeating them. " Port," says the officer. " Port it is," says the steersman. "Seek ye my face." "Thy face will I seek." The correspondence in words means the correspondence in action and the thorough-going obedience. How unlike the half-and-half seeking, the languid search, as of people listlessly looking for something which they do not much expect to find, and do not much care whether they find or no, which characterises so many so-called Christians!

They are seekers after God, are they? Yes, with less eagerness than they would seek for a sovereign if it rolled from their fingers into the mud. And so need we wonder that so may of us have but little consciousness of a found God to brighten our lives? "Seek, and ye shall find" is ever true, thank God, but it must be a whole-hearted seeking, and not the feeble, flickering desire and the listless action which mark so many of us.

Note, too, the *firm* and *decisive* resolution shining through the very brevity of the words. The original gives that brevity even more strongly. Three words suffice to hold the law which the man has made for the pole-star of his life. Fixed resolves need short professions. A Spartan brevity, as of a man with his lips tightly locked together, is fitting for such purposes. It is the waverers, who have more than one end in view, or the feeble-willed who try to brace themselves up by talking, making a fence of words around them, who are profuse in their vows. The sober temperament, that measures difficulties and knows the tenacity as well as the gravity of its determination, keeps its breath for the struggle, and does not waste it on blowing the trumpet beforehand. If we are quite resolved that our life's business is to be seeking God's face, we shall for the most part say little about it.

What a contrast that clear, self-conscious, firm resolution is to the hesitations and indecisions so common among us! How few of us could honestly crystallize the aims that guide our life into any single sentence! How much fewer there are who could do it in *that* sentence! We try the impossible feat of riding on two horses at once. We resolve and retract, and hesitate and compromise. The ship heads now one way and now another, and that not because we are wisely *tacking*—that is to say, seeking to reach one point by widely-varying courses—but because our hand is so weak on the helm that we drift wherever the wash of the waves and the buffets of the wind carry us.

Further, we have in this heart's echo to the voice of God the *conversion of a general invitation into a personal resolution.*

The call is, " Seek *ye*." The answer is, " *I* will seek." That is what we have all to do with God's words. He sows His invitations broadcast; we have to make them our own. He sends out His mercy for a world; we have to claim each our portion. He issues His commands to all; I have to make them the law for my life. The stream flows deep and broad from the throne of God, and parts into four heads, the number expressive of universal diffusion throughout the world; but I have to bring it into my own garden by my own trench, and to carry it to my own lip in my own cup. The gospel tells us that Christ died for the world; I have to "appropriate" that, as our fathers used to name it, by saying He gave Himself for *me.* So when that merciful voice comes to us there must be, each for himself, a personal response to it. "Seek ye my face." Let us each reply, " Thy face, Lord, will *I* seek."

Nothing in all the world is so blessed as to hear that wonderful beseeching call sounding in every providence, travelling to us from every corner of the universe, speaking to us in the light of setting suns and in the hush of midnight skies, sounding in the break of waves on the beach and in the rustle of leaves in the forest depths, whispering to us in the depths of our own hearts and wooing us by all things to our rest. Everything assumes a new meaning and is appareled in celestial light when we are aware that everything is a messenger from God to guide us to Himself. And nothing is so joyous as to yield to that most tender summons, while on the other hand, its non-acceptance breeds and brings discord and unrest into our whole being. To stifle it wholly is impossible, conscience will ever and again stir. When we feel most secure, and have deadened our ears most effectually, as we think, some word or look, a chance line in a book, a sunset, a phrase in a sermon, the meeting of a funeral, some fleeting gladness, sets the chords vibrating again. So there is constant inward strife, or, if not, so much the worse; for the man who has lost the capacity of discerning God's voice has lost the most of what ennobles his nature. But that is heaven on earth, nobleness, peace, and power, to stand as at the point of some great ellipse, to which converge from all sides the music of God's manifold invitations, and listening to them to say, I hear, and I obey. Thou dost call, and I answer, Lo! here am I.

III. The third bend in the stream of thought here is *the heart's cry to God founded on both the Divine voice and the human echo.*

"Hide not thy face far from me" is clearly a prayer

built upon both these elements in the past. God's invitation, and my acceptance of it, both give me the right to pray thus, and are pledges of the answer.

As to the former, "Thou saidst, Seek ye my face"—"hide not thy face from me" is but the vivid way of putting the thought that God cannot contradict Himself. His commandments are promises. "Thou shalt" is but the hard, rough shell which covers a sweet "I will" from His lips. If He bids us seek His face, He thereby pledges Himself to show us His face. He binds Himself to us by His commandments; and, in that sense too, as well as in others, His law is a covenant, placing Him under obligations, even as it does us. He recognises the force of the plea upon our lips, and owns that we prevail when we urge it. He can point with majestic self-vindication to all the records of the past, and assert, "I have never said to the seed of Jacob, Seek ye my face in vain." So we may build an unshaken confidence on His unchangeable fidelity to the obligation under which He comes by sending forth such a summons. Be sure that God never calls us to a feast and sets before us an empty table, when we take Him at His word and come. His past is the guarantee and pattern for His future. Has He bid me seek His face? Then He cannot hide His face from me, nor say me nay when I beseech Him to lift up its light upon me.

As to the second ground of this prayer, it rests on my past as well as on God's. "Thy face will I seek—hide not thy face from me." That is the confidence that because we seek we shall find. My feeblest desire brings answers correspondent to its strength and purity. It cannot be that any man ever truly longed to know God and was balked of his wish. You may have exactly as much of God as you want; as much, that is, as you can hold, as much as the ordering of your lives makes it possible that we should possess. There is no limit to our consciousness of God's loving presence and help, except that drawn by ourselves. He fills the vessels we bring, be they large or small. And there is no possibility of any longing after Him remaining unsatisfied. No hunger of heart, no aching emptiness, no eyes failing with looking for the visitor who never comes, no pining away in sick disappointment, have any place in the relation of the soul to God. So sufficient is He, so near, so infinitely desirous to impart Himself, that He needs but the narrowest opening to pour His fulness into the heart. Blessed are they who hunger and thirst after God, for they shall be filled. He does not hold out a gift with one hand and then twitch it away with the other when we try to grasp, as children do with light reflected from a looking-glass on a wall. That fair face does not elude us when we try to look on it, but to seek is to find, to wish for God is to have God.

"Seek His face evermore," and your life will be bright because you will walk in the light of His countenance always. That face will brighten the darkness of death, and "make a sunshine in that shady place." As you pass through the dark valley it will shine in upon you, as the sun looks through the savage gorge in the Himalayas, above which towers that strange mountain which is pierced right through with a circular aperture; and when you reach the land beyond you will enter it with the wonderful hope on your lips, "As for me, I shall behold thy face in righteousness," and heaven's heaven will be that "His servants serve Him and see His face."

SERMON XIV.

CITIZENS OF HEAVEN.

Philip. i. 27, 28.

Only let your conversation be as it becometh the gospel of Christ: that whether I come and see you, or else be absent, I may hear of your affairs, that ye stand fast in one spirit, with one mind striving together for the faith of the gospel; and in nothing terrified by your adversaries.

WE read in the Acts of the Apostles that Philippi was the chief city of that part of Macedonia, and a "colony." Now, the connection between a Roman colony and Rome was a great deal closer than that between an English colony and England. It was, in fact, a bit of Rome on foreign soil.

The colonists and their children were Roman citizens. Their names were enrolled on the lists of Roman tribes. They were governed not by the provincial authorities, but by their own magistrates, and the law to which they owed obedience was not that of the locality, but the law of Rome.

No doubt some of the Philippian Christians possessed these privileges. They knew what it was to live in a community to which they were less closely bound than to the great city beyond the sea. They were members of a mighty polity, though they had never seen its temples nor trod its streets. They lived in Philippi, but they belonged to Rome. Hence there is a peculiar significance in the first words of our text. The rendering, "conversation," was inadequate even when it was made. It has become more so now. The word then meant "conduct." It now means little more than words. But though the phrase may express loosely the Apostle's general idea, it loses entirely the striking metaphor under which it is couched. The Revised Version gives the literal rendering in its margin—"Behave as citizens"—though it adopts in its text a rendering which disregards the figure in the word, and contents itself with the less picturesque and vivid phrase—"let your manner of life be worthy." But there seems no reason for leaving out the metaphor; it entirely fits in with the purpose of the apostle and with the context.

The meaning is, Play the citizen in a manner worthy of the gospel. Paul does not, of course, mean, Discharge your civic duties as Christian men, though some Christian Englishmen need that reminder; but the city of which these Philippians were citizens was the heavenly Jerusalem, the metropolis, the mother city of us all. He would kindle in them the consciousness of belonging to another order of things than that around them. He would stimulate their loyalty to obedience to the city's laws. As the outlying colonies of Rome had sometimes entrusted to them the task of keeping the frontiers and extending the power of the imperial city, so he stirs them up to aggressive warfare; and as in all their conflicts the little colony felt that the Empire was at its back, and therefore looked undaunted on shoals of barbarian foes, so he would have his friends at Philippi animated by lofty courage, and ever confident of final victory.

Such seems to be a general outline of these eager exhortations to the citizens of heaven in this outlying colony of earth. Let us think of them briefly in order now.

I. *Keep fresh the sense of belonging to the mother city.*

Paul was not only writing *to* Philippi, but *from* Rome, where he might see how, even in degenerate days, the consciousness of being a Roman gave dignity to a man, and how the idea became almost a religion. He would kindle a similar feeling in Christians.

We do belong to another polity or order of things than that with which we are connected by the bonds of flesh and sense. Our true affinities are with the mother city. True, we are here on earth, but far beyond the blue waters is another community, of which we are truly members, and sometimes in calm weather we can see, if we climb to a height above the smoke of the valley where we dwell, the faint outline of the mountains of that other land, lying dream-like on the opal waves, and bathed in sunlight.

Therefore it is a great part of Christian discipline to keep a vivid consciousness that there is such an unseen order of things at present in existence. We speak popularly of "the future life," and are apt to forget that it is also the *present* life to an innumerable company. In fact, this film of an earthly life floats in that greater sphere which is all around it, above, beneath, touching it at every point.

It is, as Peter says "ready to be unveiled." Yes, behind the thin curtain, through which stray beams of the brightness sometimes shoot, that other order stands, close to us, parted from us by a most slender division, only a woven veil, no great gulf or iron barrier. And, before long His hand will draw it back, rattling with its rings as it is put aside, and *there* will blaze out what has always been, though we saw it not. It is so close, so real, so bright, so solemn, that it is worth while to try to feel its nearness; and we are so purblind, and such foolish slaves of mere sense, shaping our lives on the legal maxim that things which are non-apparent must be treated as non-existent, that it needs a constant effort not to lose the feeling altogether.

There is a present connection between all Christian men and that heavenly City. It not merely exists, but we belong to it in the measure in which we are Christians. All these figurative expressions about our citizenship being in heaven and the like, rest on the simple fact that the life of Christian men on earth and in heaven is fundamentally the same. The principles which guide, the motives which sway, the tastes and desires, affections and impulses, the objects and aims, are substantially one. A Christian man's true affinities are with the things not seen, and with the persons there, however the surface relationships knit him to the earth.

In the degree in which he is a Christian, he is a stranger here and a native of the heavens. That great City is, like some of the capitals of Europe, built on a broad river, with the mass of the metropolis on the one bank, but a wide-spreading suburb on the other. As the Trastevere is to Rome, as Southwark to London, so is earth to heaven, the bit of the city on the other side the bridge. As Philippi was to Rome, so is earth to heaven, the colony on the outskirts of the empire, ringed round by barbarians, and separated by sounding seas, but keeping open its communications, and one in citizenship.

Be it our care, then, to keep the sense of that city beyond the river vivid and constant. Amid the shows and shams of earth look ever onward to the realities, "the things which *are*," while all else only seems to be. The things which are seen are but smoke wreaths, floating for a moment across space, and melting into nothingness while we look. We do not belong to them or to the order of hings to which they belong. There is no kindred between us and them. Our true relationships are elsewhere. In this present visible world all other creatures find their sufficient and home-like abode. "Foxes have holes, and birds their roosting-places;" but man alone has not where to lay his head, nor can he find in all the width of the created universe a place in which and with which he can be satisfied. Our true *habitat* is elsewhere. So let us set our thoughts and affections on things above. The descendants of the original settlers in our colonies talk still of coming to England as going "home," though they were born in

Australia, and have lived there all their lives. In like manner we Christian people should keep vigorous in our minds the thought that our true home is there where we have never been, and that here we are foreigners and wanderers.

Nor need that feeling of detachment from the present sadden our spirits, or weaken our interest in the things around us. To recognise our separation from the order of things in which we "move," because we belong to that majestic unseen order in which we really "have our being," makes life great and not small. It clothes the present with dignity beyond what is possible to it if it be not looked at in the light of its connection with "the regions beyond." From that connection life derives all its meaning. Surely nothing can be conceived more unmeaning, more wearisome in its monotony, more tragic in its joy, more purposeless in its efforts, than man's life, if the life of sense and time be all. Truly it is "like a tale told by an idiot, full of sound and fury, signifying nothing." "The white radiance of eternity" streaming through it from above gives all its beauty to the "dome of many-coloured glass" which men call life. They who feel most their connection with the city which hath foundations should be best able to wring the last drop of pure sweetness out of all earthly joys, to understand the meaning of all events, and to be interested most keenly, because most intelligently and most nobly, in the homeliest and smallest of the tasks and concerns of the present.

So, in all things, act as citizens of the great Mother of

heroes and saints beyond the sea. Ever feel that you belong to another order, and let the thought, "Here we have no continuing city," be to you not merely the bitter lesson taught by the transiency of earthly joys and treasures and loves, but the happy result of "seeking for the city which hath the foundations."

II. Another exhortation which our text gives is, *Live by the laws of the city.*

The Philippian colonists were governed by the code of Rome. Whatever might be the law of the province of Macedonia, they owed no obedience to it. So Christian men are not to be governed by the maxims and rules of conduct which prevail in the province, but to be governed from the capital. We ought to get from on-lookers the same character that was given to the Jews, that we are "a people whose laws are different from all people that be on earth," and we ought to reckon such a character our highest praise. Paul would have these Philippian Christians act "worthy of *the gospel.*" That is our law.

The great good news of God manifest in the flesh, and of our salvation through Christ Jesus, is not merely to be believed, but to be obeyed. The gospel is not merely a message of deliverance, it is also a rule of conduct. It is not merely theology, it is also ethics. Like some of the ancient municipal charters, the grant of privileges and proclamation of freedom is also the sovereign code which imposes duties and shapes life. A gospel of laziness and mere exemption from hell was not Paul's gospel. A gospel of doctrines, to be investigated, spun into a system of theology, and accepted by the understanding, and there an end, was not Paul's gospel. He believed that the great facts which he proclaimed concerning the self-revelation of God in Christ would unfold into a sovereign law of life for every true believer, and so his one all-sufficient precept and standard of conduct are in these simple words, "worthy of the gospel."

That law is all-sufficient. In the truths which constituted Paul's gospel, that is to say, in the truths of the life, death, and resurrection of Jesus Christ, lies all that men need for conduct and character. In Him we have the "realised ideal," the flawless example, and instead of a thousand precepts, for us all duty is resolved into one —be like Christ. In Him we have the mighty motive, powerful enough to overcome all forces that would draw us away, and like some strong spring to keep us in closest contact with Right and Goodness. Instead of a confusing variety of appeals to manifold motives of interest and conscience, and one knows not what beside, we have the one all-powerful appeal, "If ye love me, keep my commandments," and that draws all the agitations and fluctuations of the soul after it, as the rounded fullness of the moon does the heaped waters in the tidal wave that girdles the world. In Him we have all the helps that weakness needs, for He Himself will come and dwell with us and in us, and be our righteousness and our strength.

Live "worthy of the gospel," then. How grand the unity and simplicity thus breathed into our duties and through our lives! All duties are capable of reduction to this one, and though we shall still need detailed instruction and specific precepts, we shall be set free from the pedantry of a small scrupulous casuistry, which fetters men's limbs with microscopic bands, and shall joyfully learn how much mightier and happier is the life which is shaped by one fruitful principle, than that which is hampered by a thousand regulations.

Nor is such an all-comprehensive precept a mere toothless generality. Let a man try honestly to shape his life by it; and he will find soon enough how close it grips him, and how wide it stretches and how deep it goes. The greatest principles of the gospel are to be fitted to the smallest duties. Indeed that combination— great principles and small duties—is the secret of all noble and calm life, and nowhere should it be so beautifully exemplified as in the life of a Christian man. The tiny round of the dew-drop is shaped by the same laws that mould the giant sphere of the largest planet. You cannot make a map of the poorest grassfield without celestial observations. The star is not too high nor too brilliant to move before us and guide simple men's feet along their pilgrimage. "Worthy of the gospel" is a most practical and stringent law.

And it is an exclusive commandment too, shutting out obedience to other codes, however common and fashionable they may be. We are governed from home, and we give no submission to provincial authorities. Never mind what people say about you, nor what may be the maxims and ways of men around you. These are no guides for you. Public opinion (which only means for most of us the hasty judgments of the half-dozen people who happen to be nearest us), use and wont, the customs of our set, the notions of the world about duty, all these we have nothing to do with. The censures or the praise of men need not move us. We report to headquarters, and subordinates' estimate need be nothing to us. Let us then say, "With me it is a very small matter that I should be judged of men's judgment. He that judgeth me is the Lord." When we may be misunderstood or harshly dealt with, let us lift our eyes to the lofty seat where the Emperor sits, and remove ourselves from men's sentences by our "appeal unto Cæsar," and, in all varieties of circumstances and duty, let us take the gospel which is the record of Christ's life, death, and character, for our only law, and labour that, whatever others may think of us, we "may be well pleasing to him."

III. Further, our text bids the colonists *fight for the advance of the dominions of the city*.—Like the armed colonists whom Russia and other empires had on their frontier, who received their bits of land on condition of holding the border against the enemy, and pushing it forward a league or two when possible, Christian men are set down in their places to be "wardens of the marches," citizen soldiers who hold their homesteads on a military tenure, and are to "*strive together for the faith of the gospel.*"

There is no space here and now to go into details of the exposition of this part of our text. Enough to say in brief that we are here exhorted to "stand fast;" that is, as it were, the defensive side of our warfare, maintaining our ground and repelling all assaults; that this successful resistance is to be "in one spirit," inasmuch as all resistance depends on our poor feeble spirits being ingrafted and rooted in God's Spirit, in vital union with whom we may be knit together into a unity which shall oppose a granite breakwater to the on-rushing tide of opposition; that in addition to the unmoved resistance which will not yield an inch of the sacred soil to the enemy, we are to carry the war onwards, and, not content with holding our own, are with one mind to strive together for the faith of the gospel. There is to be discipline, then, and compact organisation, like that of the legions whom Paul, from his prison among the Prætorian guards, had often seen shining in steel, moving like a machine, grim, irresistible. The cause for which we are to fight is the faith of the gospel, an expression which almost seems to justify the opinion that "the faith" here means, as it does in later usage, the sum and substance of that which is believed. But even here the word may have its usual meaning of the subjective act of trust in the gospel, and the thought may be that we are unitedly to fight for its growing power in our own heart, and in the hearts of others. In any case the idea is plainly here that Christian men are set down in the world, like the frontier guard, to push the conquests of the empire, and to win more ground for their King.

Such work is ever needed, never more needed than now. In this day when a wave of unbelief seems passing over society, when material comfort and worldly prosperity are so dazzlingly attractive to so many, the solemn duty is laid upon us with even more than usual emphasis, and we are called upon to feel more than ever the oneness of all true Christians, and to close up our ranks for the fight. All this can only be done after we have obeyed the other injunctions of this text. The degree in which we feel that we belong to another order of things than this around us, and the degree in which we live by the Imperial laws, will determine the degree in which we can fight with vigour for the growth of the dominion of the city. Be it ours to cherish the vivid consciousness that we are here dwelling not in the cities of the Canaanites, but, like the father of the faithful, in tents pitched at their gates, nomads in the midst of a civic life to which we do not belong, in order that we may breathe a hallowing influence through it, and win hearts to the love of Him whom to imitate is perfection, whom to serve is freedom.

IV. The last exhortation to the colonists is, *Be sure of victory.*

"In nothing terrified by your adversaries," says Paul. He uses a very vivid, and some people might think, a very vulgar metaphor here. The word rendered *terrified* properly refers to a horse shying or plunging at some object. It is generally things half seen and mistaken for something more dreadful than themselves that make horses shy; and it is usually a half-look at adversaries, and a mistaken estimate of their strength, that make Christians afraid. Go up to your fears and speak to them, and as ghosts are said to do, they will generally fade away. So we may go into the battle, as the rash French minister said he did into the Franco-German war, "with a light heart," and that for good reasons. We have no reason to fear for ourselves. We have no reason to fear for the ark of God. We have no reason to fear for the growth of Christianity in the world. Many good men in this time seem to be getting half-ashamed of the gospel, and some preachers are preaching it in words which sound like an apology rather than a creed. Do not let us allow the enemy to overpower our imaginations in that fashion. Do not let us fight as if we expected to be beaten, always casting our eyes over our shoulders, even while we are advancing, to make sure of our retreat, but let us trust our gospel, and trust our King, and let us take to heart the old admonition, "Lift up thy voice with strength; lift it up, be not afraid."

Such courage is a prophecy of victory. Such courage is based upon a sure hope. "Our citizenship is in heaven, from whence also we look for the Lord Jesus as Saviour." The little outlying colony in this far-off edge of the empire is ringed about by wide-stretching hosts of dusky barbarians. Far as the eye can reach their myriads cover the land and the watchers from the ramparts might well be dismayed if they had only their own resources to depend on. But they know that the Emperor in his progress will come to this sorely beset outpost, and their eyes are fixed on the pass in the hills where they expect to see the waving banners and the gleaming spears. Soon, like our countrymen in Lucknow, they will hear the music and the shouts that tell that He is at hand. Then when He comes, He will raise the siege and scatter all the enemies as the chaff of the threshing-floor, and the colonists who held the post will go with Him to the land which they have never seen, but which is their home, and will, with the Victor, sweep in triumph " through the gates into the city."

SERMON XV.

MOSES AND HOBAB.

NUMBERS x. 29, 31.

And Moses said unto Hobab . . . Leave us not, I pray thee; forasmuch as thou knowest how we are to encamp in the wilderness, and thou mayest be to us instead of eyes.

THE fugitives whom Moses led reached Sinai in three months after leaving Egypt. They remained there for at least nine months, and amidst the solitude of these wild rocks they kept the first Passover—the anniversary of their deliverance. "On the twentieth day of the second month" they began again their march through the grim, unknown desert.

One can fancy their thoughts and fears as they looked forward to the enemies and trials which might be awaiting them. In these circumstances this story comes in most naturally. Some time before the encampment broke up from Sinai, a relative of Moses by marriage, whose precise connection with him need not trouble us now, Hobab by name, had come into camp on a visit. He was a Midianite by race, one of the wandering tribes from the south-east of the Arabian peninsula. He knew every foot of the ground, as such men do. He knew where the springs were and the herbage, the camping places, the short cuts, and the safest routes. So Moses, who had no doubt forgotten much of the little desert skill he had learned in keeping Jethro's flock, prays Hobab to remain with them and give them the benefit of his practical knowledge—" to be to us instead of eyes."

The free, wild wanderer does not care to leave the black tents of his tribe to link his fortunes with those of the unwieldy hosts of fugitives, and flatly refuses. Then Moses presses the proposal on him, with judicious compliments and large promises of sharing in all their prosperity.

It is noteworthy that the narrative does not tell whether the persistent request succeeded or not. We find, indeed, his descendants enrolled in the great Doomsday Book of the Conquest as possessing land and probably incorporated among the Israelites. It may, therefore, be supposed that either then or afterwards Hobab forsook his country and his father's house to shelter himself beneath the wings of the God of Jacob.

But, at all events, the silence of the record is significant, especially if taken in connection with the verses immediately following. The historian does not think it worth while to tell whether Moses' attempt to secure the help of a pair of sharp Bedouin eyes succeeded or failed, but passes on to describe at once how "the ark of the covenant of the Lord went before them to search out a resting-place for them," and how "the cloud was upon them when they went out of the camp." He puts the two things side by side, not calling on us to notice the juxtaposition, but surely expecting that we shall not miss what is so plain. He would teach us that it mattered little whether Israel had Hobab or not, if they had the ark and the cloud. Perhaps he meant us to ask ourselves whether it was not a wavering of faith in Moses to be so anxious to secure a human guide when he had a Divine leader. So, at least, it appears to us, and from that point of view we purpose to view the incident now.

I. There are times and moods in which our forward look brings with it a painful sense of the *unknown* wilderness before us.

The general complexion of the future may be roughly estimated. We soon outlive the illusions which dance before us at the beginning, and cease to expect such surprising delights and radiant flashes of unexpected good fortune as young dreams spread before us. We know very early in life, unless we are wonderfully frivolous and credulous, that the thread of our days is a mingled strand, and the prevailing tone a sober, neutral tint. The main characteristics of what we shall meet we know well enough. "That which is to be hath already been." But the particular events are hid, and it is strange and impressive when we come to think how Providence, working with the same uniform materials in all human lives, can yet, like some skilful artist, produce endless novelty and surprises in each life. All men tread substantially the same road. "There hath nothing befallen us but such as is common to men," and yet for every one of us the road is new day by day. Some of us go on for years in an unbroken monotony of the same duties and circumstances, and know that in all probability we shall be doing the same things till we die, and yet every morning we come to our work with some feeling of novelty which is not all illusion. "We have not passed this way heretofore," is always true of each new day's tasks and incidents ; for even if they be the same as those of a thousand days before, yet we who tread the road are not quite the same, and the bearing of the events on us is somewhat different.

The solemn ignorance of the next moment is sometimes stimulating and joyous. To young life it gives zest and buoyancy, and secures many a joyful surprise. But to all there come times—and perhaps they are more frequent as life goes on, and the consciousness increases that changes now will generally be losses—when the blank curtain between us and the next beat of the pendulum is felt to be very near us and very thick, and when the ignorance is saddening, and when the shapes that we paint on its black folds are gloomy and threatening. Terrors come to us all, and we are apt to clasp our treasures with a spasmodic grasp, as much anguish as love, when we think of what must be some day, and may be any day. In some moods, and thinking of some things which are certainties as to the fact, and contingencies only as to the time, each of us must say—

> "Forward though I cannot see,
> I guess and fear."

It is a libel on God's goodness to speak of the world as a wilderness. He has not made it so; and if anybody finds that "all is vanity and vexation of spirit," it is his own fault. But still one aspect of life is truly represented by that figure. There are dangers and barren places, and a great solitude in spite of love and companionship, and many marchings and lurking foes, and grim rocks, and fierce suns, and parched wells, and shadeless sand wastes enough in every life to make us quail often and look grave always when we think of what may be before us. Who knows what we shall see when we top the next hill, or round the shoulder of the cliff that bars our way? What shout of an enemy may crash in upon the sleeping camp; or what stifling gorge of barren granite—blazing in the sun and trackless to our feet—shall we have to march through to-day?

The great crises and trials of our lives mostly come unlooked for. There is nothing so certain as the unexpected. The worst thunder comes on us out of a clear sky. Our Waterloos have a way of crashing into the midst of our feasts, and generally it is when all goes "merry as a marriage bell" that the cannon shot breaks in upon the mirth, which tells that the enemy have crossed the river and the battle is begun.

II. We have here an illustration of *the weakness that clings to human guides.*

Most commentators excuse, or even approve of this effort by Moses to secure Hobab's help, and draw from the story the lesson that supernatural guidance does not make human guidance unnecessary. That, of course, is true in a fashion; but it appears to us that the true lesson of the incident, considered, as we have already remarked, in connection with the following section, is much rather that for men who have God to guide them, it argues weakness of faith and courage to be much solicitous of any Hobab to show them where to go and where to camp.

Of course we are meant to depend on one another. No man can safely isolate himself, either intellectually or in practical matters. The self-trained scholar is usually incomplete. Crotchets take possession of the solitary thinker, and peculiarities of character that would have been kept in check, and might have become aids in the symmetrical development of the whole man, if they had been reduced and modified in society, get swollen into deformities in solitude. The highest and the lowest blessings for life both of heart and mind—blessedness and love, and wisdom and goodness—are ministered to men through men, and to live without dependence on human help and guidance is to be either a savage or an angel. God's guidance does not make man's needless, for a very large part of God's guidance is ministered to us through men. And wherever a man's thoughts and words teach us to understand God's thoughts and words more clearly, to love them more earnestly, or to obey them more gladly, there human guidance is discharging its noblest function. And wherever the human guide turns us away from himself to God, and says, " I am but a voice, I am not the light that guides," there it is blessed and safe to cherish and to prize it.

But we are ever apt to feel that we cannot do without the human leader. Our hearts crave for earthly love, and that craving is, as it were, an open channel, through which the purest water of life which this world can yield is poured into our hearts. But how close to the joy and the blessedness does the temptation lie! Are we not ever in danger of giving the very choicest of our love to the dear ones of earth, lavishing on them the precious juice which flows from the freshly-gathered grapes, and putting God off with the last impoverished and scanty drops which can be squeezed from the husks? How we rejoice over the love of earth, and cherish it, and feel ourselves rich and strong by reason of it! How we sink in utter despair and hopeless sorrow when it passes from us, and feel "they have taken away my gods, and what have I more?" How we follow the counsel of those whom we love, cherishing their lightest word, and feeling glad and free when we are carrying out their faintest wishes! And, alas, how often, in a very real and tragical sense, " a man's foes are they of his own household," and their love and tenderness more deadly than their hate could ever be, because it keeps us back from God, and blinds our eyes to the pointing finger of our true Guide and Lover!

We are meant to get much of our belief and practice from human teachers and examples. But our weakness of faith in the unseen is ever tending to pervert the relation between teacher and taught into practical forgetfulness that the promise of the new covenant is, "They shall all be taught of God." So we are all apt to pin our faith on some trusted guide, and many of us in these days will follow some teacher of negations with an implicit submission which we refuse to give to Jesus Christ. We put the teacher between ourselves and God, and give to the glowing colours of the painted window the admiration that is due to the light which shines through it. The teacher, be he preacher or author, has succeeded in his work when he has taught his pupils to do without him, having led them to the place where they can draw at first hand from the depths of God; and the highest eulogium that he can receive is when his scholars say to him, "Now we believe, not because of thy saying, for we have heard him ourselves."

There are a thousand ways in which our poor weak hearts cry out in their sense-bound unbelief for visible stays to lean upon, and guides to direct us. In so far as that is a legitimate longing, God, who never "sends mouths, but He sends meat to feed them," will not leave us to cry unheard. But let us guard against that ever-present weakness which clings tremblingly to creatures and men for help and guidance, and, in proportion as it is rich when it possesses them, trembles at the prospect of losing them, and is crushed and desolate when they go. Do not put them as barriers between you and God, nor yield your own clearness of vision to them, nor say to any, "Be to us instead of eyes," nor be over anxious to secure any Hobab to show you where to camp or how to match.

III. The contrast which is brought into prominence by the juxtaposition of this section and that which follows it, makes emphatic the thought of the *true leader of our march.*

The true leader of the children of Israel in their wilderness journey was not Moses, but the Divine Presence in the cloud with a heart of fire, that hovered over their camp for a defence and sailed before them for a guide. "The Lord went before them by day in a pillar of cloud to lead them the way." When it lay on the tent, whether it were for "two days, or a month, or a year," the march was stayed, and the moment that the cloud lifted "by day or by night," the encampment was broken up and the long procession was got into marching order without an instant's pause, to follow its gliding motion wherever it led and however long it lasted. First to follow was the ark on the shoulders of the Levites, and behind it, separated by some space, came the "standard of the camp of the children of Judah, and then the other tribes in their order." Surely there was no place here for Hobab's skill, and if Moses had remembered how their marching and their encampments were fixed, he need not have been so anxious to secure his sharp eyes.

We have the same Divine guidance, if we will; in sober reality we have God's presence; and waiting hearts which have ceased from self-will may receive leading as real as ever the pillar gave to Israel.

God's providence does still shape our paths, and God's

Spirit will direct us within, and God's word will counsel us. If we will wait and watch we shall not be left undirected. It is wonderful how much practical wisdom about the smallest perplexities of daily life comes to men who keep both their feet and their wishes still until Providence—or, as the world prefers to call it, "circumstances"—clears a path for them. No doubt in all our lives there come times when we seem to have been brought into a blind alley, and cannot see where we are to get out; but it is very rare indeed that we do not see one step in advance, the duty which lies next us. And be sure of this, that if we are content to see but one step at a time, and take it, we shall find our way made plain. The river winds, and often we seem on a lake without an exit. Then is the time to go half-speed, and, doubtless, when we get a little farther, the overlapping hills on either bank will part, and the gorge will open out. We do not need to see it a mile off; enough if we see it when we are close upon it. It may be as narrow and grim, with slippery black cliffs towering on either side of the narrow ribbon of the stream, as the cañons of American rivers, but it will float our boat into broader reaches and onwards to the great sea.

Do not seek to outrun God's guidance, to see what you are to do a year hence, or to act before you are sure of what is His will; do not let your wishes get in advance of the pillar and the ark, and you will be kept from many a mistake, and led into a region of deep peace. Our blunders mostly come from letting our wishes interpret our duties, or hide from us plain indications of unwelcome tasks. We are all apt to do like Nelson, and put the telescope to the blind eye when a signal is flying that we dislike. No doubt sometimes even docile hearts make mistakes, but no man who has not tried it would conceive how many of the highest results of practical wisdom are secured by the simple in heart, whose only skill is to wait on the Lord and be guided by Him.

The old injunction is still our duty and our wisdom: "Go after the ark, yet there shall be a space between it and you; come not near it, that ye may know the way ye ought to go." If we impatiently press too close on the heels of our guide we lose the guidance. There must be a reverent following, which allows indications of the way full time to develop themselves, and does not fling itself into new circumstances on the first blush of apparent duty. The merely worldly virtues of prudence, caution, judgment unbiassed by inclination, and the like, have all a Christian side, and are all included and glorified in the elements of that temper which religion enjoins as certain to be rewarded with the Divine guidance: "The meek will he guide in judgment, and the meek will he teach his way."

In the strength of that confidence let us turn away from dependence upon human guides, and lift our eyes to Him with the voice which is at once a prayer and a vow: "Thou shalt guide me with thy counsel." Better to take Moses for our example when he prayed, as the ark set forward and the march began, "Arise, Lord, and let thine enemies be scattered," than to follow him in eagerly seeking some Hobab or other to show us where we should go. Better to commit our resting times to

God with Moses' prayer when the ark halted, "Return, O Lord, unto the many thousands of Israel," and so to repose under the shadow of the Almighty, than to seek safety in having some man with us "who knows how we are to encamp in this wilderness." God's presence is enough for toil and enough for rest. If He journey with us by the way, He will abide with us when nightfall comes; and His companionship will be sufficient for direction on the road, and for solace and safety in the evening camp.

We have often to travel by solitary ways. Some of us have to journey all alone, with no fellow-travellers for society or for succour. Some of us have perplexed paths to tread. Some of us have sad memories of times when we journeyed in company with those who will never share our tent or counsel our steps any more, and, as we sit lonely by our watchfire in the wilderness, have aching hearts and silent nights. Some of us may be, as yet, rich in companions and helpers, whose words are wisdom, whose wishes are love to us, and may tremble as we think that one day either they or we shall have to tramp on by ourselves. But for us all, cast down and lonely, or still blessed with dear ones and afraid to live without them, there is a presence which departs never, which will move before us as we journey, and hover over us as a shield when we rest; which will be a cloud to veil the sun that it smite us not by day, and will redden into fire as the night falls, being ever brightest when we need it most, and burning clearest of all in the valley at the end, where its guidance will only cease because then "the

Lamb that is in the midst of the throne will lead them." "This God is our God for ever and ever; he will be our guide even unto death."

IV. A final thought suggested by this incident is, that *our craving for a human guide has been lovingly met in the gift of Christ.*

Moses sought to secure this Midianite guide because he was a native of the desert, and had travelled all over it. His experience was his qualification. We have a brother who has Himself travelled every foot of the road by which we have to go, and His footsteps have marked out with blood a track for us to follow, and have trodden a footpath through the else pathless waste. He knows " how to encamp in this wilderness," for He Himself has " tabernacled among us," and by experience has learned the weariness of the journey and the perils of the wilderness.

His life is our pattern. Our marching orders are brief and simple: Follow your leader, and plant your feet in His footprints.

That is the sum of all ethics, and the *vade mecum* for practical life. However diverse our duties and circumstances are, the principles which come out in the Divine record of that fair life and wondrous death will fit with equal closeness to us all; and so Divine and all comprehensive is it that it abides as the sufficient pattern for every class, for every stage, for every variety of character, for every era, and every land, till the end, and beyond the end.

Our poor weak hearts long for a brother's hand to hold us up, for a brother's voice to whisper a word of cheer, for a brother's example to animate as well as to instruct. An abstract law of right is but a cold guide, like the stars that shine keen in the polar winter. It is hard even to find in the bare thought of an unseen God guiding us by His unseen Spirit within and His unseen Providence without, the solidity and the warmth which we need. Therefore we have mercifully received God manifest in the flesh, a Brother to be our guide and the Captain of our salvation.

To Him then transfer all those feelings of confidence and affection too often lavished on men. The noblest use for the precious ointment of love, which the poorest of us bears in the alabaster-box of the heart, is to break it on His head.

Thus loving and following Him, we shall be set free from undue dependence on human helpers whilst they are with us, from eagerness to secure them, from dread of losing them, from despair when they depart. Perplexities will disappear. Duty will become plain. Life will not be a weary march through an unknown land where we have to choose our path by our own poor wisdom, and death is often the penalty of a blunder. All our duty and joy lie in the one command, "Follow me;" and if we only ask Him to be with us "instead of eyes" and accept His gentle leading, we shall not walk in darkness, but may plunge into thickest night and the most unknown land, assured that He will "lead us by a right way to the city of habitation."

SERMON XVI.

THE OBSCURE APOSTLES.

ST. MATTHEW x. 5.

These twelve Jesus sent forth.

AND half of "these twelve" are never heard of again as doing any work for Christ. Peter and James and John we know; the other James and Judas have possibly left us short letters; Matthew gives us a Gospel; and of all the rest no trace is left. Some of them are never so much as named again, except in the list at the beginning of the Acts of the Apostles; and none of them except the three who "seemed to be pillars" appear to have been of much importance in the early diffusion of the gospel.

There are many instructive and interesting points in reference to the Apostolate. The number of twelve, in obvious allusion to the tribes of Israel, proclaims the eternal certainty of the Divine promises to His people, and the dignity of the New Testament Church as their true heir. The ties of relationship which knit so many of the Apostles together, the order of the names varying, but within certain limits, in the different catalogues, the uncultivated provincial rudeness of most of them, would all afford material for important reflections. But, perhaps, not the least important fact about the Apostolate is that one which we have referred, which like the names of countries on the map, escapes notice because it is "writ" so "large"—namely, the small place which the Apostles as a body fill in the subsequent narrative, and the entire oblivion into which so many of them pass from the moment of their appointment.

It is to that fact that we wish to turn attention now. It may suggest some considerations worth pondering, and among other things, may help to show the exaggeration of the functions of the office by the opposite extremes of priests and rationalists. The one school makes it the depositary of exclusive supernatural powers; the other regards it as a master-stoke of organization, to which the early rapid growth of Christianity was largely due. The facts seem to show that it was neither.

I. The first thought which this peculiar and unexpected silence suggests is of *the True Worker in the Church's progress.*

The way in which the New Testament drops these Apostles is of a piece with the whole tone of the Bible. Throughout, men are introduced into its narratives and allowed to slip out with well-marked indifference. Nowhere do we get more vivid, penetrating portraiture, but nowhere do we see such carelessness about following the fortunes or completing the biographies even of those who have filled the largest space in its pages.

Recall, for example, the way in which the New

Testament deals with "the very chiefest" Apostles, the illustrious triad of Peter, James, and John. The first escapes from prison; we see him hammering at Mary's door in the grey of the morning, and after brief, eager talk with his friends he vanishes to hide in "another place," and is no more heard of, except for a moment in the great council, held in Jerusalem, about the admission of Gentiles to the Church. The second of the three is killed off in a parenthesis. The third is only seen twice in the Book of the Acts, as a silent companion of Peter at a miracle and before the Sanhedrim. Remember how Paul is left in his own hired house, within sight of trial and sentence, and neither the original writer of the book nor any later hand thought it worth while to add three lines to tell the world what became of him. A strange way to write history, and a most imperfect narrative, surely. Yes, unless there be some peculiarity in the purpose of the book, which explains this cold-blooded, inartistic, and tantalising habit of letting men leap upon the stage as if they had dropped from the clouds, and vanish from it as abruptly as if they had fallen through a trap-door.

Such a peculiarity there is. One of the three to whom we have referred has explained it in the words with which he closes his Gospel, words which might stand for the motto of the whole book, "These are written that ye might believe that Jesus is the Son of God." The true purpose is not to speak of men except in so far as they "bore witness to that light" and were illuminated for a moment by contact with Him. From the beginning the true "Hero" of the Bible is God; its theme is His self-revelation culminating for evermore in the Man Jesus. All other men interest the writers only as they are subsidiary or antagonistic to that revelation. As long as that breath blows through them they are music; else they are but common reeds. Men are nothing except as instruments and organs of God. He is all, and His whole fulness is in Jesus Christ. Christ is the sole worker in the progress of His Church. That is the teaching of all the New Testament. The thought is expressed in the deepest, simplest form in His own unapproachable words, unfathomable as they are in their depth of meaning, and inexhaustible in their power to strengthen and to cheer: "I am the vine, ye are the branches, without me ye can do nothing." It shapes the whole treatment of the history in the so-called "Acts of the Apostles," which by its very first sentence proclaims itself to be the Acts of the ascended Jesus, "the former treatise" being declared to have had for its subject "all that Jesus *began* to do and teach" while on earth, and this treatise being manifestly the continuance of the same theme, and the record of the heavenly activity of the Lord. So the thought runs through all the book: "The help that is done on earth, He does it all himself."

So let us think of Him and of His relation to us as well as to that early Church. His continuous energy is pouring down on us if we will accept it. *In* us, *for* us, *by* us He works. "My father worketh hitherto," said He when here, "and I work;" and now, exalted on high, He has passed into that same Divine Repose, which is at the same time the most energetic Divine Activity. He is all in all to His people. He is all their strength, wisdom, and righteousness. They are but the clouds irradiated by the sun and bathed in its brightness; He is the light which flames in their grey mist and turns it to a glory. They are but the belts and cranks and wheels; He is the power. They are but the channel, muddy and dry; He is the flashing life that fills it and makes it a joy. They are the body; He is the soul dwelling in every part to save it from corruption and give movement and warmth.

> "Thou art the organ, whose full breath is thunder;
> I am the keys, beneath thy fingers pressed."

If this be true, how it should deliver us from all over-estimate of men, to which our human affections and our feeble faith tempt us so sorely! There *is* one man, and One man only, whose biography is a "Gospel," who owes nothing to circumstances, and who originates the power which He wields—One who is a new beginning, and has changed the whole current of human history, One to whom we are right to bring offerings of the gold, and incense, and myrrh of our hearts, and wills, and minds, which it is blasphemy and degradation to lay at the feet of any others. We may utterly love, trust, and obey Jesus Christ. We dare not do so to any other. The inscription written over the whole book, that it may be transcribed on our whole nature, is, "No man any more save Jesus only."

If this thought be true, what confidence it ought to give us as we think of the tasks and fortunes of the Church! If we think only of the difficulties and of the enormous task before us, so disproportioned to our weak powers, we shall be disposed to agree with our enemies, who talk as if Christianity was on the point of perishing, as they have been doing ever since it began. But the outlook is wonderfully different when we take Christ into the account. We are very apt to leave Him out of the reckoning. But one man with Christ to back him is always in the majority. He flings his sword clashing into one scale, and it weighs down all that is in the other. The walls are very lofty and strong, and the besiegers few and weak, badly armed, and quite unfit for the assault; but if we lift our eyes high enough, we, too, shall see a man with a drawn sword over against us, and our hearts may leap up in assured confidence of victory as we recognise in Him the Captain of the Lord's Host, who has already overcome, and will make us valiant in fight and more than conquerors.

When conscious of our own weakness, and tempted to think of our task as heavy, or when complacent in our own power, and tempted to regard our task as easy, let us think of His ever-present work in and for His people till it braces us for all duty, and rebukes our easy-going idleness. Surely from that thought of the active ascended Christ may come to many of His slothful followers the pleading question, as from His own lips, "Dost thou not care that thou hast left me to serve alone?" Surely to us all it should bring inspiration and strength, courage and confidence, deliverance from man, and elevation above the reverence of blind impersonal forces. Surely we may all lay to heart the grand lesson that union with Him is our only strength, and oblivion of ourselves our highest wisdom. Surely he has best learned his true place and the worth of Jesus Christ who abides with unmoved humility at His feet, and, like the lonely lowly forerunner, puts away all temptations to self-assertion while joyfully accepting it as the law of his life to

"Fade in the light of the planet he loves,
To fade in his love and to die."

Blessed is he who is glad to say, " He must increase, I must decrease !"

II. This same silence of Scripture as to so many of the Apostles may be taken as suggesting *what the real work of these delegated workers was.*

It certainly seems very strange that if they were the possessors of such extraordinary powers as the Sacramentarian theory implies, we should hear so little of them in the narrative. The silence of Scripture about them goes a long way to discredit such ideas, while it is entirely accordant with a more modest view of the Apostolic office.

What was an Apostle's function during the life of Christ ? One of the evangelists divides it into three portions—" to be with Jesus, to preach the kingdom, to cast out devils and to heal." There is nothing in these offices peculiar to them. The seventy had miraculous powers too, and some at least were our Lord's companions and preachers of His kingdom who were simple disciples. What was an Apostle's function after the resurrection? Peter's words, on proposing the election of a new apostle, lay down the duty as simply "to bear witness" of that resurrection. Not supernatural channels of mysterious grace, not lords over God's heritage, not even leaders of the Church, but bearers of a testimony to the great historical fact, on the acceptance of which all belief in an historical Christ depended then and depends now. Each of the greater of the apostles is penetrated with the same thought. Paul disclaims anything beside in his "Not I, but the grace of God in me." Peter thrusts the question at the staring crowd, "Why look ye on us as though by *our* power or holiness *we* had made this man to walk?" John, in his calm way, tells his children at Ephesus, "Ye need not that any man teach you."

Such an idea of the Apostolic office is far more reasonable and accordant with Scripture than a figment about unexampled powers and authority in the Church. It accounts for the qualifications as stated in the same address, which merely secure the validity of their testimony. The one thing that *must* be found in an Apostle was that he should have been in familiar intercourse with Christ during his earthly life, both before and after His resurrection, in order that he might be able to say, I knew Him well; I know that He died; I know that He rose again; I saw Him go up to heaven. For such a work there was no need for men of commanding power. Plain, simple, honest men who had the requisite eye-witness were sufficient. The guidance and the missionary work of the Church need not necessarily be in their hands, and, in fact, does not seem to have been. In harmony with this view of the office and its requisites, we find that Paul rests the validity of his Apostolate on the fact that "He was seen of me also," and regards that vision as his true appointment which left him not "one whit behind the very chiefest apostles." Miraculous gifts indeed they had, and miraculous gifts they imparted; but in both instances others shared their powers with them. It was no apostle who laid his hands on the blinded Saul in that house in Damascus and said, "Receive the Holy Ghost." An apostle stood by passive and wondering when the Holy Ghost fell on Cornelius and his comrades. In reality Apostolic succession is absurd, because there is nothing to succeed to, except what cannot be transmitted, personal knowledge of the reality of the resurrection of Jesus Christ. To establish that fact as indubitable history is to lay the foundation of the Christian Church, and the twelve plain men who did that needed no superstitious mist around them to magnify their greatness.

In so far as any succession to them or any devolution of their office is possible, all Christian men inherit it, for to bear witness of the living power of the risen Lord is still the office and honour of every believing souL It is still true that the sharpest weapon which any man can wield for Christ is the simple adducing of his own personal experience. "That which we have seen and handled we declare" is still the best form into which our preaching can be cast. And such a voice every man and woman who has found the sweetness and the power of Christ filling their own souls, is bound—rather let us say is privileged—to lift up: "This honour have all the saints." Christ is the true worker, and all our work is but to proclaim Him, and what He has done and is doing for ourselves and for all men.

III. We may gather too the lesson of *how often faithful work is unrecorded and forgotten.*

No doubt those Apostles who have no place in the history toiled honestly and did their Lord's commands and oblivion has swallowed it all. Bartholomew and "Lebbæus, whose surname was Thaddæus," and the rest of them, have no place in the record, and their obscure work is faded, faithful and good as certainly it was.

So it will be sooner or later with us all. For most of us, our service has to be unnoticed and unknown, and the memory of our poor work will live perhaps for a year or two in the hearts of some few who loved us, but will fade wholly when they follow us into the silent land. Well, be it so; we shall sleep none the less sweetly, though none be talking about us over our heads. The world has a short memory, and, as the years go on, the list that it has to remember grows so crowded that it is harder and harder to find room to write a new name on it, or to read the old. The letters on the tombstones are soon erased by the feet that tramp across the churchyard. All that matters very little. The notoriety of our work is of no consequence. The earnestness and accuracy with which we strike our blow is all important; but it matters nothing how far it echoes. It is not the heaven of heavens to be talked about, nor does a man's life consist in the abundance of newspaper or other paragraphs about him. "The love of fame" is, no doubt, sometimes found in "minds" otherwise "noble," but in itself is very much the reverse of noble. We shall do our work best, and be saved from much festering anxiety which corrupts our purest service and fevers our serenest thoughts, if we once fairly make up our minds to working unnoticed and unknown, and determine that whether our post be a conspicuous or an obscure one we shall fill it to the utmost of our power; careless of praise or censure because our judgment is with our God; careless whether we are unknown or well known, because we are known altogether to Him.

The magnitude of our work in men's eyes is as little important as the noise of it. Christ gave all the Apostles their tasks—to some of them to found the Gentile churches, to some of them to leave to all generations precious teaching, to some of them none of these things. What then? Were the Peters and the Johns more highly favoured than the others? Was their work greater in His sight? Not so. To Him all service done from the same motive is the same, and His measure of excellence is the quantity of love and spiritual force in our deeds, not the width of the area over which they spread. An estuary that goes wandering over miles of shallows may have less water in it, and may creep more languidly, than the torrent that thunders through some narrow gorge. The deeds that stand highest on the records in heaven are not those which we vulgarly call great. Many "a cup of cold water only" will be found to have been rated higher there than jewelled golden chalices brimming with rare wines. God's treasures, where He keeps His children's gifts, will be like many a mother's secret store of relics of her children, full of things of no value, what the world calls "trash," but precious in His eyes for the love's sake that was in them.

All service which is done from the same motive in the same force is of the same worth in His eyes. It does not matter whether you have the gospel in a penny Testament printed on thin paper with black ink and done up in cloth, or in an illuminated missal glowing in gold and colour, painted with loving care on fair parchment, and bound in jewelled ivory. And so it matters little about the material or the scale on which we express our devotion and our aspirations; all depends on what we copy, not on the size of the canvas on which, or on the material in which, we copy it. "Small service is true service while it lasts," and the unnoticed insignificant servants may do work every whit as good and noble as the most widely known, to whom have been intrusted by Christ tasks that mould the ages.

IV. Finally we may add that *forgotten work is remembered, and unrecorded names are recorded above.*

The names of these almost anonymous apostles have no place in the records of the advancement of the Church or of the development of Christian doctrine. They drop out of the narrative after the list in the first chapter of the Acts. But we do hear of them once more. In that last vision of the great city which the seer beheld descending from God, we read that in its "foundations were the names of the twelve Apostles of the Lamb." All were graven there—the inconspicuous names carved on no record of earth, as well as the familiar ones cut deep in the rock to be seen of all men for ever.

At the least that grand image may tell us that when the perfect state of the Church is realised, the work which these twelve men did when their testimony laid its foundation, will be for ever associated with their names. Unrecorded on earth, they are written in heaven.

The forgotten work and workers are remembered by Christ. His faithful heart and all-seeing eye keep them ever in view. The world, and the Church whom these humble men helped, may forget, yet will not He forget. From whatever muster-roll of benefactors and helpers their names may be absent, they will be in His list. The Apostle Paul, in his epistle to the Philippians, has a saying in which his delicate courtesy is beautifully conspicuous, where he half apologizes for not sending his greetings "to others my fellow-workers." by name, and reminds them that however their names may be unwritten in his letter, they have been inscribed by a mightier hand on a better page, and "are in the Lamb's book of life." It matters very little from what record ours may be absent so long as they are found there. Let us rejoice that, though we may live obscure. and die forgotten, we may have our names written on the breastplate of our High Priest as He stands in the Holy Place, the breastplate which lies close to His heart of love, and is fixed to His arm of power.

The forgotten and unrecorded work lives too in the great whole. The fruit of our labour may perhaps not be separable from that of others, any more than the sowers can go into the reaped harvest-field and indentify the gathered ears which have sprung from the seed that they sowed, but it is there all the same; and whosoever may be unable to pick out each man's share in the blessed total outcome, the Lord of the Harvest knows, and his accurate proportionment of individual reward to individual service will not mar the companionship in the general gladness, when "he that soweth and he that reapeth shall rejoice together."

The forgotten work will live, too, in the blessed results to the doers. Whatever of recognition and honour we may miss here, we cannot be robbed of the blessing to ourselves, in the perpetual influence on our own character, of every piece of faithful even if imperfect service. Habits are formed, emotions deepened, principles confirmed, capacities enlarged by every deed done for Christ, which make an over-measure of reward here, and in their perfect form hereafter are heaven. Nothing done for Him is ever wasted. "Thou shalt find it after many days." We are all writing our lives, histories here, as if with one of these "manifold writers"—a black blank page beneath the flimsy sheet on which we write, but presently the black page will be taken away, and the writing will stand out plain on the page behind that we did not see. Life is the filmy unsubstantial page on which our pen rests; the black page is death; and the page beneath is that indelible transcript of our earthly actions, which we shall find waiting for us to read, with shame and confusion of face, or with humble joy, in another world.

Then let us do our work for Christ, not much careful whether it be greater or smaller, obscure or conspicuous, assured that whoever forgets us and it He will remember, and however our names may be unrecorded on earth they will be written in heaven, and confessed by Him before His Father and the holy angels.

SERMON XVII.

THE SOUL'S PERFECTION.

PHILIP. iii. 15.

Let us therefore, as many as be perfect, be thus minded: and if in anything ye be otherwise minded, God shall reveal even this unto you.

"AS many as be perfect;" and how many may they be? Surely a very short bede-roll would contain their names; or would there be any other but the Name which is above every name upon it? Part of the answer to such a question may be found in observing that the New Testament very frequently uses the word to express not so much the idea of moral completeness as that of physical maturity. For instance, when Paul says that he would have his converts to be "*men* in understanding," and when the Epistle to the Hebrews speaks of "them that are of full age," the same word is used as this "perfect" in our text. Clearly in such cases it means "full grown," as in contrast with "babes," and expresses not absolute completeness, but what we may term a relative perfection, a certain maturity of character and advanced stage of Christian attainment, far removed from the infantile epoch of the Christian life.

Another contribution to the answer may be found in observing that in this very context these "perfect" people are exhorted to cultivate the sense of not having "already attained," and to be constantly reaching forth to unattained heights, so that a sense of imperfection and a continual effort after higher life are parts of Paul's "perfect man." And it is to be still further noticed that on the same testimony "perfect" people may probably be "otherwise minded;" by which we understand not divergently minded from one another, but "otherwise" than the true norm or law of life would prescribe, and so may stand in need of the hope that God will by degrees bring them into conformity with His will, and show them "this," namely, their divergence from his Pattern for them.

It is worth our while to look at these large thoughts thus involved in the words before us.

I. Then there are people whom without exaggeration the judgment of truth calls *perfect.*

The language of the New Testament has no scruple in calling men "saints" who had many sins, and none in calling men perfect who had many imperfections; and it does so, not because it has any fantastic theory about religious emotions being the measure of moral purity, but partly for the reasons already referred to, and partly because it wisely considers the main thing about a character to be not the degree to which it has attained completeness in its ideal, but what that ideal is. The distance a man has got on his journey is of less consequence than the direction in which his face is turned. The arrow may fall short, but to what mark was it shot? In all regions of life a wise classification of men arranges them according to their aims rather than their achievements. The visionary who attempts something high and accomplishes scarcely anything of it, is often a far nobler man, and his poor, broken, foiled, resultless life far more perfect than his who aims at marks on the low levels and hits them full. Such lives as these, full of yearning and aspiration, though it be for the most part vain, are

> "Like the young moon with a ragged edge
> E'en in its imperfection beautiful."

If then it be wise to rank men and their pursuits according to their aims rather than their accomplishments, is there one class of aims so absolutely corresponding to man's nature and relations that to take them for one's own, and to reach some measure of approximation to them, may fairly be called the perfection of human nature? Is there one way of living concerning which we may say that whosoever adopts it has, in so far as he does adopt it, discerned and attained the purpose of his being? The literal force of the word in our text gives pertinence to that question, for it distinctly means "having reached the end." And if that be taken as the meaning, there need be no doubt about the answer. Grand old words have taught us long ago "Man's chief end is to glorify God and to enjoy Him for ever." Yes, he who lives for God has taken that for his aim which all his nature and all his relations prescribe, he is doing what he was made and meant to do; and however incomplete may be its attainments, the lowest form of a God-fearing, God-obeying life is higher and more nearly "perfect" than the fairest career or character against which, as a blight on all its beauty, the damning accusation may be brought, "The God in whose hand thy breath is, and whose are all thy ways, thou hast not glorified."

People sneer at "saints" and point at their failings. They remind us of the foul stains in David's career, for instance, and mock as they ask, "Is this your man after God's own heart?" Yes, he is; not because religion has a morality of its own different from that of the world (except as being higher), nor because "saints" make up for adultery and murder by making or singing psalms, but because the main set and current of the life was evidently towards God and goodness, and these hideous sins were glaring contradictions, eddies and backwaters, as it were, wept over with bitter self-abasement and conquered by strenuous effort. Better a life of Godward aspiration and straining after purity, even if broken by such a fall, so recovered, than one of habitual earthward grubbing, undisturbed by gross sin.

And another reason warrants the application of the word to men whose present is full of incompleteness, namely, the fact that such men have in them the germ of a life which has no natural end but absolute completeness. The small seed may grow very slowly in the climate and soil which it finds here, and be only a poor little bit of ragged green, very shabby and inconspicuous by the side of the native flowers of earth flaunting around it, but it has a Divine germinant virtue within, and waits but being carried to its own clime and "planted in the house of the Lord" above, to "flourish in the courts of our God," when these others with their glorious beauty have faded away and are flung out to rot.

II. We have set forth here very distinctly *two of the characteristics of this perfection.*

The apostle in our text exhorts the perfect to be "*thus* minded." How is that? Evidently the word points back to the previous clauses, in which he has been describing his own temper and feeling in the Christian race. He sets that before the Philippians as their pattern, or rather invites them to fellowship with him in the estimate of themselves and in their efforts after higher attainments. "Be thus minded" means, Think as I do of yourselves, and do as I do in your daily life.

How did he think of himself? He tells us in the sentence before, "Not as though I were already perfect. I count not myself to have apprehended." So then a leading characteristic of this true Christian perfection is a constant consciousness of imperfection. In all fields of effort, whether intellectual, moral, or mechanical, as faculty grows, consciousness of insufficiency grows with it. The farther we get up the hill the more we see how far it is to the horizon. The more we know the more we know our ignorance. The better we can do the more we discern how much we cannot do. Only people who never have done and never will do anything, or else raw apprentices with the mercifully granted self-confidence of youth, which gets beaten out of most of us soon enough, think that they can do everything.

In morals and in Christian life the same thing is true. The measure of our perfection will be the consciousness of our imperfection—a paradox, but a great truth. It is plain enough that it will be so. Conscience becomes more sensitive as we get nearer right. The worse a man is the less it speaks to him, and the less he hears it. When it ought to thunder it whispers; when we need it most it is least active. The thick skin of a savage will not be disturbed by lying on sharp stones, while a crumpled rose-leaf robs the Sybarite of his sleep. So the habit of evil hardens the cuticle of conscience, and the practice of goodness restores tenderness and sensibility; and many a man laden with crime knows less of its tingling than some fair soul that looks almost spotless to all eyes but its own. One little stain of rust will be conspicuous on a brightly polished blade, but if it be all dirty and dull a dozen more or fewer will make little difference. As men grow better they become like that glycerine barometer recently introduced, on which a fall or a rise that would have been invisible with mercury to record it takes up inches, and is glaringly conspicuous. Good people sometimes wonder, and sometimes are made doubtful and sad about themselves by this abiding and even increased consciousness of sin. There is no need to be so. The higher the temperature the more chilling would it be to pass into an ice-house, and the more our lives are brought into fellowship with the perfect life the more shall we feel our own shortcomings. Let us be thankful if our consciences speak to us more loudly than they used to do. It is a sign of growing holiness, as the tingling in a frost-bitten limb is of returning life. Let us seek to cultivate and increase the sense of our own imperfection, and be sure that the diminution of a consciousness of sin means not diminished power of sin, but lessened horror of it, lessened perception of right, lessened love of goodness, and is an omen of death, not a symptom of life. Painter, scholar, craftsman all know that the condition of advance is the recognition of an ideal not attained. Whoever has not before him a standard to which he has not reached will grow no more. If we see no faults in our work we shall never do any better. The condition of all Christian, as of all other progress, is to be drawn by that fair vision before us, and to be stung into renewed effort to reach it, by the consciousness of present imperfection.

Another characteristic to which these perfect men are exhorted is a constant striving after a further advance. How vigorously, almost vehemently, that temper is put in the context—" I follow after ; " " I press towards the mark ; " and that picturesque "reaching forth," or, as the Revised Version gives it, " stretching forward." The full force of the latter word cannot be given in any one English equivalent, but may be clumsily hinted by some such phrase as "stretching one's self out . over," as a runner might do with body thrown forward and arms extended in front, and eagerness in every strained muscle, and eye outrunning foot, and hope clutching the goal already. So yearning forward, and setting all the current of his being, both faculty and desire, to the yet unreached mark, the Christian man is to live. His glances are not to be bent backwards, but forwards. He is not to be a " praiser of the past," but a herald and expectant of a nobler future. He is the child of the day and of the morning, forgetting the things which are behind, and ever yearning towards the things which are before, and drawing them to himself. To look back is to be stiffened into a living death; only with faces set forward are we safe and well.

This buoyant energy of hope and effort is to be the result of the consciousness of imperfection of which we have spoken. Strange to many of us, in some moods, that a thing so bright should spring up from a thing so dark, and that the more we feel our own shortcomings, the more hopeful should we be of a future unlike the past, and the more earnest in our effort to make that future the present. There is a type of Christian experience not uncommon among devout people, in which the consciousness of imperfection paralyzes effort instead of quickening it; men lament their evil, their slow progress and so on, and remain the same year after year. They are stirred to no effort. There is no straining onwards. They almost seem to lose the faith that they can ever be any better. How different this from the grand, wholesome completeness of Paul's view here, which embraces both elements, and even draws the undying brightness of this forward-looking confidence from the very darkness of his sense of present imperfection !

So should it be with us, "as many as be perfect." Before us stretch indefinite possibilities of approximating to the unattainable fulness of the Divine life. We may grow in knowledge and in holiness through endless ages and grades of advance. In a most blessed sense we may have that for our highest joy which in another meaning is a punishment of unfaithfulness and indocility, that we shall be "ever learning, and never coming to the full knowledge of the truth." No limit can be put to what we may receive of God, nor to the closeness, the fulness of our communion with Him, nor to the beauty of holiness which may pass from Him into our poor characters, and irradiate our homely faces. Then, brethren, let us cherish a noble discontent with all that we at present are. Let our spirits stretch out all their powers to the better things beyond, as the plants grown in darkness will send out pale shoots that feel blindly towards the light, or the seed sown on the top of a rock will grope down the bare stone for the earth by which it must be fed. Let the sense of our own weakness ever lead to a buoyant confidence in what we, even we, may become if we will only take the grace we have. To this touchstone let us bring all claims to higher holiness—they who are perfect are most conscious of imperfection, and most eager in their efforts after a further progress in the knowledge, love, and likeness of God in Christ.

III. We have here also distinctly brought out the *co-existence with these characteristics of their opposites.*

"If in anything ye are otherwise minded," says Paul.

I have already suggested that this expression evidently refers not to difference of opinion among themselves, but to a divergence of character from the pattern of feeling and life which he has been proposing to them. If in any respects ye are unconscious of your imperfections, if there be any "witch's mark" of insensibility in some spot of your conscience to some plain transgressions of law, if in any of you there be some complacent illusion of your own stainlessness, if to any of you the bright vision before you seem faint and unsubstantial, God will show you what you do not see. Plainly then he considers that there will be found among these perfect men states of feeling and estimates of themselves opposed to those which he has been exhorting them to cherish. Plainly he supposes that a good man may pass for a time under the dominion of impulses and theories which are of another kind from those that rule his life.

He does not expect the complete and uninterrupted dominion of these higher powers. He recognises the plain facts that the true self, the central life of the soul, the higher nature, "the new man," abides in a self which is but gradually renewed, and that there is a long distance so to speak, from the centre to the circumference. That higher life is planted, but its germination is a work of time. The leaven does not leaven the whole mass in a moment, but creeps on from particle to particle. "Make the tree good" and in due time its fruit will be good. But the conditions of our human life are conflict, and these peaceful images of growth and unimpeded natural development, "first the blade, then the ear, after that the full corn in the ear," are not meant to tell all the truth. Interruptions from external circumstances, struggles of flesh with spirit, and of imagination and heart and will against the better life implanted in the spirit, are the lot of all, even the most advanced here, and however a man may be perfect, there will always be the possibility that in something he may be "otherwise minded."

Such an admission does not make such interruptions less blameworthy when they occur. The doctrine of averages does not do away with the voluntary character of each single act. The same number of letters are yearly posted without addresses. Does anybody dream of not scolding the errand boy who posted them, or the servant who did not address, because he knows that? We are quite sure that we could have resisted each time that we fell. That piece of sharp practice in business, or that burst of bad temper in the household which we were last guilty of—could we have helped it or not? Conscience must answer that question, which does not depend at all on the law of averages. Guilt is not taken away by asserting that sin cleaves to men, "perfect men."

But the feelings with which we should regard sin and contradictions of men's truest selves in ourselves and others, should be so far altered by such thoughts, that we should be very slow to pronounce that a man cannot be a Christian because he has done so and so. Are there any sins which are clearly *incompatible* with a Christian character? All sins are *inconsistent* with it, but that is a very different matter. The uniform direction of a man's life being godless, selfish, devoted to the objects and pursuits of time and sense, is incompatible with his being a Christian—but, thank God, no single act, however dark, is so, if it be in contradiction to the main tendency impressed upon the character and conduct. It is not for us to say that any single deed shows a man cannot be Christ's nor to fling ourselves down in despair saying, "If I were a Christian, I could not have done that." Let us remember that "all unrighteousness is sin," and the least sin is in flagrant opposition to our Christian profession; but let us also remember, and that not to blunt our consciences or weaken our efforts, that Paul thought it possible for perfect men to be "otherwise minded" from their deepest selves and their highest pattern.

IV. The crowning hope that lies in these words is the certainty of a *gradual but complete attainment* of all the Christian's aspirations after God and goodness.

The ground of that confidence lies in no natural tendencies in us, in no effort of ours, but solely in that great name which is the anchor of all our confidence, the name of God. Why is Paul certain that "God will reveal even this unto you"? Because He is God. The apostle has learned the infinite depth of meaning that lies in that name. He has learned that God is not in the way of leaving off His work before He has done His work, and that none can say of Him, that "He began to build, and was not able to finish." The assurances of an unchangeable purpose in redemption, and of inexhaustible resources to effect it; of a love that can never fade, and of a grace that can never be exhausted—are all treasured for us in that mighty name. And such confidence is confirmed by the manifest tendency of the principles and motives brought to bear on us in Christianity to lead on to a condition of absolute perfection, as well as by the experience which we may have, if we will, of the sanctifying and renewing power of His Spirit in our Spirit.

By the discipline of daily life, by the ministry of sorrow and joy, by merciful chastisements dogging our steps when we stray, by duties and cares, by the teaching of His word coming even closer to our hearts and quickening our consciences to discern evil where we had seen none, as well as kindling in us desires after higher and rarer goodness, by the reward of enlarged perceptions of duty and greater love towards it, with which He recompenses lowly obedience to the duty as yet seen, by the secret influences of His Spirit of Power and of Love and of a sound Mind breathed into our waiting spirits, by the touch of His own sustaining hand and glance of His own guiding eye, He will reveal to the lowly soul all that is yet wanting in its knowledge, and communicate all that is lacking in character.

So for us, the true temper is confidence in His power and will, an earnest waiting on Him, a brave forward yearning hope blended with a lowly consciousness of imperfection, which is a spur not a clog, and vigorous increasing efforts to bring into life and character the fulness and beauty of God. Presumption should be as far from us as despair—the one because we have not already attained, the other because "God will reveal even this unto us." Only let us keep in mind the caution which the apostle, knowing the possible abuses which might gather round His teaching, has here attached to it, "Nevertheless"—though all which I have been saying is true, it is only true on this understanding—"whereto we have already attained, by the same let us walk." God will perfect that which concerneth you if—and only if—you go on as you have begun, if you make your creed a life, if you show what you are. If so, then all the rest is a question of time. A has been said, and Z will come in its proper place. Begin with humble trust in Christ, and a process is commenced which has no natural end short of that great hope with which this chapter closes, that the change which begins in the deepest recesses of our being, and struggles slowly and with many interruptions, into partial visibility in our character, shall one day triumphantly irradiate our whole nature out to the very finger tips, and "even the body of our humiliation shall be fashioned like unto the body of Christ's glory, according to the working whereby He is able even to subdue all things to Himself."

SERMON XVIII.

THE FIRST PREACHING AT ANTIOCH.

Acts xi. 20, 21.

And some of them were men of Cyprus and Cyrene, which, when they were come to Antioch, spake unto the Grecians, preaching the Lord Jesus. And the hand of the Lord was with them: and a great number believed, and turned unto the Lord.

THUS simply does the historian tell one of the greatest events in the history of the Church. How great it was will appear if we observe that the weight of authority among critics and commentators sees here an extension of the message of salvation to Greeks, that is, to pure heathens, and not a mere preaching to Hellenists, that is, to Greek-speaking Jews born outside Palestine.

If that be correct, this was a great stride forward in the development of the Church. It needed a vision to overcome the scruples of Peter, and impel him to the bold innovation of preaching to Cornelius and his household, and, as we know, his doing so gave grave offence to some of his brethren in Jerusalem. But in the case before us, some Cypriote and African Jews—men of no note in the Church, whose very names have perished, with no official among them, with no vision nor command to impel them, with no precedent to encourage them, with nothing but the truth in their minds and the impulses of Christ's love in their hearts—solve the problem of the extension of Christ's message to the heathen, and, quite unconscious of the greatness of their act, do the thing about the propriety of which there had been such serious question in Jerusalem.

This boldness becomes even more remarkable if we notice that the incident of our text may have taken place before Peter's visit to Cornelius. The verse before our text, "They which were scattered abroad upon the persecution that arose about Stephen travelled, . . . preaching the word to none but unto the Jews only," is almost a verbatim repetition of words in an earlier chapter, and evidently suggests that the writer is returning to that point of time, in order to take up another thread of his narrative cotemporaneous with those already pursued. If so, three distinct lines of expansion appear to have started from the dispersion of the Jerusalem church in the persecution —namely Philip's mission to Samaria, Peter's to Cornelius, and this work in Antioch. Whether prior in time or no, the preaching in the latter city was plainly quite independent of the other two. It is further noteworthy that this, the effort of a handful of unnamed men, was the true "leader"—the shoot that grew. Philip's work, and Peter's so far as we know, were side branches, which came to little; this led on to a church at Antioch, and so to Paul's missionary work, and all that came of that.

The incident naturally suggests some thoughts bearing

on the general subject of Christian work, which we now briefly present.

I. Notice the *spontaneous impulse* which these men obeyed.

Persecution drove the members of the Church apart, and, as a matter of course, wherever they went they took their faith with them, and, as a matter of course, spoke about it. The coals were scattered from the hearth in Jerusalem by the armed heel of violence. That did not put the fire out, but only spread it, for wherever they were flung they kindled a blaze. These men had no special injunction " to preach the Lord Jesus." They do not seem to have adopted this line of action deliberately, or of set purpose. They believed, and therefore spoke. A spontaneous impulse, and nothing more, leads them on. They find themselves rejoicing in a great Saviour-Friend. They see all around them men who need Him, and that is enough. They obey the promptings of the voice within, and lay the foundations of the first Gentile church.

Such a spontaneous impulse is ever the natural result of our own *personal possession* of Christ. In regard to worldly good the instinct, except when overcome by higher motives, is to keep the treasure to oneself. But even in the natural sphere, there are possessions which to have is to long to impart, such as truth and knowledge. And in the spiritual sphere, it is emphatically the case that real possession is always accompanied by a longing to impart. The old prophet spoke a universal truth when he said: "Thy word was as a fire shut up in my bones, and I was weary with forbearing, and I could not stay." If we have found Christ for ourselves, we shall undoubtedly wish to speak forth our knowledge of his love. Convictions which are deep demand expression. Emotion which is strong needs utterance. If our hearts have any fervour of love to Christ in them, it will be as natural to tell it forth, as tears are to sorrow or smiles to happiness. True, there is a reticence in profound feeling, and sometimes the deepest love can only "love and be silent," and there is a just suspicion of loud or vehement protestations of Christian emotion, as of any emotion. But for all that, it remains true that a heart warmed with the love of Christ needs to express its love, and will give it forth, as certainly as light must radiate from its centre, or heat from a fire.

Then, true *kindliness of heart* creates the same impulse. We cannot truly possess the treasure for ourselves without pity for those who have it not. Surely there is no stranger contradiction than that Christian men and women can be content to keep Christ as if He were their special property, and have their spirits untouched into any likeness of his Divine pity for the multitudes who were as sheep having no shepherd. What kind of Christians must they be who think of Christ as "a Saviour for me," and take no care to set Him forth as "a Saviour for you?" What should we think of men in a shipwreck who were content to get into the life-boat, and let everybody else drown? What should we think of people in a famine feasting sumptuously on their private stores, whilst women were boiling their children for a meal and men fighting with dogs for garbage on the dunghills? "He that withholdeth bread, the people shall curse him." What of him who withholds the Bread of Life, and all the while claims to be a follower of the Christ, who gave his flesh for the good of the world?

Further, *loyalty to Christ* creates the same impulse. If we are true to our Lord, we shall feel that we cannot but speak up and out for Him, and that all the more where His name is unloved and unhonoured. He has left His good fame very much in our hands, and the very same impulse which hurries words to our lips when we hear the name of an absent friend calumniated should make us speak for Him. He is a doubtfully loyal subject who, if he lives among rebels, is afraid to show his colours. He is already a coward, and is on the way to be a traitor. Our Master has made us his witnesses. He has placed in our hands, as a sacred deposit, the honour of his name. He has entrusted to us, as His selectest sign of confidence, the carrying out of the purposes for which on earth His blood was shed, on which in heaven His heart is set. How can we be loyal to Him if we are not forced by a mighty constraint to respond to His great tokens of trust in us, and if we know nothing of that spirit which said: "Necessity is laid upon me; yea, woe is unto me, if I preach not the gospel!" I do not say that a man cannot be a Christian unless he knows and obeys this impulse. But, at least, we may safely say that he is a very weak and imperfect Christian who does not.

II. This incident suggests the *universal obligation* on all Christians to make known Christ.

These men were not officials. In these early days the Church had a very loose organisation. But the fugitives in our narrative seem to have had among them none even of the humble office-bearers of primitive times. Neither had they any command or commission from Jerusalem. No one there had given them authority, or, as would appear, knew anything of their proceedings. Could there be a more striking illustration of the great truth that whatever varieties of function may be committed to various officers in the Church, the work of telling Christ's love to men belongs to every one who has found it for himself or herself? "This honour have all the saints."

Whatever may be our differences of opinion as to church order and offices, they need not interfere with our firm grasp of this truth. "Preaching Christ," in the sense in which that expression is used in the New Testament, implies no one special method of proclaiming the glad tidings. A word written in a letter to a friend, a sentence dropped in casual conversation, a lesson to a child on a mother's lap, or any other way by which, to any listeners, the great story of the cross is told, is as truly—often more truly—preaching Christ as the set discourse which has usurped the name.

We profess to believe in the priesthood of all believers, we are ready enough to assert it in opposition to sacerdotal assumptions. Are we as ready to recognise it as laying a very real responsibility upon us, and involving a very practical inference as to our own conduct? We all have the power, therefore we all have the duty. For what purpose did God give us the blessing of knowing Christ ourselves? Not for our own well-being alone, but that through us the blessing might be still farther diffused.

> "Heaven doth with us as men with torches do,
> Not light them for themselves."

"God hath shined into our hearts that we might give to others the light of the knowledge of the glory of God in the face of Jesus Christ." Every Christian is solemnly bound to fulfil this Divine intention, and to take heed to the imperative command, "Freely ye have received, freely give."

III. Observe, further, *the simple message* which they proclaimed.

"Preaching the Lord Jesus," says the text—or, more accurately perhaps—preaching Jesus as Lord. The substance then of their message was just this—proclamation of the person and dignity of their Master, the story of the human life of the Man, the story of the Divine sacrifice and self-bestowment by which He had bought the right of supreme rule over every heart; and the urging of His claims on all who heard of His love. And this, their message, was but the proclamation of their own personal experience. They had found Jesus for themselves to be lover and Lord, friend and Saviour of their souls, and the joy they had received they sought to share with these Greeks, worshippers of gods and lords many.

Surely anybody can deliver that message who has had that experience. All have not the gifts which would fit for public speech, but all who have tasted that the Lord is gracious can tell somehow how gracious He is. The first Christian sermon was very short, and it was very efficacious, for it "brought to Jesus" the whole congregation. Here it is: "He first findeth his brother Simon, and saith unto him, We have found the Messias." Surely we can all say that, if we have found Him. Surely we shall all long to say it, if we are glad that we have found Him, and if we love our brother.

Notice, too, how simple the form as well as the substance of the message. "They *spake.*" It was no set address, no formal utterance, but familiar, natural talk to ones and twos, as opportunity offered. The form was so simple that we may say there was none. What we want is that Christian people should speak anyhow. What does the shape of the cup matter? What does it matter whether it be gold or clay? The main thing is that it shall bear the water of life to some thirsty lip. All Christians have to preach, as the word is here, that is, to tell the good news. Their task is to carry a message—no refinement of words is needed for that—arguments are not needed. They have to tell it simply and faithfully, as one who only cares to repeat what he has had given to him. They have to tell it confidently, as having proved it true. They have to tell it beseechingly, as loving the souls to whom they bring it. Surely we can all do that if we ourselves are living on Christ and have drunk into His spirit. Let His mighty salvation, experienced by yourselves, be the substance of your message, and let the form of it be guided by the old words, "It shall be, when the Spirit of the Lord is come upon thee, that thou shalt do as occasion shall serve thee."

IV. Notice, lastly, the *mighty Helper* who prospered their work.

"The hand of the Lord was with them." The very keynote of this book of the Acts is the work of the ascended Christ in and for his Church. At every turning point in the history, and throughout the whole narratives, forms of speech like this occur bearing witness to the profound conviction of the writer that Christ's active energy was with His servants, and Christ's hand the origin of all their security and of all their success.

So this is a statement of a permanent and universal fact. We do not labour alone; however feeble our hands, that mighty Hand is laid on them to direct their movements and to lend strength to their weakness. It is not our speech which will secure results, but his presence with our words which shall bring it about that even through them a great number shall believe and turn to the Lord. There is our encouragement when we are despondent. There is our rebuke when we are self-confident. There is our stimulus when we are indolent. There is our quietness when we are impatient. If ever we are tempted to think our task heavy, let us not forget that He who set it helps us to do it, and from His throne shares in all our toils, the Lord still, as of old, working with us. If ever we feel that our strength is nothing, and that we stand solitary against many foes, let us fall back upon the peacegiving thought that one man against the world, with Christ to help him, is always in the majority, and let us leave issues of our work in his hands, whose hand will guard the seed sown in weakness, whose smile will bless the springing thereof.

How little any of us know what shall become of our poor work, under His fostering care! How little these men knew that they were laying the foundations of the great change which was to transform the Christian community from a Jewish sect into a world-embracing Church! So is it ever. We know not what we do when simply and humbly we speak His name. The far-reaching issues escape our eyes. Then sow the seed, and He will "give it a body as it pleaseth Him." On earth we may never know the results of our labours. They will be among the surprises of heaven, where many a solitary worker shall exclaim with wonder as he looks on the hitherto unknown children whom God hath given him, "Behold, I was left alone; these, where had they been?" Then, though our names may have perished from earthly memories, like those of the simple fugitives of Cyprus and Cyrene, who "were the first that ever burst" into the night of heathendom with the torch of the gospel in their hands, they will be written in the Lamb's book of life, and He will confess them in the presence of His Father in heaven.

SERMON XIX.

THE MASTER AND HIS SLAVES.

2 PETER ii. 1.

Denying the Lord that bought them.

THERE were three great stains on the civilisation of the world into which Christianity came: war, the position of woman, and slavery. With the two first of these we have nothing to do with at present, but the relation of the New Testament to the last of these great evils naturally connects itself with the words before us. That relation is at first sight very singular. There can be no doubt that the atrocious system of slavery is utterly irreconcileable with the principles and spirit of the Gospel. It dies in the light of Christianity, like some foul fungus that can only grow in the dark. And yet there is not a word of condemnation of it in the book. The writers of the New Testament found that evil institution which makes the slaves chattels and their masters fiends in full force, and they said nothing against it. Paul recognises it in several of his letters, regulates it, gives counsels to Christians standing to each other in the extraordinary relation of owner and slave; sends back the runaway

Onesimus to his master, and shows no consciousness of the revolutionary force of his own words, "In Christ Jesus there is neither bond nor free." Whether he foresaw the effect of the gospel in breaking every yoke or no, the fact remains that Christianity at its beginning ran no tilt against even the most execrable social iniquities, but was guided by the wisdom which said, "Make the tree good, and its fruit good." The only way to mend institutions is by mending individuals. Elevate the tone of society by lifting the moral nature of the units, and evil things will drop away and become impossible. Other ways are revolutionary and imperfect.

In like manner, this same wicked thing, slavery, is used as an illustration of the highest, sacredest, noblest relationship possible to men—their submission to Jesus Christ. With all its vileness, it is still not too vile to be lifted from the mud, and to stand as a picture of the purest and loftiest tie that can bind the soul. The apostles glory in calling themselves "slaves of Jesus Christ." That title of honour heads each epistle. And here in this text we have the same figure expressed with Peter's own energy, and carried out in detail. The word in our text for "Lord," is an unusual one, selected to put the idea in the roughest, most absolute form. It is the root of our word "despot," and conveys, at any rate, the notion of unlimited, irresponsible authority. We might read "owner" with some approach to the force of the word.

Nor is this all. One of the worst and ugliest features of slavery is that of the market, where men and women and children are sold like cattle. And that has its parallel too, for this Owner has bought men for His.

Nor is this all; for, as there are fugitive slaves, who "break away every man from his master," and when questioned will not acknowledge that they are his, so men flee from this Lord and Owner, and by words and deeds assert that they owe Him no obedience, and were never in bondage to Him.

So, then, there are these three points brought out in the words before us: Christ's absolute *ownership* of men; the *purchase* on which it depends; and the *fugitives* who deny his authority.

I. The strong expression of the text asserts *Christ's absolute ownership.* If a word had been sought to convey the hardest possible representation of irresponsible, unlimited authority, bound by no law but its own will, the word in our text would have been chosen. Such authority can never be really exercised by men over men. For thought and will are ever free. To claim it would be blasphemy, to allow it would be degradation. But such an authority, in comparison with which the most absolute that man can exercise over man is slight and superficial, this peasant of Nazareth claims, and not in vain. Proud hearts have bowed to his authority, and through the centuries the whole being of thousands upon thousands has gloried in submission—utter and all-embracing—to Him. "What manner of man is this," it was said of old, "that even the winds and the sea obey Him?" But the question opens a deeper depth of wonder, and a higher stretch of power: "What manner of man is this that even the hearts and wills of men obey Him?" His autocratic lips spake, and it was done, when He was here on earth—rebuking disease, and it fled; the wild storm, and there was a great calm; demons, and they came out; death itself, and its dull cold ear heard, and Lazarus came forth. To material things and forces He spake as their great Imperator and Commander, saying to this one "Go," and he went, and showing his Divinity, as even the pagan centurion had learned, by the power of His word, the bare utterance of His will.

But His rule in the region of man's spirit is as absolute and authoritative, and there too "His word is with power." The correlative of Christ's ownership is our entire submission of will, our complete acceptance of the law of his lips, our practical recognition that we are not our own. Loyola demanded from his black-robed militia obedience to the general of the order so complete that they were to be "just like a corpse," or "a staff in a blind man's hand." Such a requirement made by a man is of course the crushing of the will, and the emasculation of the whole nature. But such a demand yielded to from Christ is the vitalising of the will and the ennobling of the spirit. To give myself up to Him is to become not "like a corpse"—but to be as alive from the dead. We then first find our lives when we surrender them to Him.

The owner of the slave could set him to any work he thought fit. So our Owner gives all His slaves their several tasks. As in some despotic eastern monarchies the sultan's mere pleasure makes of one slave his vizier, and of another his slipper-bearer, our King chooses one man to a post of honour, and another to a lowly place; and none have a right to question the allocation of work. What corresponds on our parts to that sovereign freedom of appointment? Cheerful acceptance of our task, whatever it be. What does it matter whether we are set to do things which the vulgar world calls "great," or things which the blind world calls "small?" They are equally set us by Him to whom all service is alike that is done from the same motive, and all that we need care about is to give glad obedience and unmurmuring honest work. Nobody knows what is important service, and what not. We have to wait till another day far ahead, before we can tell that. All work that contributes to a great end is great; as the old rhyme has it, "for the want of a nail a kingdom was lost." So, whatever our tasks, let us say, "Lord, what wilt thou have me to do?"

The slave's hut, and little patch of garden ground, and few bits of furniture, whose were they—his or his master's? If he was not his own, nothing else could be his own. And whose are our possessions? If we have no property in ourselves, still less can we have property in our property. These things were His before, and are His still. The first claim on them is our Master's, not ours. We have not the right to do what we like with our own. So, if we rightly understand our position, we shall feel that we are trustees, not possessors. When, like prodigal sons, we "waste our substance," we are unfaithful stewards, also, "wasting our Lord's goods."

Such absolute submission of will, and recognition of

Christ's absolute authority over us, our destiny, work, and possessions, is ennobling and blessed. So to bow before a man would be degrading were it possible, but so to bow before Him is our highest honour, and liberates us from all other submission. The king's servant is every other person's master. We learn from historians that the origin of nobility in some Teutonic nations is supposed to have been the dignities enjoyed by the king's household —of which you find traces still. The king's master of the horse, or chamberlain, or cupbearer, becomes noble. Christ's servants are lords, free because they serve Him, noble because they wear His livery and bear the mark of Jesus as their Lord.

II. The text brings into view the *purchase* on which that ownership is founded.

This master has acquired men by right of purchase. That abomination of the auction-block may suggest the better "merchandise of the souls of men," which Christ has made, when He bought us with His own blood as our ransom.

That purchase is represented in two forms of expression. Sometimes we read that He has bought us with His "blood;" sometimes that He has given "Himself" for us. Both expressions point to the same great fact—His death as the price at which He has acquired us as His own.

There are far deeper thoughts involved in this statement than can be dealt with here, but let me note one or two plain points. First, then, that is a very beautiful and profound one, that Christ's lordship over men is built upon His mighty and supreme sacrifice for men. Nothing short of His utter giving up of himself for them gives Him the right of absolute authority over them; or, as Paul puts it, "He gave himself for us," that He might "purchase for himself a people." He does not found His kingdom on His Divinity, but on His suffering. His cross is His throne. It seems to me that the recognition of Christ's death as our ransom is absolutely essential to warrant the submission to Him which is the very heart of Christianity. I do not know why any man who rejects that view of the death of Christ should call to Him, "Lord! Lord!" We are justified in saying to Him, "O Lord, truly I am thy servant," only when we can go on to say, "Thou hast loosed my bonds."

Then, consider that the figure suggests that we are bought from a previous slavery to some other master. Free men are not sold into slavery, but slaves pass from one master to another, and sometimes are bought into freedom as well as into bondage. Hebrew slavery was a very different thing from Roman or American slavery— but such as it was, there was connected with it that peculiar institution of the *Goel*, by which, under certain circumstances, if an Israelite had sold himself into slavery, he could be redeemed. As the law has it, "One of his kinsmen may redeem him." So our Kinsman buys us back from our bondage to sin and guilt and condemnation, from the slavery of our tyrant lusts, from the slavery to men's censures and opinions, from the dominion of evil and darkness, and making us His, makes us free.

He that committeth sin is the slave of sin. If the Son therefore make you free, ye shall be free indeed.

III. Our text also brings to view the *Runaways*. We do not care to enquire here what special type of heretics the apostle had in view in these solemn words, nor to apply them to modern parallels which we may fancy we can find. It is more profitable to notice how all godlessness and sin may be described as denying the Lord. *All* sin, I say, for it would appear very plain that the people spoken of here were not Christians at all, and yet the apostle believes that Christ had bought them by His sacrifice, and so had a right over them, which their conduct and their words equally denied.

How eloquent that word "denying" is on Peter's lips. Did the old man travel back in memory to that cold morning, when he was shivering beside the coal-fire in the high priest's palace, and a flippant serving-maid could frighten him into lying? Is it not touching to notice that he describes the very worst aspect of the sin of these people in the words that recall his own? It is as if he were humbly acknowledging that no rebellion could be worse than his, and were renewing again his penitence and bitter weeping after all those years.

All sin is a denial of Christ's authority. It is in effect saying, "We will not have this man to reign over us." It is at bottom the uprising of our own self-will against his rule, and the proud assertion of our own independence. It is as foolish as it is ungrateful, as ungrateful as it is foolish.

That denial is made by deeds which are done in defiance or neglect of his authority, and it is done too by words and opinions. It is not for us to bring such a grave charge against individuals, but at least we may exhort our readers to beware of all forms of teaching which weaken Christ's absolute authority or which remove the very foundation of His throne by weakening the power and meaning of His sacrifice.

Finally, let us beware lest the fate of many a runaway slave be ours, and we be lost in trackless bogs and perish miserably. Casting off His yoke is sure to end in ruin. Rather, drawn by the cords of love, and owning the blessed bonds in which willing souls are held by the love of Christ, let us take Him for our Lord, who has given himself for our ransom, and answer the pleading of His cross with our glad surrender. Then shall He say, "I call you not servants but friends."

SERMON XX.

A PRISONER'S DYING THOUGHTS.

2 TIMOTHY iv. 6–8.

I am now ready to be offered, and the time of my departure is at hand. I have fought a good fight, I have finished my course, I have kept the faith: henceforth there is laid up for me a crown of righteousness.

PAUL'S long day's work is nearly done. He is a prisoner in Rome, all but forsaken by his friends, in hourly expectation of another summons before Nero. To appear before him was, he says, like putting his head into " the mouth of the lion." His horizon was darkened by sad anticipations of decaying faith and growing corruptions in the church. What a road he had travelled since that day when, on the way to Damascus, he saw the living Christ, and heard the words of his mouth!

It had been but a failure of a life, if judged by ordinary standards. He had suffered the loss of all things, had thrown away position and prospects, had exposed himself to sorrows and toils, had been all his days a poor man and solitary, had been hunted, despised, laughed at by Jew and Gentile, worried and badgered even by so-called brethren, loved the less, the more he loved. And now the end is near. A prison and the headsman's sword are the world's wages to its best teacher. When Nero is on the throne, the only possible place for Paul is the dungeon opening on to the scaffold. Better to be the martyr than the Cæsar!

These familiar words of our text bring before us a very sweet and wonderful picture of the prisoner, so near his end. How beautifully they show his calm waiting for the last hour and the bright forms which lightened for him the darkness of his cell! Many since have gone to their rest with their hearts stayed on the same thoughts, though their lips could not speak them to our listening ears. Let us be thankful for them, and pray that for ourselves, when we come to that hour, the same quiet heroism and the same sober hope mounting to calm certainty may be ours.

These words refer to the past, the present, the future. "I have fought—the time of my departure is come—henceforth there is laid up."

I. So we notice first. *The quiet courage which looks death full in the face without a tremor.*

The language implies that Paul knows his death hour is all but here. As the revised version more accurately gives it, "I am already being offered"—the process is begun, his sufferings at the moment are, as it were, the initial steps of his sacrifice—"and the time of my departure is *come*." The tone in which he tells Timothy this is very noticeable. There is no sign of excitement, no tremor of emotion, no affectation of stoicism in the simple sentences. He is not playing up to a part, nor pretending to be anything which he is not. If ever language sounded perfectly simple and genuine, this does.

And the occasion of the whole section is as remarkable as the tone. He is led to speak about himself at all, only in order to enforce his exhortation to Timothy to put his shoulder to the wheel, and do his work for Christ with all his might. All he wishes to say is simply, Do your work with all your might, for I am going off the field. But having begun on that line of thought, he is carried on to say more than was needed for his immediate purpose, and thus inartificially to let us see what was filling his mind.

And the subject into which he subsides after these lofty thoughts is as remarkable as either tone or occasion. Minute directions about such small matters as books and parchments, and perhaps a warm cloak for winter, and homely details about the movements of the little group of his friends immediately follow. All this shows with what a perfectly unforced courage Paul fronted his fate, and looked death in the eyes. The anticipation did not dull his interest in God's work in the world, as witness the warnings and exhortations of the context. It did not withdraw his sympathies from his companions. It did not hinder him from pursuing his studies and pursuits, nor from providing for small matters of daily convenience. If ever a man was free from any taint of fanaticism or morbid enthusiasm, it was this man waiting so calmly in his prison for his death.

There is great beauty and force in the expressions

which he uses for death here. He will not soil his lips with its ugly name, but calls it an offering and a departure. There is a wide-spread unwillingness to say the word "Death." It falls on men's hearts like clods on a coffin —so all people and languages have adopted euphemisms for it, fair names which wrap silk round his dart and somewhat hide his face. But there are two opposite reasons for their use—terror and confidence. Some men dare not speak of death because they dread it so much, and try to put some kind of shield between themselves and the very thought of it by calling it something less dreadful to them than itself. Some men, on the other hand, are familiar with the thought, and though it is solemn, it is not altogether repellent to them. Gazing on death with the thoughts and feelings which Jesus Christ has given them concerning it, they see it in new aspects, which take away much of its blackness. And so they do not feel inclined to use the ugly old name, but had rather call it by some which reflect the gentler aspect that it now wears to them. So "sleep," and "rest" and the like are the names which have almost driven the other out of the New Testament—witness of the fact that in inmost reality Jesus Christ "has abolished death," however the physical portion of it may still remain master of our bodies.

But looking for a moment at the specific metaphors used here, we have first, that of an *offering*, or more particularly of a drink offering, or *libation*, "I am already being poured out." No doubt the special reason for the selection of this figure here is Paul's anticipation of a violent death. The shedding of his blood was to be an offering poured out like some costly wine upon the altar, but the power of the figure reaches far beyond that special application of it. We may all make our deaths a sacrifice, an offering to God, for we may yield up our will to God's will, and so turn that last struggle into an act of worship and self surrender. When we recognize His hand, when we submit our wills to His purposes, when "we live unto the Lord," if we live, and "die unto Him," if we die, then Death will lose all its terror and most of its pain, and will become for us what it was to Paul, a true offering up of self in thankful worship. Nay we may even say, that so we shall in a certain subordinate sense be "made conformable unto his death" who committed His spirit into His Father's hands, and laid down His life, of His own will. The essential character and far-reaching effects of this sacrifice we cannot imitate, but we can so yield up our wills to God and leave life so willingly and trustfully as that death shall make our sacrifice complete.

Another more familiar and equally striking figure is next used, when Paul speaks of the time of his "departure." The thought is found in most tongues. Death is a going away, or, as Peter calls it (with a glance, possibly, at the special meaning of the word in the Old Testament, as well as its use in the solemn statement of the theme of converse on the Mountain of Transfiguration), an Exodus. But the well-worn image receives new depth and sharpness of outline in Christianity. To those who have learned the meaning of Christ's resurrection, and feed their souls on the hopes that it warrants,

Death is merely a change of place or state, an accident affecting locality, and little more. We have had plenty of changes before. Life has been one long series of departures. This is different from the others mainly in that it is the last, and that to go away from this visible and fleeting show, where we wander aliens among things which have no true kindred with us, is to go home, where there will be no more pulling up the tent-pegs, and toiling across the deserts in monotonous change. How strong is the conviction, spoken in that name for death, that the essential life lasts on quite unaltered through it all! How slight the else formidable thing is made. We may change climates, and for the stormy bleakness of life may have the long still days of heaven, but we do not change ourselves. We lose nothing worth keeping when we leave behind the body, as a dress not fitted for home, where we are going. We but travel one more stage, though it be the last, and part of it be in pitchy darkness. Some pass over it as in a fiery chariot, like Paul and many a martyr. Some have to toil through it with slow steps and bleeding feet and fainting heart; but all may have a Brother with them, and holding His hand may find that the journey is not so hard as they feared, and the home from which they shall remove no more, better than they hoped when they hoped the most.

II. We have here too, *the peaceful look backwards*.

There is something very noteworthy in the threefold aspect under which his past life presents itself to the apostle, who is so soon to leave it. He thinks of it as a contest, as a race, as a stewardship. The first suggests the tension of a long struggle with opposing wrestlers who have tried to throw him, but in vain. The world, both of men and things, has had to be grappled with and mastered. His own sinful nature and especially his animal nature has had to be kept under by sheer force, and every moment has been resistance to subtle omnipresent forces that have sought to thwart his aspirations and hamper his performances. His successes have had to be fought for, and everything that he has done has been done after a struggle. So is it with all noble life; so will it be to the end.

He thinks of life as a race. That speaks of continuous advance in one direction, and more emphatically still, of effort that sets the lungs panting and strains every muscle to the utmost. He thinks of it as a stewardship. He has kept the faith (whether by that word we are to understand the body of truth believed or the act of believing) as a sacred deposit committed to him, of which he has been a good steward, and which he is now ready to return to his Lord. There is much in these letters to Timothy about keeping treasures entrusted to one's care. Timothy is bid to "keep that good thing which is committed to thee," as Paul here declares that he has done. Nor is such guarding of a precious deposit confined to us stewards on earth, but the apostle is sure that his loving Lord, to whom he has entrusted himself, will with like tenderness and carefulness "keep that which he has committed unto Him against that day." The confidence in that faithful Keeper made it possible for Paul to be faithful to his trust, and as a steward who was bound by all ties to his Lord, to guard His possessions and administer His affairs. Life was full of voices urging him to give up the faith. Bribes and threats, and his own sense-bound nature, and the constant whispers of the world had tempted him all along the road to fling it away as a worthless thing, but he had kept it safe; and now, nearing the end and the account, he can put his hand on the secret place near his heart where it lies, and feel that it is there, ready to be restored to his Lord, with the thankful confession, "Thy pound hath gained ten pounds."

So life looks to this man in his retrospect as mainly a field for struggle, effort and fidelity. This world is not to be for us an enchanted garden of delights, any more than it should appear a dreary desert of disappointment and woe. But it should be to us mainly a palæstra, or gymnasium and exercising ground. You cannot expect many flowers or much grass in the place where men wrestle and run. We need not much mind though it be bare, if we can only stand firm on the hard earth, nor lament that there are so few delights to stay our eyes from the goal. We are here for serious work; let us not be too eager for pleasures that may hinder our efforts and weaken our vigour, but be content to lap up a hasty draught from the brooks by the way, and then on again to the fight.

Such a view of life makes it radiant and fair while it lasts, and makes the heart calm when the hour comes to leave it all behind. So thinking of the past, there may be a sense of not unwelcome lightening from a load of responsibility when we have got all the stress and strain of the conflict behind us, and have at any rate not been altogether beaten. We may feel like a captain who has brought his ship safe across the Atlantic, through foul weather and past many an iceberg, and gives a great sigh of relief as he hands over the charge to the pilot, who will take her across the harbour bar and bring her to her anchorage in the landlocked bay where no tempests rave any more for ever.

Prosaic theologians have sometimes wondered at the estimate which Paul here makes of his past services and faithfulness, but the wonder is surely unnecessary. It is very striking to notice the difference between his judgment of himself while he was still in the thick of the conflict, and now when he is nearing the end. Then, one main hope which animated all his toils and nerved him for the sacrifice of life itself was "that I might finish my course with joy." Now, in the quiet of his dungeon, that hope is fulfilled, and triumphant thoughts, like shining angels, keep him company in his solitude. Then he struggles, and wrestles, touched by the haunting fear lest after that he has preached to others he himself should be rejected. Now the dread has passed, and a meek hope stands by his side.

What is this change of feeling but an instance of what, thank God, we so often see, that at the end the heart which has been bowed with fears and self-depreciation is filled with peace? They who tremble most during the conflict are most likely to look back with solid satisfaction, while they who never knew a fear all along the course will often have them surging in upon their souls too late, and will see the past in a new lurid light, when they are powerless to change it. Blessed is the man who thus feareth always. At the end he will have hope. The past struggles are joyful in memory, as the mountain ranges, which were all black rock and white snow while we toiled up their inhospitable steeps, lie purple in the mellowing distance, and burn like fire as the sunset strikes their peaks. Many a wild winter's day has a fair cloudless close, and lingering opal hues diffused through all the quiet sky. "At eventide it shall be light." Though we go all our lives mourning and timid, there may yet be granted us ere the end some vision of the true significance of these lives, and some humble hope that they have not been wholly in vain.

Such an estimate has nothing in common with self-complacency. It coexists with a profound consciousness of many a sin, many a defeat, and much unfaithfulness. It belongs only to a man who, conscious of these, is "looking for the mercy of the Lord Jesus Christ unto eternal life," and is the direct result, not the antagonist, of lowly self-abasement, and contrite faith in Him by whom alone our stained selves and poor broken services can ever be acceptable. Let us learn too that the only life that bears being looked back upon is a life of Christian devotion and effort. It shows fairer when seen in the strange cross lights that come when we stand on the boundary of two worlds, with the white radiance of eternity beginning to master the vulgar oil lamps of earth, than when seen by these alone. All others have their shabbiness and their selfishness disclosed then. I remember once seeing a mob of revellers streaming out from a masked ball in a London theatre in the early morning sunlight; draggled and heavy-eyed, the rouge showing on the cheeks, and the shabby tawdriness of the foolish costumes pitilessly revealed by the pure light. So will many a life look when the day dawns, and the wild riot ends in its unwelcome beams.

The one question for us all, then, will be, Have I lived for Christ, and by Him? Let it be the one question for us now, and let it be answered, Yes. Then we shall have at the last a calm confidence, equally far removed from presumption and from dread, which will let us look back on life, though it be full of failures and sins, with peace, and forward with humble hope of the reward which we shall receive from His mercy.

III. The climax of all is *the triumphant look forward.* "Henceforth there is laid up for me a crown of righteousness." In harmony with the images of the conflict and the race, the crown here is not the emblem of sovereignty, but of victory, as indeed is almost without exception the case in the New Testament. The idea of the royal dignity of Christians in the future is set forth rather under the emblem of association with Christ on his throne, while the wreath on their brows is the coronal of laurel, "meed of mighty conquerors," or the twine of leaves given to him who, panting, touched the goal. The reward then which is meant by the emblem, whatever be its essence, comes through effort and conflict. "A man is not crowned, except he strive."

That crown, according to other words of Scripture, consists of "life," or "glory"— that is to say, the issue and outcome of believing service and faithful stewardship here is the possession of the true life, which stands in union with God, in measure so great, and in quality so wonderous that it lies on the pure locks of the victors like a flashing diadem, all ablaze with light in a hundred jewels. The completion and exaltation of our nature and characters by the illapse of "life" so sovereign and transcendant that it is "glory" is the consequence of all Christian effort here in the lower levels, where the natural life is always weakness and sometimes shame, and the spiritual life is at the best but a hidden glory and a struggling spark. There is no profit in seeking to gaze into that light of glory so as to discern the shapes of those who walk in it, or the elements of its lambent flames. Enough that in its gracious beauty transfigured souls move as in their native atmosphere! Enough that even our dim vision can see that they have for their companion "One like unto the Son of Man." It is Christ's own life which they share; it is Christ's own glory which irradiates them.

That crown is "a crown of righteousness" in another sense from that in which it is "a crown of life." The latter expression indicates the material, if we may say so, of which it is woven, but the former rather points to the character to which it belongs or is given. Righteousness alone can receive that reward. It is not the struggle or the conflict which wins it, but the character evolved in the struggle, not the works of strenuous service, but the moral nature expressed in these. There is such a congruity between righteousness and the crown of life, that it can be laid on none other head but that of a righteous man, and if it could, all its amaranthine flowers would shrivel and fall when they touched an impure brow. It is, then, the crown of righteousness, as belonging by its very nature to such characters alone.

But whatever is the essential congruity between the character and the crown, we have to remember too that, according to this apostle's constant teaching, the righteousness which clothes us in fair raiment, and has a natural right to the wreath of victory, is a gift, as truly as the crown itself, and is given to us all on condition of our simple trust in Jesus Christ. If we are to be "found of Him in peace, without spot and blameless," we must be " found *in* Him, not having our own righteousness, but that which is ours through faith in Christ." Toil and conflict, and anxious desire to be true to our responsibilities, will do much for a man, but they will not bring him that righteousness which brings down on the head the crown of life. We must trust to Christ to give us the righteousness in which we are justified, and to give us the righteousness by the working out of which in our life and character we are fitted for that great reward. He crowns our works and selves with exuberant and unmerited honours, but what he crowns is His own gift to us, and His great love must bestow both the righteousness and "the crown."

The crown is given at a time called by Paul "at that day," which is not the near day of his martyrdom, but that of His Lord's appearing. He does not speak of the fulness of the reward as being ready for him at death, but as being "henceforth laid up for him in heaven." So he looks forward beyond the grave. The immediate future after death was to his view a period of blessedness indeed, but not yet full. The state of the dead in Christ was a state of consciousness, a state of rest, a state of felicity, but also a state of expectation. To the full height of their present capacity they who sleep in Jesus are blessed, being still in his embrace, and their spirits pillowed on his heart, nor so sleeping that, like drowsy infants, they know not where they lie so safe, but only sleeping in so much as they rest from weariness, and have closed their eyes to the ceaseless turmoil of this fleeting world, and are lapped about for ever with the sweet, unbroken consciousness that they are "present with the Lord." What perfect repose, perfect fruition of all desires, perfect union with the perfect End and Object of all their being, perfect exemption from all sorrow, tumult and sin can bring of blessedness, that they possess in over measure unfailingly. And, in addition, they still know the joy of hope, and have carried that jewel with them into another world, for they wait for "the redemption of the body," in the reception of which, "at that day," their life will be filled up to a yet fuller measure, and gleam with a more lustrous "glory." Now they rest and wait. Then shall they be crowned.

Nor must self-absorbed thoughts be allowed to bound

our anticipations of that future. It is no solitary blessedness to which Paul looked forward. Alone in his dungeon, alone before his judge when "no man stood by" him, soon to be alone in his martyrdom, he leaps up in spirit at the thought of the mighty crowd among whom he will stand in that day, on every head a crown, in every heart the same love to the Lord whose life is in them all and makes them all one. So we may cherish the hope of a social heaven. Man's course begins in a garden, but it ends in a city. The final condition will be the perfection of human society. There all who love Christ will be drawn together, and old ties, broken for a little while here, be reknit in yet holier form, never to be parted more.

Ah, friends, the all-important question for each of us is how may we have such a hope, like a great sunset light shining into the western windows of our souls? There is but one answer—Trust Christ. That is enough. Nothing else is. Is your life built on Jesus Christ? Are you trusting your salvation to Him? Are you giving Him your love and service? Does your life bear looking at to-day? Will it bear looking at in death? Will it bear His looking at in Judgment?

If you can humbly say, To me to live is Christ, then is it well. Living by Him we may fight and conquer, may win and obtain. Living by Him, we may be ready quietly to lie down when the time comes, and may have all the future filled with the blaze of a great hope that glows brighter as the darkness thickens. That peaceful hope will not leave us till consciousness fails, and then when it has ceased to guide us Christ himself will lead us, scarcely knowing where we are, through the waters, and when we open our half-bewildered eyes in brief wonder, the first thing we see will be his welcoming smile, and his voice will say, as a tender surgeon might to a little child waking after an operation, " It is all over." We lift our hands wondering and find wreaths on our poor brows. We lift our eyes, and lo ! all about us a crowned crowd of conquerors,

> "And with the morn those angel faces smile
> Which we have loved long since, and lost awhile."

THE END.

www.ingramcontent.com/pod-product-compliance
Lightning Source LLC
Chambersburg PA
CBHW021213240426
43667CB00038B/463